STRANGE ATTRACTORS

STRANGE ATTRACTORS
Literature, culture and
chaos theory

HARRIETT HAWKINS

PRENTICE HALL
HARVESTER WHEATSHEAF

NEW YORK LONDON TORONTO SYDNEY TOKYO SINGAPORE

First published 1995 by
Prentice Hall/Harvester Wheatsheaf
Campus 400, Maylands Avenue
Hemel Hempstead
Hertfordshire, HP2 7EZ
A division of
Simon & Schuster International Group

Typeset in 10/12pt Sabon
by Dorwyn Ltd, Rowlands Castle, Hants

Printed and bound in Great Britain by
Biddles Limited, Guildford

Library of Congress Cataloging in Publication Data

Hawkins, Harriett.
  Strange attractors : literature, culture, and chaos theory / by
Harriett Hawkins.
    p.   cm.
  Includes bibliographical references and index.
  ISBN 0-7450-1141-1 : $22.00
    1. Literature, Modern—20th century—History and criticism.
  2. Chaotic behavior in systems in literature. 3. Literature and
  science.   I. Title.
  PN771.H348   1995
  820.9'355—dc20   94-35486
                                                          CIP

British Library Cataloguing in Publication Data

A catalogue record for this book is available from
the British Library ˙

ISBN 0-13-355355-8

1   2   3   4   5   99   98   97   96   95

Contents

List of illustrations

Preface

Chaos is persistent instability.
Ian Percival, 'Chaos: a science for the real world'

Chaos is exciting because it opens up the possibility of simplifying complicated phenomena. Chaos is worrying because it introduces new doubts about the traditional model-building procedures of science. Chaos is fascinating because of its interplay of mathematics, science and technology. But above all chaos is beautiful. This is no accident. It is visible evidence of the beauty of mathematics ... which here spills over into the everyday world of human senses. The striking computer graphics of chaos have resonated with the global consciousness; the walls of the planet are papered with the famous Mandelbrot sets.

Ian Stewart, 'Portraits of chaos'

The main point made throughout this book is that concepts and metaphors from chaos science, most notably 'the butterfly effect', 'fractals' and 'the strange attractor', as they have been appropriated by modern artists of altogether different kinds, also provide important *theoretical* perspectives on the persistent instability that characterizes the dynamical interaction between order and disorder both in canonical and popular fictions.

Chaos science is concerned with nature's dynamical (non-linear) systems that change radically through feedback and therefore – although their newly emergent configurations are characterized by self-similarity – will never return to their initial state. To illustrate this process in mathematics, the result of a calculation is input back into the equation, and the equation is run again – and so on. With the use of computers, which allow for millions of repetitions (iterations) of this feedback process, scientists can see chaos and can understand its laws, but they cannot exert control over it. The long-term behaviour of nonlinear systems is humanly unpredictable because tiny differences in input can very soon result in enormous differences in output, and systems fraught with a variety of positive feedback will often undergo sudden and revolutionary changes in behaviour. Very like certain characters in mythic literature, nonlinear systems tend to behave in a regular, orderly way until something sets them off, a critical point is passed, and they suddenly become chaotic. Conversely, the outlines of these unpredictable configurations are ruled entirely by physical laws, and the operative combination of order and chaos thus seems cognate to a complex work of art such as *Paradise Lost* (or to a personification of omnipotence *within* a work of art – witness Milton's God) that *simultaneously* ordains, contains, and orders chaos into intricate, unfolding patterns. These and other dynamical correspondences explain why so many artists have found chaos science especially congenial, and why chaos scientists so frequently illustrate their precepts with references to mythic portrayals of the interaction between order and disorder in ancient theologies and in classic works of art.

The theoretical implications of chaos science are very important culturally as well as scientifically, and some of the works involved are extremely complex, but the classic and popular examples (for instance, *Paradise Lost* and *Jurassic Park*) that I have used to illustrate the major concepts of chaos theory were chosen because they are the most conspicuous and amusing ones. Certain literary as well as obvious scientific oversimplifications are therefore inevitable: for instance, the terms 'chaos' and 'turbulence' have different technical meanings for scientists, but here as in literature, they are used interchangeably. For that matter, as Katherine Hayles observes (in *Chaos and Order: Complex dynamics in literature and science*, The University of Chicago Press, Chicago and London,

1991, p. 2), the mythic and historical as well as the new scientific meanings associated with the word 'chaos' allow it to serve as 'a cross-roads, a juncture', a matrix where various cultural associations interact and converge, and that is the way I use chaos theory here. My central arguments – that in literature, as in life, momentous, tragic and unforeseeable results often come from very small causes ('the butterfly effect'); that the interaction between order and disorder in certain complex works has inevitably generated diverse and unpredictable responses and imitations as well as critical efforts to stabilize their persistent instabilities; and that certain forces metaphorically embodied in certain figures in literature generate instability in ways markedly comparable to the 'strange attractors' (magnetic basins or points of instability at the heart of a chaotic system) – may well be technically challenged, since they range far afield from the exact mathematics involved in chaos theory. Yet their ubiquity in past and present works of art might in turn suggest that there *could* be some underlying unity in the dynamical processes that 'nonlinear' literature and science alike enable us at least to recognize or, metaphorically, to comprehend, albeit never, finally, to predict or to control. Certainly, as citations from artists and scientists alike may serve to demonstrate, by suggesting that comparable laws are operative both in art and in nature, chaos theory currently provides the most fruitful of all conceptual bridges between 'the two cultures'.

Chaos science also raises interesting questions (and therefore could provoke fruitful disagreements) about *why* certain dynamical processes in art that seem markedly cognate to comparable processes in nature, have proved, quite independently and subjectively, to be both experientially resonant and aesthetically pleasing in altogether different historical and cultural contexts. No one would deny that certain canons of 'beauty' are historically and culturally restrictive, but the transcultural and transhistorical appeal of certain works of art suggests that there may also be some common ground: witness the way the nonlinear dynamics of jazz have spread across the globe.

I am particularly indebted, throughout this book, to the seminal work on chaos theory, modern critical theory and postmodern literature by N. Katherine Hayles. And while my discursive use of their perceptions concerning deterministic chaos is obviously appropriative rather than technical, I have based my central arguments on direct quotations from chaos scientists and historians themselves. Because individual chapters were designed to be reasonably self-contained, some repetition of the major tenets of chaos theory seemed justifiable, since they take on new relevance in differing literary and critical contexts. I have kept the style as simple as possible and the references to modern popular works as eclectic as possible, in the hope that this book may be of use to readers who are not specialists in Shakespeare or Milton or popular culture, and who are unfamiliar with chaos theory.

Shakespeare references are to *The Complete Works*, edited by Stanley Wells and Gary Taylor, Clarendon Press, Oxford, 1986, and Milton quotations are from *John Milton: Complete Poems and Major Prose*, edited by Merritt Y. Hughes, Odyssey Press, New York, 1957. Gustave Doré's depiction of Milton's Satan surveying Paradise is reproduced from *Doré's Illustrations to Paradise Lost*, 1993, by courtesy of Dover Publications Inc., New York, and Merion C. Cooper's cinematic imitation of it in *King Kong* is reproduced from *David O'Selznick's Hollywood*, by Ronald Haven, Bonanza Books, New York, 1985. A brief extract from chapter 2 has been published in *Textual Practice* (edited by Terence Hawkes) 8, 2 (Summer 1994), 255–67. I owe special thanks to Tom Mullin for an informal interview. For criticism, references, and offprints, I am grateful to R. M. Adams, Catherine Belsey, Eric Buckley, John Carey, Robert Clare, Hazel Lessey Corey, Manuel Gomez-Lara, Cecily Palser Havely, Jackie Jones, Paulina Kewes, Allen Michie, Sarah Poynting and John Rumrich. The careless-and-reckless driving (while intoxicated), on this joy-ride through literature in chaos theory's custom-designed Lamborghini, is all my own.

Chaos in classical myth and modern science

Myth is all about what never happened and what always is.
Sallustius, fourth century AD

Before the ocean was, or earth, or heaven,
Nature was all alike, a shapelessness,
Chaos, so-called . . .
Heat fought with cold, wet fought with dry, the hard
Fought with the soft, things having weight contended
With weightless things. Till God, or kindlier Nature
Settled all argument, and separated
Heaven from earth, water from land, our air
From the high stratosphere . . .
But these, by the Creator's order, held
No general dominion; even as it is,
These brothers brawl and quarrel; though each one
Has his own quarter, still, they come near tearing
The universe apart.
Ovid, *Metamorphoses*, first century BC

Before their eyes in sudden view appear
The secrets of the hoary deep, a dark
Illimitable Ocean without bound,
Without dimension, where length, breadth and height,
And time and place are lost; where eldest *Night*
And *Chaos*, Ancestors of Nature, hold
Eternal Anarchy amidst the noise
Of endless wars, and by confusion stand.
Milton, *Paradise Lost*, 1674

Nowadays, the 'chaology' of classical mechanics is an intensively active area of research – chaology is a revival of a term used by theologians two centuries ago to mean the study of what existed before the Creation. It has applications ranging from the irregular tumbling of Saturn's satellite Hyperion to the intricate orbits of food particles in a liquidizer.

Michael Berry, 'Quantum physics on the edge of chaos', 1992

It is undoubtedly true that chaos is a very popular subject in recent years judging by the media attention and the production of scientific papers . . . However, chaos seems to have survived the fashionable phase, and perhaps one reason is that the natural world is inherently nonlinear.

Tom Mullin, *The Nature of Chaos*, 1993

CHAPTER ONE

Introduction: chaos, classics and modern culture

The framing of this circle on the ground
Brings whirlwinds, tempests, thunder and lightning.
                    Christopher Marlowe, *Dr Faustus*

'A butterfly flaps its wings in Peking, and the weather in New York is different . . . thunderstorms instead of sunshine.'
            Ian Malcolm, the chaos mathematician in *Jurassic Park*

Small changes lead to bigger changes later. This behaviour is the signature of chaos. Chaos is found everywhere in nature.
            Ian Percival, 'Chaos: a science for the real world'

Deterministic chaos

From Tom Stoppard's recent play, *Arcadia*, and Charles Wuorninin's musical composition, 'Bamboula Squared', to Robert Littell's thriller, *The Visiting Professor*, and Michael Crichton's blockbuster, *Jurassic Park*, modern chaos theory is currently influential everywhere in the creative arts. In turn, chaos scientists themselves illustrate their theories with reference to Shakespeare, Milton, Pope, Goethe, Blake, Keats and other past masters of art. For in art, as in nature, 'Deterministic laws can produce behaviour that appears random. Order can breed its own kind of chaos'.[1]

The new scientific accounts of the dynamics of 'deterministic chaos' clearly differ from previous scientific and ideological paradigms by insisting that randomness, irregularity, unpredictability are not just occasional. Occurring everywhere in nature's nonlinear systems and operating in humanly unforeseeable ways, deterministic chaos is the context, the medium we inhabit in everyday life, ubiquitously allowing for, and indeed mandating individuality as well as unpredictability within a physically determined order, as in the case of a snowflake or a snowstorm. The most famous example of deterministic chaos that is cited by scientists is only half-jokingly termed 'the butterfly effect'. As its discoverer, Edward Lorenz observed, incalculable effects are built into nature's 'nonlinear' systems:

> There is no question that the chains of events through which chaos can develop out of regularity, or regularity out of chaos, are essential aspects of families of dynamical systems . . . Sometimes a nearly imperceptible change in a constant will produce a qualitative change in the system's behaviour: from steady to periodic, from steady or periodic to almost periodic, or from steady, periodic, or almost periodic to chaotic. Even chaos can change abruptly to more complicated chaos, and, of course, each of these changes can proceed in the opposite direction. Such changes are called *bifurcations*.

Thus the atmosphere, which is governed by physical laws, is '*unstable* with respect to perturbations of small amplitude' and therefore long-term weather predictions are impossible. If a single flap of a butterfly's wings can be instrumental in generating or preventing a tornado, 'so can all the previous and subsequent flaps of its wings, as can the flaps of the wings of millions of other butterflies, not to mention the activities of innumerable more powerful creatures, including our own species'. And although Lorenz's discovery of the butterfly effect blows certain previous deterministic paradigms sky high, as everyone has noted, nature is very much like *art* in that respect. A state of persistent instability could serve as an accurate description of many literary works, situations and characters. After he had written his original paper, Lorenz was reminded of Ray Bradbury's classic science fiction short story, 'A sound of thunder', wherein the death of a prehistoric butterfly, caused by a time-travelling human, irrevocably influences the subsequent course of history.[2]

And so, as the fictional chaos scientist observes in Tom Stoppard's *Arcadia*:

> The unpredictable and the predetermined unfold together to make everything the way it is. It's how nature creates itself, on every scale, the snowflake and the snowstorm. It makes me so happy . . . People

were talking about the end of physics. Relativity and quantum looked as if they were going to clean out the whole problem between them. A theory of everything. But they only explained the very big and the very small. The universe, the elementary particles. The ordinary-sized stuff which is our lives, the things people write poetry about – clouds – daffodils – waterfalls – and what happens in a cup of coffee when the cream goes in – these things are full of mystery, as mysterious to us as the heavens were to the Greeks. We're better at predicting events at the edge of the galaxy or inside the nucleus of an atom than whether it'll rain on auntie's garden party three Sundays from now. Because the problem turns out to be different. We can't even predict the next drip from a dripping tap when it gets irregular. Each drip sets up the conditions for the next, the smallest variation blows prediction apart, and the weather is unpredictable the same way, will always be unpredictable. When you push the numbers through the computer you can see it on the screen. The future is disorder. A door like this has cracked open five or six times since we got up on our hind legs. It's the best possible time to be alive, when almost everything you thought you knew is wrong.[3]

Compare the conclusions arrived at by Ian Malcolm, the fictional chaos theorist in Michael Crichton's *Jurassic Park*: ' "In the past", Malcolm observed, science offered a vision "of total control" '. It was believed

'that prediction was just a function of keeping track of things. If you knew enough, you could predict anything. That's been a cherished scientific belief since Newton, but in the twentieth century it has been shattered beyond repair. Chaos theory throws it right out the window. It says that you can never predict certain phenomena at all . . . Because in fact there are great categories of phenomena that are inherently unpredictable.'

This ' "implies large consequences for human life. Much larger than Heisenberg's principle or Gödel's theorem" ':

'Heisenberg's uncertainty principle set limits on what we could know about the subatomic world. Oh well, we say. None of us lives in a subatomic world. It doesn't make any practical difference as we go through our lives. Then Gödel's theorem set similar limits to mathematics. [But] now chaos theory proves that unpredictability is built into our daily lives. It is as mundane as the rainstorm we cannot predict.'[4]

And of course an unpredicted rainstorm (deterministically assured by the structure of Crichton's novel) is what prevents the engineer from returning to reactivate the electric fences controlling the dinosaurs in the theme park. In their hubristic attempts to control chaos in nature (as personified by the cloned dinosaurs) the Faustian billionaire John Hammond and his associates turn out to be not its masters, but its prey.

As a scientific concept, deterministic chaos cannot conceivably be described in moral terms. Its frame of reference is mundane, not metaphysical. But it has obvious affinities with ancient as well as modern philosophical and theological metaphors involving synergistic interactions, as well as oppositions, between order and disorder. Compare, for instance, the medieval personification of sublunary chaos, the Goddess Fortuna as described by Boethius in *The Consolation of Philosophy* and subsequently portrayed by Chaucer as a governing principle operative everywhere in this world down here. Or compare existentialism's emphasis on 'the absurd'. Modern theories of deterministic chaos likewise have clear affinities with portrayals of order and disorder in premodern as well as postmodern art. Indeed, one could argue that in seeing a deterministic order ordaining as well as containing chaos, art got there before science did. Plato recognized (and deplored) Greek art's chaotic components before Aristotle attempted to regularize, moralize and rationalize them.

Looked at from an artistic as well as a theological angle, very like Mephistopheles, the 'son of Chaos' ('*Das Chaos wunderlicher Sohn*'), who is described in Goethe's *Faust* as 'a portion of that power who always works for Evil and effects the Good',[5] chaos in nature (as in art) likewise may be seen to serve a higher order as a creative force that may produce beauty, freedom and growth as well as catastrophe. Thus the modern scientist Otto Rössler saw in the dynamics that give rise to chaos a self-organizing principle generally operative in the world as if, 'like the devil in medieval history' chaotic energy in nature 'is doing something productive' as it were 'against its will', and 'by self-entanglement produces beauty'.[6]

Moreover, in the dynamics of classical and popular art as in nature, chaos is a creative necessity. This is why, in their portrayal of chaotic energies, artists of all kinds are (as Blake famously observed of Milton) likewise of the Devil's party. And so is their audience: where, for instance, would *Paradise Lost* be without

Satan, or *Othello* without Iago, or *The Tempest* without its own, deterministically ordained, tempest, or a modern 'disaster' movie without a disaster? In art, as well as life, a desire to experience chaos coexists and competes with a will to order. Their obvious conceptual and dynamical affinities explain why state-of-the-art science fictions such as *Jurassic Park* simultaneously refer to chaos theory and to myths and character types in the highest of 'high' literature, even as artists are constantly cited in books by and about modern chaos theorists themselves. To give only a few examples: David Ruelle cites Dante's Hell and the bargains of Faust; Benoit Mandelbrot cites Shakespeare (see below, p. 12); and Mitchell Feigenbaum cites Mahler, Van Gogh, Turner and Ruysdale, paying special homage to Goethe's theories about the universal recognizability of the colour red.[7]

This book focuses on the strange attraction and creative interaction between chaos theory, popular modern fictions and classic works of English literature by Shakespeare and Milton. Its main literary concern is with the reasons why certain works survive over the centuries in their own right as metaphorically or structurally resonant with the way people generally perceive and experience the world and, *simultaneously*, inspire contradictory critical interpretations as well as successive works of altogether different kinds. Art's complex nonlinear systems are, it is argued, inherently chaotic and therefore at odds with comparatively linear critical, aesthetic, moralistic and ideological ideals of order. Indeed, the signature of a complex nonlinear work of art may be that it not only inspires diverse imitations and dialectically opposite critical interpretations but, in effect, elicits successive artistic and critical efforts to smooth out and impose order (either ideologically, or morally, or structurally) on its structurally, ideologically and morally chaotic components.

Although the examples used to illustrate the relevance of chaos theory to canonical and popular literature in succeeding chapters were chosen because they are the most immediately obvious (or amusing) ones, the complex interactions between them are of critical importance in theoretically allowing for a contemporary, and reciprocally creative interaction between art and science, as well as providing a new conceptual framework from which to view the continuing interaction between premodern and postmodern and popular and classic works. It is not unusual for contemporary art to reflect contemporary scientific theories, but it is very unusual for the insights of modern experimental sciences to resonate with primal mythic fictions. Witness, for instance, the mythically resonant scenario that serves to illustrate the movement of a system from order to chaos in a popular introduction to chaos theory:

> The systems of nature are like animals that have been caged all their lives. Let out of the cage, they tend at first to move in a restricted way, not venturing too far, prowling around and around, performing a variety of repetitive movements. It's only when a slightly more adventurous animal breaks this pattern that it gets out of sight of its home cage, discovers a whole universe to explore, and runs away in an entirely unpredictable direction. As we'll soon see, nature's systems will often undergo rigid, repetitive movements and then, at some critical point, evolve a radical new behaviour.[8]

Recognize the cognate transitions from order to chaos in Genesis and *Paradise Lost*, or in *The Island of Doctor Moreau*, and in *Jurassic Park* when the dinosaurs are loosed from their confines in a man-made Eden? Not surprisingly (see chapter 2, below), the structure of Michael Crichton's bestselling novel was based both on modern chaos theory and on the primal 'paradise lost' paradigm for the obvious reason that they reciprocally reflect comparable transitions from order to chaos observable everywhere in nature today as yesterday. After all, as Roger Lewin concludes in his book, *Complexity: Life on the edge of chaos*, 'If anyone still believes that systems may not be toppled from a poised, quasi-stable condition into sudden chaos, they should start reading the newspapers'.[9] Alternatively, they could have a look back at Milton's epic.

For obviously, some of the concepts involved in chaos science are very old, as its practitioners and historians everywhere acknowledge. They cite interactions between chaos and order in Eastern religions, as well as the perennial theological and literary questions raised by a determinism that not only allows for, but in effect ordains chaos in nature, as in art:

> And when the stars threw down their spears,
> And water'd heaven with their tears,
> Did he smile his work to see?
> Did he who made the Lamb make thee?

Thus Blake *simultaneously* asks the identical rhetorical questions of himself, as the creator of its poetic embodiment ('In what distant deeps or skies/Burnt the fire of thine eyes?'); and intertextually (he echoes questions raised in the Book of Job as well as specific questions Milton raised with reference to Satan: 'what strength, what art?'); and extratextually, of the God or force of nature (comparable to deterministic chaos) that first created 'The Tyger': 'What immortal hand or eye/Dare frame thy fearful symmetry?' All these frames of reference interact on every scale (linguistic, conceptual, symbolic, psychological, emotional) throughout the poem. Exactly the same holds true of the nonlinear geometry of nature as described in chaos theory: it is likewise operative, and contains a comparable complexity of informational content and detail, on every scale. *Fearful Symmetry: Is God a geometer?* was therefore the perfect title for a book by the chaos mathematicians, Ian Stewart and Martin Golubitsky. Appropriately, their illustrative frontispiece is Blake's painting of 'The Ancient of Days', with the caption, 'The Geometer God plans his universe'.[10]

The implications of the current interaction between chaos scientists and artists of very different times, as well as very different kinds, are both culturally and critically significant. For modern audiences, the mutuality of insight operates retroactively as well as reciprocally, so that portrayals of deterministic chaos in current works based on modern science lend new relevance to past works, just as past works lend their mythic force and resonance to present works of art – and to the cognate insights of chaos theory itself. This explains why comparable mythic and theological concepts are so often referred to *by* chaos theorists and *in* modern fictions based on chaos theory. Finding an ultimate order (like Shakespeare's Prospero, or Milton's God) overseeing chaos, some of the most up-to-date scientific theories not only allow people familiar with mythic literature to say 'we knew it all along', they also enable us to see in new ways the nonlinear dynamics operative in certain premodern classics.

For instance, through its creative fusion of literary and scientific, and popular and classical, and ancient and modern perspectives on the ways of the world, chaos theory opens up broader perspectives on canonical literature than do certain comparatively restrictive critical perspectives which currently assign, say *Paradise Lost*, to its historically or generically or ideologically restricted place. Thus metaphorically (so to speak) chaos theory liberates some formidable literary dinosaurs from their designated pens in criticism's methodologically ordered Jurassic Parks. It also helps to explain why, after centuries, certain works maintain their operational fangs and claws and terrible beauty. They are the artistic equivalents of deterministic chaos, and as such evoke chaotic responses, contradictory interpretations, altogether different generic adaptations. Therefore, as in the artistic tradition itself, their complex metaphorical signifiers keep on floating around in the minds of individual readers (and generations) long after the text was first read or the show was first seen, and centuries after *Paradise Lost* was first published and *The Tempest* was first staged (see chapters 2 and 3, below). Moreover, in so far as their structures not only contain but mandate chaos on every scale, they in effect encourage adventurous readers, as well as adventurous characters within them, to wander off in differing directions, and so break out of their own artistically determined confines.

Chaos science and the 'real world'

The mathematics of chaos science may be formidably difficult, but the basic precepts of chaos theory are easy to grasp, even as its metaphorical relevance to cognate processes in art will be immediately apparent. For instance, as John Briggs has observed, 'the most fertile area of chaos study' lies along the edge of chaos, which is the 'ferociously active frontier that has been found to exist between stability and incomprehensible disorder' – and is of course the frontier that has proved most fertile in major artistic portrayals of the ways of the world. In the emergent science of complexity, 'the edge of chaos' defines a point of interactive order and instability. For example, as Mitchell Waldrop notes, in the global stock markets, 'Millions of individual decisions to buy or not to buy can reinforce each other, creating a boom or a recession. And that economic climate can fold back to shape the very buying decisions that produced it'. Likewise, Waldrop concludes, 'Except for the very simplest physical systems, virtually everything and everybody in the world is caught up in a vast, nonlinear web of incentives and constraints and connections. The slightest change in one place causes tremors everywhere else. We can't help but disturb the Universe, as

T. S. Eliot almost said. The whole is almost always equal to a good deal more than the sum of its parts.'[11]

And so, as Nina Hall observes in her useful editorial introduction to The 'New Scientist' Guide to Chaos, 'chaos theory depicts a universe that is deterministic, obeying the fundamental physical laws, but with a predisposition for disorder, complexity and unpredictability.' The computer can visually illustrate the complex behaviour of nonlinear systems because it can follow their trajectories over many millions of steps, 'revealing the substructure that characterizes the nature of chaos, and indicating when predictability breaks down'. The exquisite computer graphics that have contributed so much to the popular appeal of chaos theory serve to demonstrate how 'quite simple equations can produce breathtaking patterns of ever increasing complexity'. Within their alternatively abstract, yet often lifelike forms, there are patterns that repeat themselves on smaller and smaller scales. Benoit Mandelbrot coined the word 'fractal' for such shapes and established their immediate link with nature, for trees and mountains and cloud formations and coastlines are likewise examples of fractals. Conceptually speaking, Hall continues, 'Scientists now have an interpretive tool for describing many of the complexities of this world, from weather systems and population dynamics to brain rhythms and gold futures'.[12] 'Chaos stalks every scientific discipline', concludes the mathematician Ian Percival, in an essay he pointedly subtitled 'a science for the real world'.[13]

For that matter, the practitioners of chaos science, in a whole spectrum of once discrete disciplines ranging from mathematics and physics to biology and engineering, unanimously stress the fact that deterministic chaos is not *just* a theoretical metaphor. In his book on *Chance and Chaos*, David Ruelle emphatically notes that

> The way we do mathematics is human, very much so. But mathematicians have no doubt that there is a mathematical reality beyond our puny existence. We discover mathematical truth, we do not create it . . . We don't understand why the world of mathematical truth is accessible to us. Yet, wonderfully, it is.

'Chaos *does* occur in nature', Ian Stewart insists:

> In fact, I find it amazing how much Nature seems to know about the mathematics of chaos. And presumably knew it long before the

mathematicians did. Not only does the idea of chaotic dynamics work – it works far better than anyone could have hoped . . . We'd *like* it to be true – and in defiance of all experience, it is. There is a mystery here. But not one that has to be resolved before we can take advantage of the wonderful miracle that it *works*.[14]

In his introduction to *The Nature of Chaos*, the physicist Tom Mullin likewise observes that there are, on the one hand, 'many splendid abstract mathematical ideas in discussions of dynamical systems and chaos, and on the other there are so-called "real world" phenomena'.[15] And certainly by now, both its mathematical insights and its 'real world' ramifications, as well as its aesthetically evocative metaphors and dynamical processes, have proved irresistibly attractive to modern artists of all kinds. 'Chaos is beautiful and develops itself in fantastic patterns and shapes' ('Chaos ist schön, und es entwickelt sich in phantastischen Mustern und Formen'), proclaims the German newsmagazine *Der Spiegel* in a prominent feature on the international 'Cult of Chaos' ('*Kult um das Chaos*', 27 September 1993, pp. 156–64), citing T-shirts and popular posters displaying Mandelbrot's fractals alongside John Cage and György Ligeti as two examples of the innumerable ('*ungezählten*') musicians who have incorporated the mathematical insights of chaos science into their own compositions. Looked at from any angle, the impact of the processes and concepts of chaos science on the creative arts and the global village of modern popular culture is by now so widespread that it should not be ignored by critical or cultural theorists, students and teachers of literature.

The immediate historical relevance of chaos theory to postmodern literature and poststructuralist theory can be taken for granted here, since it has already been demonstrated. For instance, in her groundbreaking discussions of their affinities, N. Katherine Hayles has shown that chaos theory 'provides a new way to think about order, conceptualizing it not as a totalized condition but as the replication of symmetries that also allows for asymmetries and unpredictabilities'. She continues:

> In this it is akin to poststructuralism, where the structuralist penchant for replicating symmetries is modified by the postmodern turn towards fragmentation, rupture and discontinuity. The science of chaos is like other postmodern theories also in recognizing the importance of scale.[16]

As will be discussed in more detail in the next two chapters, the same holds true of the affinities between deterministic chaos (in theory and in nature) and premodern works by Shakespeare and Milton involving comparable symmetries, asymmetries, ruptures, iterations, recursions and bifurcations. Chaos theory also confirms modern critical arguments that in works by these authors subversion and resistance can be shown to be co-present with containment (not alternatives to it);[17] thus some people may admire (or disapprove of) their works as affirmations of a given ideology, religious orthodoxy or political order, and others may applaud (or deplore) them for their chaotic disruptions and defiance of it. But in either event, in ways cognate to chaos theory, their frames of reference and their dynamical interactions between order and chaos, are neither internally nor externally limited to *artistic* intertextuality in the restrictive ways theoretically associated with postmodern art, or with frequent oversimplifications of Derrida's assertion that there is nothing outside, no outside to the text (*'il n'y pas de hors-texte'*). Indeed Shakespeare and Milton repeatedly suggest that there is more outside their texts than any text can conceivably contain or fully communicate – any more than our own experience of, say, music, is deterministically contained, or can be fully communicated by our own linguistic constructions about it. Likewise, the chemist Peter Coveney concludes that, 'as physicists have already found through quantum mechanics, the full structure of the world is richer than our language can express and our brains comprehend'.[18]

In arguments as it were diametrically opposed to those of some of the most influential modern literary theorists, the most influential chaos theorists everywhere acknowledge and indeed insist that there is 'something' of far more importance than their texts, outside their texts. For instance, as Ian Stewart observes (of symmetry-breaking in mathematics): 'It isn't the long-sought Theory of Everything . . . but we believe it to be a Theory of Something, which may be a better idea.' Moreover, 'once you've become sensitized to that something, to the role that symmetry-breaking plays in nature's patterns, then you'll see the world around you with new eyes.'[19] Compare their *constant*, mystified repetition of the word 'something', as well as the combination of wonder, liberation and exhilaration evinced by the differing scientists quoted by James Gleick in his historical account of the development of chaos theory:

'It's the paradigm shift of paradigm shifts.' 'It's not the same as the old vision at all – it's much broader.' What was 'striking to us' was that 'if you take regular physical systems which have been analyzed to death in classical physics, but you take one little step away in parameter space, you end up with something to which all of this huge body of analysis does not apply.' 'You can't appreciate the kind of revelation [we experienced] unless you've been brainwashed by six or seven years of a typical physics curriculum. You're taught that there are classical models where everything is determined by initial conditions. And then there are quantum mechanical models where things are determined but you have to contend with a limit on how much initial information you can gather.' 'The idea that all these classical deterministic systems could generate *randomness* led to the realization that there was a whole realm of physical experience that did *not* fit into the current framework: It seemed like something out of nothing.' 'We at last had a chance to look around at the immediate world – a world so mundane it was wonderful – and understand something!'[20]

Complex dynamics in nature and art

Their shared conceptual and structural concern with the complex interaction between order and chaos in nature, as in our lives – which is the traditional stuff that fictions are made of – clearly explains why so *many* scientists so often refer to comparable portrayals of this dynamic in literary classics as well as in painting, music and architecture. For instance, Benoit Mandelbrot aptly described, as 'The Merchant of Venice syndrome', the 'fractal' structure nature devised for the circulation of the blood which works so efficiently that in most tissue no cell is ever more than three or four cells away from a blood vessel: 'Not only can't you take a pound of flesh without spilling blood, you can't take a milligram.' Thus Mandelbrot pointedly paraphrases Shylock: 'If you prick us, do we not bleed?'[21]

What Mandelbrot originally termed the 'fractal' geometry of nature involves the iteration of comparably complex details on every scale. The coastline of Great Britain is a case in point. Seen on a large scale from far above it has an irregular outline; looked at more closely, more details of the same irregular coastline-outline will emerge, and so on down to the smallest scale. Its length seems finite and measurable, easily mapped, but followed through to a microscopic scale it becomes virtually infinite: its promontories and crannies contain their own promontories and crannies, symmetries and asymmetries, and so do these, and so on.

Thus, when a fractal is viewed on any scale, comparably complex details emerge. And comparably complex details likewise emerge in individual lines, books, actions, and characterizations, as well as on the mythic, narrative and temporal scales of a complex nonlinear work such as *Paradise Lost* (see chapter 2, below). But this nonlinear complexity on every scale is clearly *not* apparent in 'Space Seed', a *Star Trek* episode based on Milton's portrayal of Satan. Thus, a definition of complexity which involves our apprehension of the pleasures and difficulties involved in works manifesting a comparable richness of informational content and detail on all scales allows us to distinguish between, yet simultaneously relish, both a complex work like *The Tempest* and a science fiction spin-off such as *The Forbidden Planet* that mimics its outline and character-types without attempting to offer comparably detailed complexity on more than one clearly designated scale.

In chaos science, the term 'complexity' may be technically used 'to indicate the length of a set of instructions that one would have to follow to depict or construct a system'.[22] Publishers of romantic novels, for instance, can send their authors a brief set of instructions from which they can construct successive novels. By comparison, a set of instructions informing authors how to construct a work on the order of *Paradise Lost* or *The Tempest* would be virtually interminable, requiring volumes far far longer than the word-count of either work. Individual facets can be replicated (even as a map of Great Britain replicates the immediately recognizable outline of its coastline), but to get the whole complex of detail and informational content that interact throughout the original, it would be necessary to replicate *The Tempest* in its entirety. But, of course, the self-same coastline-outline (as well as the comparably recognizable inhabitants of Prospero's enchanted island) has served as the primary point of *departure* for works as dramatically different from each other as *The Enchanted Island* by Dryden and Davenant, *A Tempest*, the policitized, anti-imperialist adaptation by Aimé Cesaire, and the light-hearted postmodern rock musical, *Return to the Forbidden Planet* (see chapter 3, below).

Also like older literary classics (is *The Tempest* a romance? a musical? a comedy? a tragi-comedy? it has inspired works of all these kinds) chaos theory raises transgeneric as well as transtemporal questions about the dynamic interaction between the forces of order and disorder, and between regularities and irregularities in nature and art. For instance, the identical definition of order 'not as a totalized condition, but allowing for the replication of symmetries and asymmetries' that Katherine Hayles cites with reference to postmodernism, and that I use with reference to works by Shakespeare and Milton, could likewise serve to describe the dynamics of Bach's 'Goldberg Variations' and of 'Dixieland', as well as avant-garde jazz. Moreover, chaos theory is ideologically unrestrictive as well as multidisciplinary. Its pioneers working in differing scientific disciplines in the communist Soviet Union and in the capitalist United States quite independently achieved cognate results. Indeed, the manifest ubiquity of its relevance clearly accounts for the international vogue for chaos in popular culture and the fine arts as well as in specialized scientific publications. And to my mind, its ubiquity of appeal – across history, cultures, generations, genres, art and science – makes chaos theory of special, perhaps crucial, and timely importance to our increasingly Balkanized world.

But will it survive? For that matter, why do some works of art, like some scientific theories, inspire others and survive, while others die out? *Paradise Lost*, for instance, has survived critically fashionable and unfashionable phases (remember when it was deemed, by F. R. Leavis and others, to have been dislodged with remarkably little fuss?) in part because its character types and action continue to resonate in the artistic tradition and partly because they seem emblematic images of certain ways of the world – or so it will be argued later. As cited in an epigraph to this book, Tom Mullin likewise concludes that in scientific circles worldwide, 'chaos has by now survived its fashionable phase, and perhaps one reason is that the natural world is inherently nonlinear.'[23] If the natural world subsequently proves – as in practice if not in theory it has hitherto conspicuously failed to prove – to be inherently *linear*, then chaos science will die out. But if not, its correspondence to sublunary nature will assure that its influence continues to spread outside as well as inside the scientific community. For instance, in an essay on 'The chaotic rhythms of life', the biologist Robert May concludes that:

One thing is certain. Biological systems, from communities and populations to physiological processes are governed by nonlinear mechanisms. This means that we must expect to see chaos as often as we see cycles or steadiness. The message that I urged more than 10 years ago is even more true today: 'not only in research, but also in the everyday world of politics and economics, we would all be better off if more people realized that simple nonlinear systems do not necessarily possess simple dynamical properties'.[24]

In a time of collapsing explanatory and ideological paradigms and certainties, a theory which stresses built-in unpredictabilities seems both necessary and congenial to a post-Newtonian, post-Freudian, post-Marxist and post-postmodern world view: 'If Newton could not predict the behaviour of three balls, could Marx predict that of three people?' asks Ian Stewart. He could not possibly have done so (nor could Freud), any more than anyone could have predicted the sudden disintegration of the Soviet Empire or the outbreak of ethnic war in Bosnia. For 'the "inexorable laws of physics" on which Marx tried to model his laws of history were never really there.' Likewise, many of Freud's dicta which he originally introduced as *clinically* valid (not just as fruitful literary metaphors) have proved as useless in predicting psychological catastrophe as 'a spider web against an avalanche'.[25] For the reason that the world demonstrably contains a wide range of chaotic, as well as linear systems: 'Those that are chaotic have severely limited predictability, and even one such system would rapidly exhaust the entire Universe's capacity to compute its behaviour.'[26]

Butterflies are free

As chaos science demonstrates, whether it occurs in a computer, a weather system, or a human being, a difference in input, so small as to be imperceptible at the time when it occurs, can ultimately produce a huge difference in output. Thus, the long-term behaviour of weather systems (to say nothing of historical events, or how a given child will turn out as an adult) can never be certainly predicted. Likewise a scientific insight (like Mendel's work) that initially produces a small ripple on the surface may produce a huge effect later on. The potential sources of major impacts are too varied ever to be humanly calculable. Although there is order in chaos, and systems behave according to fixed laws (and therefore all conceivable variables and the interactions between all conceivable variables could conceivably be calculated), it would require an omniscient supercomputer (like Milton's God) that is far larger than any conceivable universe to calculate them. Thus deterministic chaos 'sets limits on the intellectual control' that human beings have 'on the evolution of the world.'[27]

By contrast, there has long been a powerful tendency in scientific, literary, historical and biographical studies to seek calculably linear and correspondingly great determinisms for great (tragic, biographical, and historical) consequences and effects. Because of the terrible catastrophes and suffering meted out to them, linear-minded moralists have sought to charge tragic heroes and heroines with *correspondingly* great (*quid pro quo*) crimes, vices, sins and fatal flaws. But as chaos theory demonstrates, and as has long been obvious in ordinary life (as in comic as well as tragic art) very small, morally neutral, individual effects – a chance encounter, an undelivered letter (as in *Romeo and Juliet*), or an inadvertent dropping of a handkerchief, or someone else's otherwise insignificant incapacity to tolerate alcohol (as in *Othello*) – can exponentially compound with other effects and give rise to disproportionate impacts. 'What mighty contests rise from trivial things', Pope observed in lines not exclusively applicable to *The Rape of the Lock*.

As quoted above, real (as well as fictional) chaos scientists repeatedly remind us that deterministic chaos crucially differs from previous scientific uncertainties because it is so much broader. From day to day, we *all* live on the edge of chaos since 'butterfly' effects – unforeseen, haphazard, trivial, mundane events that can both positively and negatively influence an unlimited number of other variables – are everywhere. In nature, art and personal experience alike they are equally unpredictable, sometimes equally imperceptible, but equally pervasive. Witness the unidentified lines a drama student once gave me:

> Everything that we see or hear
> Can add to or increase us in some way,
> And so it might be with this play.
> Some seeds have drifted from our stage. A few
> May even have entered and taken root in you.

But what these seeds are – even though
In your darkest places they feed and grow,
Whatever these seeds are – you will never know.[28]

Obviously, in ordinary life, as in chaos theory, a small change in one variable can have a disproportional effect on other variables that in turn affect others, and so on. Thus, even if we could, initially, calculate all the possible variables, we could not predict how all of them would interact on all the others, much less predict all the possible future interactions all possible present interactions might give rise to. This seems cognate to the old Socratic view acknowledging our ultimate ignorance. But the discoverer of the butterfly effect, Edward Lorenz, did not stop with an image of predictability giving way to pure randomness. He saw that the butterfly effect itself was no accident: 'To produce the rich repertoire of real earthly weather, the beautiful multiplicity of it, you could hardly wish for anything better than a Butterfly Effect.'[29]

As in art, deterministic chaos in nature serves to create as well as destroy. Likewise, when personally experienced, it may prove creative or prove destructive, but we cannot foresee which way it will operate on us: metaphorically speaking, the impact of a butterfly's wings is as uncontrollable as the force that framed the Tyger. The world as we experience it and, arguably, as it is portrayed in some of the greatest and most popular past and present works of art is inherently nonlinear. The butterfly effect is not a rare exception, but a rule.

Its immediate, as well as ubiquitous relevance explains why, as Tom Mullin observes, there has 'naturally' been a tendency to extend the precepts of chaos theory 'into fields where there is no rigorous scientific justification for doing so' (as is obviously the case in this book) and 'one penalty of a scientific subject gaining such popularity' is that it may be seized on as 'the answer to everything'. But, as we shall see with reference to literature (as in life and in science), chaos theory raises at least as many questions as it answers, including questions about art's extratextual relevance and impact as well as its intertextual frames of reference. In any event, Mullin concludes that 'if new insights into difficult ideas are obtained through its use, then a great deal has been achieved.'[30]

Critical consequences, conflicts and continuities

It should be stated here at the outset that although this book has
absolutely no quarrel with the new historicism, or with any other
form of historical or critical insight into literature, chaos theory
does pose a challenge to the more linear (*exclusively* historical,
ideological, and cultural) determinisms that have been theoretically
imposed on art – just as it challenged comparably restrictive tend-
encies in science. Its holistic view of nature's nonlinear systems
gives new relevance to Wordsworth's observation that 'we murder
to dissect' and to the ironic advice the devil Mephistopheles gives to
the student in Goethe's *Faust*:

> Who wants to see and circumscribe a living thing
> must first expel the living spirit,
> for then he has the separate parts in hand . . .
> It will come easier by and by
> when you learn how to reduce
> and duly classify all things. (ll. 1935–40)

Goethe, is, for obvious reasons, one of the artists most frequently
cited by chaos scientists in opposition to disciplinary reductivisms.
And chaos theory in turn is cited for cognate reasons in a brilliant
essay on 'Literature, complexity, interdisciplinarity', where William
Paulson first quotes the chaos scientist, James Crutchfield and his
collaborators:

> 'Chaos brings a new challenge to the reductionist view that a system
> can be understood by breaking it down and studying each piece . . .
> The interaction of components on one scale can lead to complex
> global behaviour on a larger scale that in general cannot be deduced
> from knowledge of the individual components'.[31]

Likewise, Paulson observes, 'many of the theoretical efforts characteristic of modern literary studies are in effect attempts to define a
narrower disciplinary formation by privileging a particular level of
phenomena and establishing methodological principles for its in-
vestigation.' Thus, he continues:

> Differing schools of theorists work on procedures for describing
> different, virtually separate domains: rhetoric, narrative structure,

intertextuality, the reading process, psychoanalytic structures, socio-political significations . . . The list could grow long. There is a risk that these critical schools, each believing itself to be providing disciplinary rigor, could have less and less to say to each other.

Moreover, the structural nature of complex literary texts 'argues against such exclusionary reductionism'. 'The test is not fully determined by the linguistic features of which we know it to be made.'[31] For (and here chaos theory gains strong support from poststructuralism) neither the author nor the reader nor the critic can finally control how all the variables operative in a complex text will interact, or predict exactly how they will combine to produce meanings that may differ from reader to reader in impact, inspiration, and so on.[32] But, as differing, contradictory, chaotic artistic and literary responses to *Paradise Lost* and *The Tempest* can serve to illustrate, even as chaos theory calls into question comparatively *exclusive* critical paradigms, it also allows for a retroactive, retrospective understanding of earlier artistic and critical insights commonly brushed aside as outmoded or as too obvious to need further thought.

Like mathematics, literature and literary criticism are full of channels and byways that seem to lead nowhere in one era and become major areas of study in another. 'In his antiquarian mode', Benoit Mandelbrot, for instance, 'came across so much good mathematics that was ready to be dusted off' that he described himself as an explorer in the 'trash cans' of scientific theory. Likewise Mitchell Feigenbaum broke new ground in part because he had 'managed not to purge himself of some seemingly unscientific ideas from eighteenth-century Romanticism' – most notably Goethe's ideas.[33] So I have not hesitated to forage in the dustbins of criticism of the relevant canonical texts while pillaging the writings of chaos theorists for new insights into the nonlinear structures of art and nature alike.

The main critical argument of the next chapter, which deals with structural similarities between the chaotic disruption of an ordered environment in *Paradise Lost* and *Jurassic Park*, is that chaos theory allows for a new way of discussing time-transcending forms and text-transcending relevance. For while the obvious differences between these works may be explained historically, the continuing appeal of markedly similar structures over centuries cannot. By the same token, their obvious differences in *genre* need not preclude adiscussion of the equally obvious structural similarities between an epic poem based on a sacred text, and a modern blockbuster based on up-to-the-minute scientific theory.

Chapter 3 is primarily concerned with self-similarities, replications, bifurcations, symmetries and asymmetries that occur throughout Shakespeare's nonlinear plays just as they occur, according to chaos theory, in nature's nonlinear systems. By now, as Katherine Hayles has observed, chaotic irregularities, replications, self-similarities, symmetrical asymmetries, self-references and intertextual references comparable to Shakespeare's occur everywhere, to such an extent that they are deemed characteristic of postmodern art.[34] But there is a difference between the way Shakespeare's systems directly refer to the extratextual dynamic of nature, and the way self-consciously postmodern works refer solely to other works of art. The difference betwen *The Tempest* and *Return to the Forbidden Planet*, the amusing, but exclusively intertextual musical directly based on it, is a case in point.

In chaos theory, a 'strange attractor' (a magnetic basin or point of instability) is a source of information as well as disorder, rather like the apple in the garden of Eden – or like Shakespeare's strangest of strange attractors, the witches in *Macbeth* or his Lord of Misrule, Falstaff, who describes himself as 'a cause of wit in others'. Chapter 4 deals with individual characters explicitly identified with chaos, and inevitably concentrates on the irresistibly fascinating women most alluringly associated with its strange attraction, from Milton's Eve and Shakespeare's Cleopatra to (and so we come full circle) 'Eve Sylvan' in *The Strange Attractors*, a fantasy for adolescents based on chaos theory.

In conclusion, it is argued that by illuminating contrasts, as well as comparisons, between major and minor works of differing periods and genres, chaos theory can offer at least a partial, if not a final, answer to the conundrum Karl Marx (who was a card-carrying Shakespearian) posed about the continuing impact of certain works of art. As Marx observed, it is, comparatively speaking, not at all difficult to see *any* work of art as the product of a given social, historical and technological stage of development, or in terms of a reigning ideology:

> The difficulty is not in grasping the idea that Greek plays [compare Shakespeare's plays or *Paradise Lost*] are bound up with certain

forms of social development. It lies rather in understanding why they still constitute for us a source of aesthetic enjoyment and in certain respects prevail as the standard and model beyond attainment.[35]

Complex works that display a primal and permanent interaction between chaos and order may in turn appeal, in differing as well as markedly similar ways, to cultures in various stages of technological development and with altogether different ideologies. Enduring sources of inspiration and information as well as controversy, they are themselves 'strange attractors', mirroring on every scale our own, most strange estate. As such, they remain among the richest literary sources of insight into the deterministically chaotic ways of our world that are communally available to successive generations.

Notes

1. See Ian Stewart, *Does God Play Dice? The new mathematics of chaos*, Penguin, London, 1990, p. 2. See also Stewart 'Portraits of chaos' in *The 'New Scientist' Guide to Chaos* (ed. Nina Hall), Penguin, London, 1992, pp. 44–58.
2. See Edward Lorenz, *The Essence of Chaos*, UCL Press, London, 1993, pp. 69, 181. Lorenz's groundbreaking paper, 'Predictability: does the flap of a butterfly's wings in Brazil set off a tornado in Texas?' (pp. 181–4), was originally presented at the 139th meeting of the American Association for the Advancement of Science on 29 December 1972. See also p. 118: Henri Poincaré (1854–1912) had mathematically anticipated certain conclusions arrived at by chaos scientists: '*La prediction devient impossible*'.

    Some of Lorenz's correspondents subsequently called his attention to Ray Bradbury's short story, 'A sound of thunder', written long before the Washington meeting. Before the meeting, Lorenz had sometimes used a seagull to illustrate his points, and the switch was made by the session convener, who was not aware of Bradbury's story: 'Perhaps the butterfly, with its seeming frailty and lack of power is a natural choice for a symbol of the small that can produce the great' (p. 15). 'A sound of thunder' appears in *The Stories of Ray Bradbury*, Alfred A. Knopf, New York, 1980, pp. 231–41. 'Chaos', as a standard term for nonperiodic behaviour, emerged with the appearance of a paper by Tien Yien Li and James Yorke entitled 'Period three implies chaos' in *American Mathematical Monthly*, 82 (1975), 985–92.
3. See Tom Stoppard, *Arcadia*, Faber & Faber, London, 1993, pp. 47–8. To Hannah's objection that 'The weather is fairly predictable in the

Sahara', Valentine replies that 'The scale is different but the graph goes up and down the same way. Six thousand years in the Sahara looks like six months in Manchester, I bet you.' Hannah: 'How much?' Valentine: 'Everything you have to lose.' Hannah [*pause*]: 'No.' Valentine: 'Quite right. That's why there was corn in Egypt.'

4. See Michael Crichton, *Jurassic Park*, Arrow, London, 1991, pp. 159–60, 312–13.

5. See Johann Wolfgang von Goethe, *Faust* (first part), translated by Peter Salm, Bantam World Drama, New York, 1967, ll. 1336–7, 1384, pp. 85–7. Subsequent line references to this edition of *Faust* are cited parenthetically in the text.

6. James Gleick cites Rössler's conclusions in his historical survey *Chaos: Making a new science*, Cardinal, London, 1989 (first published in Great Britain by Heinemann, 1988), pp. 141–2.

7. David Ruelle, *Chance and Chaos*, Penguin, London, 1993 (originally published by Princeton University Press, 1991), pp. 125, 129. For Feigenbaum's discussion of art and chaos, see Gleick, *Chaos* (n. 6, above), pp. 186–7.

8. See John Briggs and F. David Peat, *Turbulent Mirror: An illustrated guide to chaos theory*, Harper & Row, New York, 1989, p. 33.

9. Roger Lewin, *Complexity: Life on the edge of chaos*, Orion, London, 1993, p. 200.

10. See Ian Stewart and Martin Golubitsky, *Fearful Symmetry: Is God a geometer?*, Penguin, London, 1993 (first published by Blackwell, 1992), pl. 1, p. 3.

11. Quotations are from John Briggs, *Fractals: The patterns of chaos*, an illustrated discussion of 'the new aesthetic of art, science and nature', Thames & Hudson, London, 1992, p. 21, and M. Mitchell Waldrop, *Complexity: The emerging science at the edge of order and chaos*, Penguin, London, 1992, p. 65.

12. See Nina Hall in N. Hall (ed.), *The 'New Scientist' Guide to Chaos*, Penguin, London, 1992, pp. 8–9.

13. See Ian Percival, 'Chaos: a science for the real world' in *The 'New Scientist' Guide to Chaos* (n. 12, above), pp. 11–21. The quotation is from p. 15 and appears in the following context:

> The theory of deterministic chaos mixes determinism and probability in a totally unexpected way. Understanding the subtle unfolding of chaos in a system is helping us to describe not only the behaviour of the floating leaf, the irregular heartbeat and the dripping tap, but many aspects of our complex Universe, on both a small and a grand scale. Chaos stalks every scientific discipline.

14. See David Ruelle, *Chance and Chaos*, Penguin, London, 1993, p. 161, and Ian Stewart, *Does God Play Dice?* (n. 1, above), p. 185. See also Lewis Wolpert, 'Science as practice and culture', *TLS*, 22 October

1993, p. 17: 'A strong case can be made for science approaching nearer and nearer to the "true" nature of the physical world' and 'there is no question that some ideas in science have lasted rather well – Archimedes would have good reason to be pleased'. 'We will, of course, never understand everything' and there are 'important problems in the sociology of science'. But the sociologists' approach 'is doomed' if they believe (as was argued in Harry Collins' letter to the *TLS* of 15 October 1993) that 'the natural world has a small or non-existent role in the construction of scientific knowledge'.

15. See Tom Mullin's editorial introduction to *The Nature of Chaos*, Oxford Scientific Publications, Clarendon Press, Oxford, 1993, pp. x, xvii.

16. See N. Katherine Hayles (ed.), *Chaos and Order: Complex dynamics in literature and science*, University of Chicago Press, Chicago and London, 1991, pp. 10–11. This seminal collection of essays on chaos theory and literature includes an attack on many arguments made here (as well as by Hayles and her other contributors), most notably the argument made by scientists that deterministic chaos in nature is a matter of fact, not a metaphor. For the argument that any chaos which can be written or spoken of must be no more than a trope, see Maria L. Assad, 'Michael Serres: In search of a tropography' (*Chaos and Order*, pp. 278–98). For further discussion of chaos theory, poststructuralism and postmodernism in particular, see Hayles, *Chaos Bound: Orderly disorder in contemporary literature and science*, Cornell University Press, Ithaca, New York, 1990, and 'Chaos as orderly disorder: shifting ground in contemporary literature and science', *New Literary History* 20 (1989), 305–22. In a book published while this one was at press, *Chaosmos: Literature, science and theory* (State University of New York Press, Albany, NY, 1994), Philip Kuberski argues that certain works of literature, theory and science forecast and confirm the shift from a modern to a truly postmodern culture.

17. As portrayed dramatically, 'ideology may afford the ground of its own critique'. For a succinct summary of these and opposed critical arguments, see Alan Sinfield, 'Untune that string: Shakespeare and the scope for dissidence' in the *Times Literary Supplement*, 22 April 1994, pp. 4–5. In an article on 'Chaos, entropy and the arrow of time' in *The 'New Scientist' Guide to Chaos* ((see n. 12, above), p. 209) the physical chemist Peter Coveney describes chaos as an especially interesting 'form of self-organization when there is an overload of order'. This view would seem to support Sinfield's argument that the overload of an educational order – the force-feeding of Shakespeare to school students through thought-stultifying tests – may have chaotic consequences unanticipated in governmental philosophy, in so far as 'containment provokes dissidence'.

18. See Coveney's essay, cited in n. 17, above, p. 212 and compare the conclusions previously arrived at by the biologist J. B. S. Haldane in his essay on 'Possible worlds' (1927) – as well as by Hamlet:

> Now, my own suspicion is that the universe is not only queerer than we suppose, but queerer than we can suppose. I have read and heard many attempts at a systematic account of it, from materialism and theosophy to the Christian system or that of Kant, and I have always felt that they were much too simple. I suspect that there are more things in heaven and earth than are dreamed of, or can be dreamed of, in any philosophy.

19. See Stewart and Golubitsky, *Fearful Symmetry* (n. 10, above), p. xix.
20. See James Gleick, *Chaos* (n. 6, above), pp. 52, 230–1. See also p. 39, citing Thomas Kuhn's account of a paradigm shift: 'It is rather as if the professional community had been suddenly transported to another planet where familiar objects are seen in a different light and are joined by unfamiliar ones as well.'
21. See James Gleick's interviews with Mandelbrot and Feigenbaum in *Chaos* (n. 6, above), pp. 108–14, 164–6; and see also Benoit Mandelbrot, 'Fractals: a geometry of nature' in *The 'New Scientist' Guide to Chaos* (n. 12, above), pp. 122–35: 'Fractal geometry plays two roles. It is the geometry of deterministic chaos and it can also describe the geometry of mountains and clouds.' See also Mandelbrot, *The Fractal Geometry of Nature*, W. H. Freeman, San Francisco, 1982. For a fabulous display of computer graphics portraying this geometry, the most famous of which is the 'Mandelbrot set', see H. O. Peitgen and P. H. Richter, *The Beauty of Fractals*, Springer-Verlag, Berlin, 1986. See also John Briggs' book graphically illustrating the 'new aesthetic of art, science and nature', *Fractals: The patterns of chaos*, Thames & Hudson, London, 1992.
22. See Edward Lorenz, *The Essence of Chaos* (n. 2, above), p. 167.
23. See Tom Mullin, *The Nature of Chaos* (n. 15, above), p. xvii.
24. See Robert May, 'The chaotic rhythms of life', in *The 'New Scientist' Guide to Chaos* (n. 12, above), pp. 82–95; the quotation is from p. 95. Robert May served as a scientific advisor and wrote the programme note on chaos theory to Tom Stoppard's *Arcadia*.
25. See Ian Stewart, *Does God Play Dice?* (n. 1, above), pp. 40, 44.
26. See Paul Davies, 'Is the universe a machine?' in *The 'New Scientist' Guide to Chaos* (n. 12, above), pp. 213–21; the quotation is from p. 220.
27. See David Ruelle, *Chance and Chaos* (n. 7, above), pp. 80, 163. Moreover, even if human beings could calculate them, their calculations of a given system's behaviour might have an unforeseen effect – or counter-effect – and so on. For a philosophical anticipation of these conclusions see K. R. Popper, 'On the sources of knowledge and ignorance' and 'Prediction and prophecy in the Social Sciences', in *Conjectures*

and Refutations, Routledge & Kegan Paul, London, 1963, pp. 3–30, 336–46.

28. A note scrawled on the margin of this poem names 'Peter Weiss, *The Murder of Marat* and Strindberg', but I've never tracked it down in either one.

29. The quotation is from James Gleick, *Chaos* (n. 5, above), pp. 22–3.

30. Tom Mullin, *The Nature of Chaos* (n. 15, above), p. xvii.

31. See William Paulson, 'Literature, complexity, interdisciplinarity', in Hayles, *Chaos and Order* (n. 16, above), pp. 37–53. Paulson observes that 'In an apparent paradox, the current literature–science dialogue . . . is made possible by the very [chaotic, nonlinear, irregular] properties of literature that long made it seem the antithesis of a scientific object' (p. 41).

32. The process operates rather like bifurcating variations on a set text in jazz. For examples of critical variations on Shakespearian meanings, see Terence Hawkes, *That Shakespeherian Rag: Essays on a critical process*, Methuen, London, 1986 and *Meaning by Shakespeare*, Routledge, London, 1992.

33. See James Gleick, *Chaos* (n. 5, above), pp. 110, 113, 158, 165.

34. See N. Katherine Hayles, *Chaos Bound: Orderly disorder in contemporary literature and science* (n. 16, above), p. 295: 'Postmodern texts do not have a monopoly' on the literary strategies deemed their primary characteristics: 'What could be more self-referential than the end of *A Midsummer Night's Dream*?'

35. See *Grundrisse*, in *Karl Marx: Selected Writings*, ed. David McLellan, Oxford University Press, Oxford, 1977, p. 360.

CHAPTER TWO

Paradigms lost: chaos theory, Milton's Eden and *Jurassic Park*

> *Chaos* Umpire sits,
> And by decision more imbroils the fray
> By which he Reigns . . . [over his] wild Abyss,
> The Womb of nature and perhaps her Grave,
> Of neither Sea, nor Shore, nor Air, nor Fire,
> But all these in their pregnant causes mixt
> Confus'dly, and which thus must ever fight.
> John Milton, *Paradise Lost*, 1674

Physics has had great success at describing certain kinds of behaviour: planets in orbit, spacecraft going to the moon . . . the regular movements of objects. But there is another kind of behaviour,
which physics handles badly. For example, anything to do with turbulence. Water coming out of a spout. Air moving over an airplane
wing. Weather. Blood flowing through the heart. Turbulent events
are described by nonlinear equations. They're hard to solve – in fact,
they're usually impossible to solve. So physics has never understood
this whole class of events. Until about ten years ago. The new theory
that describes them is called chaos theory.
Michael Crichton, *Jurassic Park*, 1991

Portrayed as 'Ancestor of nature', primordial ruler over Sea, Shore,
Air, Fire, Tumult, Confusion and Chance, imperial Chaos entered
classic English literature in Milton's *Paradise Lost*. Milton drew his
image of the turbulent abyss ruled by Chaos from the Biblical account of the void from which God created the cosmos, as well as
from the opening lines of Hesiod's *Theogeny* and Ovid's *Metamorphoses*. And Chaos appears as a crowned Monarch/Anarch
who is both its personification and its ruler in Boccaccio's *Geneal-
ogy of the Gods*. But Milton expanded on his sources to make
Chaos a ruling principle throughout his epic. 'In the Beginning, the

26

Heavens and Earth/Rose out of Chaos' (I, 9–10). The eternal Anarch reigned 'when this world was not' and 'where these Heavens now roll' (V, 577–9). Our 'frail World' is suspended over Chaos, the vast abyss that lies between Heaven and Hell (II, 1030), even as chaotic forces unleashed as a consequence of the Fall still (and now) contend in nature, as in the human psyche. Moreover, Milton suggests that Chaos may be not only the state of things from which everything emerged, but the state of things to which nature as we know it will ultimately return: 'The Womb of nature and perhaps her Grave'.[1] And of course successive poets have followed Milton, as Alexander Pope famously did from the beginning to the end of *The Dunciad* (1743):

> Lo, thy dread empire, Chaos! is restor'd;
> Light dies before thy uncreating word;
> Thy hand, great Anarch! lets the curtain fall,
> And universal darkness buries all.

But compare also Pope's portrayal of 'Man' as a 'Chaos of Thought and Passion all confus'd', 'Created half to rise, and half to fall;/ Great lord of all things, yet a prey to all.'[2] As in Milton's portrayals of Adam and Eve, the 'Chaos' involved in the condition of human beings that seem to have been '*created*' half to rise and half to fall is here placed in the context of a larger determinism.

In ways cognate to the overall order of his epic, the overall (cosmic, long-term) order of Milton's God ultimately encompasses Chaos:

> Within appointed bounds be Heav'n and Earth,
> Boundless the Deep, because I am who fill
> Infinitude, nor vacuous the space
> Though I uncircumscrib'd myself retire,
> And put not forth my goodness, which is free
> To act or not, Necessity and Chance
> Approach not mee, and what I will is Fate. (VII, 167–73)

Eternal providence is thus deemed operative in Milton's portrayal of the Abyss of Chaos and the Fall of man, as in the fall of a sparrow – or the flap of a butterfly's wing. Likewise, in modern theories of 'deterministic chaos', a comparable paradox emerges. As Ian Stewart observes, 'Deterministic behaviour is ruled by exact and unbreakable law', while 'stochastic' (random, chaotic) processes are 'lawless and irregular'. So deterministic chaos 'is lawless behaviour governed entirely by law'.[3] And in so far as they likewise insist that there is an order ultimately ruling, as well as allowing, disorder, modern chaos theory fits *Paradise Lost* like a glove.

Three centuries after Milton published *Paradise Lost*, chaos theory has entered modern popular culture in a big way, perhaps most conspicuously through the crash course offered to the mass readership of Michael Crichton's *Jurassic Park* and then through the simplified version of it in Steven Spielberg's hugely successful film adaptation of Crichton's fable. And significantly, in incident as well as in its imagery and outline, Crichton's best seller structurally replicates *Paradise Lost* which in turn replicates Genesis. For instance, in an introductory chapter pointedly entitled 'Almost Paradise', an innocent little girl gets bitten when she tries to play with an unusually intelligent and friendly little reptile that can, astonishingly, walk upright on its hind legs.[4] It is a mini-dinosaur, and the scene so strikingly comparable to Eve's meeting with the friendly, talking serpent in *Paradise Lost*, is the first of our close encounters with the megaserpents re-created to inhabit a high-tech Eden. Comparable mythic correspondences are emphasized throughout the novel.

Jurassic Park and the paradise paradigm

As by now practically everyone ever likely to read this book (along with their kids) may know, on a carefully controlled, patrolled and isolated island off the coast of Central America, Crichton's grandfather-*would-be*-god-figure, the billionaire John Hammond, oversees the creation of 'new life forms' in 'a very short time'. Although 'they have an intelligence of their own' and 'may not do [his] bidding', he expects them to because he 'made them' (p. 305). 'Dear God . . .' exclaims the chaos theorist, Ian Malcolm, who correctly anticipates that the dinosaurs will not behave according to Hammond's plan.

Everywhere in Hammond's theme park, 'extensive and elaborate planting' emphasized the impression of a dawn-of-creation world (p. 86), and when Hammond's voice boomed commandments over the intercom, it 'sounded like the voice of God' (p. 252).

' "My God", said Ellie softly' upon first glimpsing one of Hammond's re-creations through the mists – 'Her first thought was that the dinosaur was extraordinarily beautiful' – ' "My God", Ellie said again.' 'These animals were so big', Gennaro thought: 'He hoped to God the island was safe' (p. 81). Of course, as anyone familiar with Milton's epic or the Book of Genesis – or with chaos theory – could have foreseen, the denizens of *Jurassic Park* will inevitably fail to behave as obediently as their creator originally planned for them to do. In spite of all precautions, dinosaurs programmed not to breed or escape do both. Hammond's theme park is no more secure than Milton's Paradise. His high-tech sensors and electric fences are no more effective against disruption than Eden's guardian angels or the confines of Hell.

Milton's majestic, menacing *Tyrannosaurus rex*, Satan – who wilfully revolted against God's authority – then Adam and Eve, whose violation of God's will was comparatively unpremeditated, then the morally blameless (albeit threatening to man) reptiles that escape from Hammond's confines (thus we come full circle from Satan) seem likewise summoned up from time immemorial to ensure chaos. On a metaphysical level (Satan), a human level (Adam and Eve) and a natural (animal) scale alike, ensuing turbulence is effectively programmed into the total scheme of things – exactly as Satan originally promised Chaos and his consort Night that it would be:

> No mean recompence it brings
> To your behoof, if I that Region lost [by Chaos to cosmos]
> All usurpation thence expell'd reduce
> To her original darkness and your sway
> (Which is my present journey) and once more
> Erect the Standard there of *ancient Night*;
> Yours be th'advantage all, mine the revenge. (II, 982–7)

Thus, the foreordained outline of *Paradise Lost* assures that Chaos will reign on earth, even as Hammond's seemingly impregnable island inevitably proceeds to behave in chaotic ways exactly as Ian Malcolm had predicted it would (p. 77). But why on earth should this 'inevitably' be the pattern in ancient and modern *fictions* as well as in chaos theory? Why should events in a three-hundred-year-old epic poem which was based on the most primal of Biblical parables, and a late twentieth-century blockbuster based on state-of-the-art scientific theory, follow an identical pattern? *Unless* theory and mythic fictions alike are reflecting a comparable reality even as (in chaos theory) 'fractal geometry' appears to describe 'real objects' and events 'in the natural world' that 'look almost identical at different scales' (see *Jurassic Park*, p. 171):

> 'For example', Malcolm said, 'a big mountain, seen from far away has a certain rugged mountain shape. If you get closer, and examine a small peak of the big mountain, it will have the same mountain shape. In fact, you can go all the way down the scale to a tiny speck of rock, seen under a microscope – it will have the same basic fractal shape as the big mountain . . . And this sameness also occurs for events.'

A cognate 'sameness' of shape and event would seem to occur in art exactly as it does in nature and in chaos theory: 'Of all the possible pathways of disorder, nature favours just a few'.[5] And so, apparently, does art. Looked at mythically, *Jurassic Park* can not only be seen as cognate to *Paradise Lost*, but to the legends of Faust and Frankenstein, who, like John Hammond, thought they could be as gods and were likewise headed for a fall, even as (in the novel) Hammond is devoured by dinosaurs of his own creation and thus brought down by the chaos theory that Crichton uses as a metaphor for things as they really are. Conversely, in the film version, as in *Paradise Lost*, the grandfather/god figure survives the rebellions of his own creations – so we may have *Jurassic Park II* as well as *Paradise Regained*.

But in any event, as in Milton's epic, where the Argument of the opening lines (to say nothing of foreknowledge of the Genesis myth) gives us certain knowledge that the earthly paradise is bound to be lost, Ian Malcolm's confident predictions assure that the suspense involved in *Jurassic Park* lies not in finding out *whether* but *how* things on Hammond's island will go wrong. That, Malcolm informs us, we cannot know, until they inevitably do. Or, as Doyne Farmer – a real-life member of the 'Chaos Cabal' – describes the process, the overall system 'is deterministic, but you can't say what it's going to do next.' 'On a philosophical level, it struck me as an operational way to define free will, in a way that allowed you to reconcile free will with determinism' (*Chaos*, p. 251). Arguably the same processes are operative in chaos theory, in fact, and in Milton's predetermined mythic fiction about eternal providence and free will.

Sensitive dependence on initial conditions

Michael Crichton introduces his fictional exponent of chaos theory as 'one of the most famous of the new generation of mathematicians' who were 'openly interested in "how the real world works" ' (p. 73). In contrast to linear equations describing the regular, and therefore predictable movements of planets and comets, these mathematicians were concerned with apparently simple and mundane systems (like the movement of a billiard ball) as well as extremely complex systems (like the weather) that are likewise so 'sensitive to initial conditions' that they will *inevitably* operate in humanly *unpredictable* ways.

Thus, as Ian Malcolm puts it, 'Chaos theory says two things. First, that complex systems like weather have an underlying order. Second, the reverse of that – simple systems can produce complex behaviour.' Take the example of pool balls. Although 'you can know the force and the mass of a ball' and 'can calculate the force with which it will strike the walls', you cannot predict the ball's course for 'more than a few seconds into the future' since, 'almost immediately, very small effects – imperfections in the surface of the ball, tiny indentations in the wood of the table – start to make a difference. And it doesn't take long before they overpower your careful calculations' (pp. 76–7). 'Hammond's project', Malcolm adds, 'is another apparently simple system – animals within a zoo environment – that will eventually show unpredictable behaviour.'

'You know this because of . . .'
'Theory.' Malcolm said.
'But hadn't you better see the island, to see what he's actually done?'
'No. That is quite unnecessary. The details don't matter. Theory tells me that the island will quickly proceed to behave in an unpredictable fashion.'
'And you're confident of your theory.'
'Oh, yes,' Malcolm said, 'Totally confident.' He sat back in the chair. 'There is a problem with that island. It is an accident waiting to happen.' (p. 77)

For neither in theory nor in practice can John Hammond – nor any geneticist, nor any student of dinosaurs, nor any computer – possibly predict *what* small effects or imperfections might become, or were presently being amplified, as they were when amphibian DNA introduced to correct a deficiency enabled certain cloned dinosaurs to mate independently; or what human miscalculations or misdeeds might mess things up, as when a computer engineer temporarily shut off the electrified fences that controlled the dinosaurs, and on account of an unanticipated storm which overpowers all his careful calculations, did not get back to turn them on again and so allowed a wholesale escape.

Whether they are looked at structurally or thematically, inevitability (determinism) and instability (divergence, disruption, chaos, turbulence) are simultaneously and systematically built into the form and content of *Paradise Lost* and *Jurassic Park* alike. Ian Malcolm's account of the way weather systems are so 'sensitively dependent on initial conditions' that 'one will wander off and rapidly become very different from the first' and so you get 'thunderstorms instead of sunshine' (p. 76) could serve as a theoretical gloss on Milton's portrayal of the falls of Eve and Adam. In chaos science 'initial conditions' need not be the ones that existed when a system was created; they are the conditions at the beginning of a given time of action, or a stretch of time that interests an investigator, as when a billiard ball begins to move. But the conditions in Milton's Eden are metaphorically, primally 'initial'. Individually sensitive to 'initial conditions' within their carefully controlled environment, Adam and Eve (first introduced to us hand in hand) soon begin to show increasingly divergent and amplified traits.

Created as lord of the animals but lesser than the angels, Adam had initially experienced acute loneliness and therefore asked God for a mate of his own kind. He first sees his golden Eve, 'adorn'd/With what all Earth or Heaven could bestow/To make her amiable' when he watches her creation in a dreamlike trance. Compared to that vision, 'what seem'd fair in all the World, seem'd now/Mean, or in her summ'd up, in her contain'd' (VIII, 472–3). At the end of his dream,

> Shee disappear'd, and left me dark, I wak'd
> To find her, or for ever to deplore
> Her loss, and other pleasures all abjure
> When out of hope, behold her, not far off,
> Such as I saw her in my dream . . . (VIII, 478–82)

Subsequently, Adam fears losing Eve again more than he fears anything else, including God or Satan:

> How can I live without thee, how forgo
> Thy sweet Converse and Love so dearly join'd,
> To live again in these wild Woods forlorn? (IX, 908–10)

He finally eats the apple because he cannot bear the thought of life without her.

Conversely Eve, who had no experience of life without Adam as her better half, subsequently eats the apple because she desires independence, freedom, autonomy: 'Was I to have never parted from thy side?/As good have grown there still a lifeless rib' (IX, 1153–4). She simultaneously aspires to the intellectual equality and comparatively superior status apparently denied her by her gender – 'their sex not equal seem'd' (IV, 296). After she has eaten the Fruit of the Tree of Knowledge, she debates with herself:

> Shall I to him make known
> As yet my change, and give him to partake
> Full happiness with mee, or rather not,
> But keep the odds of Knowledge in my power
> Without Copartner? So to add what wants
> In Female Sex, the more to draw his Love,
> And render me more equal, and perhaps,
> A thing not undesirable, sometime
> Superior: for inferior who is free? (IX, 816–25)

By now, Eve has come a very long way from truly believing hers the 'happier Lot' because her 'Guide' and 'Head' is intellectually 'Preeminent by so much odds'. Or considering Adam's lot less happy because he has no 'like consort' for himself, no earthly peer (IV, 445–8).

Earlier on the morning before the Fall, the divergence between Adam and Eve amplifies with great rapidity when Eve suggests to Adam that they might work alone for a time: 'Let us divide our labors, thou where choice/Leads thee . . . while I/In yonder Spring of Roses intermixt/With Myrtle, find what to redress till Noon' (IX, 214–19). He prefers togetherness, and pleads with her to stay with him, but in his responses to her request he seems to question her capacity to resist external temptation alone. She takes his worry as an insult to her integrity and intelligence. And even though he has been forewarned of the danger from Satan, and justifiably fears what might befall her severed from him, Adam permits Eve to go because he fears alienating her even more by insisting that she stay against her will. If she would really prefer to be without him for a while – 'If much converse perhaps/Thee satiate' – he tells her to 'Go, for thy stay, not free, absents thee more' (IX, 247–8, 372). Promising to be back by noon, 'from her husband's hand her hand/Soft she withdrew' (IX, 385–6). From thence the loss of Eden.

Thus the bifurcations resulting from their individual sensitivity to initial conditions are amplified with such rapidity that all hell breaks loose in fewer than 1000 lines of verse beginning with Milton's harmonious portrayal of 'the human pair' on the morning of the Fall, as the sacred light began to dawn in Eden and their voices joined the choir 'of all things that breathe' in praising their creator (IX, 191–201). Here, in contrast, is Milton's account of the cosmic and psychological turbulence ensuing afterwards:

> Nor only Tears
> Rained at their Eyes, but high Winds worse within
> Began to rise, high Passions, Anger, Hate
> Mistrust, Suspicion, Discord, and shook sore
> Their inward State of Mind, calm Region once,
> And full of Peace, now toss't and turbulent. (IX, 1121–6)

As this conflation of psychic and climatic turbulence suggests, the reign of Chaos now encompasses life as we know it on earth.

'Et sine fine Chaos & sine fine Deus', says S. B. in one of the two poems dedicatory to *Paradise Lost* (second edition, 1674): 'without end Chaos and without end God'.[6] In human time, the two powers are co-extensive. Yet in the cosmic games God plays, the odds are with the house. Thus, to Einstein's question raised in the title of Ian Stewart's book about the new mathematics of chaos, *Does God Play Dice?*, the answer offered on the last page is 'If God played dice, He'd win'. Likewise, when asked by another character 'Is chaos all just random and unpredictable? Is that it?' Crichton's Ian Malcolm emphatically answers 'No. We actually find regularities within the complex variety of [an increasingly turbulent] system's behaviour' (p. 76). As if to exemplify his process, Milton's Chaos is personified as 'Umpire' who 'by decision more embroils the fray by which he reigns' (II, 908–9). Portrayed as a process and a place as well as a state of mind (the mind is its own place) the wild dominion of Chaos, the eternal Anarch is in turn contained within the larger cosmic order over which God (the eternal Monarch) presides as ultimate umpire, and by decision rules. Likewise finding order-in-chaos, modern chaos theory ultimately even deconstructs its own deconstructions – and so does *Paradise Lost*, whose author is, simultaneously, of the Devil's party and on the side of the angels. Indeed, recent discussions of chaos theory and of Milton's epic alike suggest that perhaps God's continuing struggle with chaos may, metaphorically, be seen as an internal one.[7] For in chaos theory, as in *Paradise Lost*, the act of playing the game has a way of changing the rules, but does not annihilate deterministic order: Satan's fall results in a newly ordered system (earth); the falls of Adam and Eve result in a different, but inexorably operative set of rules, as death and chaos enter earth's deterministic equations.

In any event, like the first chapters of Genesis, *Paradise Lost* and *Jurassic Park* enact comparable processes through which an externally controlled and newly created environment (cosmos) of order and maximum security gives rise to forces of chaos that are in turn contained within the larger order of 'external Providence' – of Art, of Nature – of chaos theory itself. 'Almost Paradise', the initial chapter stressing Crichton's mythic sequence of events, is balanced by the title of a concluding chapter, 'Almost Paradigm', that stresses his ordering of incidents according to the principles of chaos theory. And comparably conflated scientific and literary allusions such as 'paradigms lost' and 'chaos is come again' would provide equally appropriate subtitles for Crichton's science-fiction and for Milton's epic.

Thus, when looked at in terms of the boldest claim of chaos theory itself, which is that it accurately reflects the ways of our world, *Paradise Lost*, *Jurassic Park*, Genesis, and other high and low, ancient and modern portrayals of comparable dissolutions of an initially ordered environment into chaos not only reveal the same outline and sequence of events: they can also be said to reflect the same, simultaneously ordered and chaotic reality. This is why chaos theory may prove as challenging to certain axioms of literary theory as it did to cherished scientific assumptions. For in marked contrast to many influential literary theorists, the most influential chaos theorists and practitioners repeatedly insist (see above, pp. 11–12), that whether we like it or not, there is 'something' of universal (not exclusively culture-based) relevance that lies outside their texts, and for which their texts themselves are but approximations, symbolic images, metaphors. So does Milton:

> What surmounts the reach
> Of human sense, I shall delineate so,
> By lik'ning spiritual to corporal forms,
> As may express them best, though what if Earth
> Be but the shadow of Heav'n, and things therein
> Each to each other like, more than on Earth is thought? (V, 571–6)

Through his unrivalled range of intertextual allusions (to Pandora, Proserpina, Venus, Samson, Orpheus, Homer, Virgil, Dante) Milton reveals the manifold myths underlying his epic attempt to encompass them all. In his commendatory poem 'On *Paradise Lost*' Andrew Marvell in turn stressed its 'sacred truths' along with its 'infinite' scale, its 'vast Design': 'God's Reconcil'd Decree,/ Rebelling Angels, the Forbidden Tree,/Heav'n, Hell, Earth, Chaos, All' (see *Paradise Lost*, ed. Hughes, p. 3); and he appropriately evokes another myth, another 'Mighty Poet', another prophet:

> Where couldst thou words of such a compass find?
> Whence furnish such a vast expense of mind?
> Just Heav'n thee like *Tiresias* to requite
> Rewards with Prophecy thy loss of sight.

The point is that in Marvell's tribute, as in the poem he pays tribute to, poetic fictions are explicitly used to point to truths that lie outside the cited texts.[8]

Like enduring mythic fictions, modern chaos theory may ultimately doom to extinction the by now tired old critical axiom that there is no such thing as a universal truth, which if true, *must*, paradoxically, be false (compare the classical 'paradox of the liar') but nevertheless (again paradoxically) seems to be the only universal 'truth' acknowledged as such in certain critical circles. By contrast, chaos theory makes strong claims about its universality: 'The laws of complexity hold universally, caring not at all for the details of a system's constituent atoms', 'No matter what the medium, the behaviour obeys the same newly discovered laws'. 'It was a very happy and shocking discovery that there were [dynamical] structures in nonlinear systems that are always the same if you looked at them the right way' (Gleick, *Chaos*, pp. 5, 183, 304). Compare *Jurassic Park*, pp. 171–2:

> 'I guess [chaos theory] is one way to look at things', Grant said.
> 'No,' Malcolm said, 'It's the *only* way to look at things. At least, the only way that is true to reality . . . We have soothed ourselves into imagining sudden change as something that happens outside the normal order of things. An accident, like a car crash . . . We do not conceive of sudden, radical, irrational change as built into the very fabric of existence. Yet it is. And chaos theory teaches us,' Malcolm said, 'that straight linearity, which we have come to take for granted in everything from physics to fiction, simply does not exist. Linearity is an artificial way of viewing the world. Real life isn't a series of interconnected events occurring one after the other like a string of beads on a necklace. Life is actually a series of encounters in which one event may change those that follow it, in a wholly unpredictable, even devastating way.'

Again, Malcolm insists that in contrast to comparatively linear and limited, and therefore conceivably controllable determinisms, chaos theory corresponds to certain inherently unpredictable and uncontrollable ways of the world.

Although every reviewer agreed that Steven Spielberg's cinematic dinosaurs are fabulous, many objected to the film's watered down version of scientific theories. But in his *Daily Mail* review (13 July 1993, p. 9) Christopher Tookey persuasively argued that:

> Spielberg may have simplified Crichton's novel, but he's retained its most interesting concepts: about dinosaurs having much in common with birds, about scientific research falling into the hands of irresponsible commerce, about Chaos Theory – which holds that life is too complicated ever to be totally controlled.
> And at a time when the old world order has disintegrated, a film which explains Chaos Theory in terms that a child can understand is extraordinarily well timed.

Likewise, the novel's more detailed and complex account of chaos theory, structurally functional though it may be, serves not just as an exercise in authorial ingenuity. Chaos theory is Crichton's 'extraordinarily well timed' metaphor for the way things are *outside* his fiction. For instance, the axiom whereby 'intelligent animals' with 'diverse traits' (like the dinosaurs in *Jurassic Park*, or like Adam and Eve) will inevitably behave in chaotic ways makes it impossible to base accurate predictions of individual behaviour, including how our own creations/children will turn out, on a comparatively reductive model, such as Freud's family drama, or on biological determinism, or on ideological indoctrination – or what you will: 'You can't study a living economy, or a nation, or a mind by isolating a small part. Your experimental subsystem will be constantly perturbed by unexpected and uncontrollable outside influences', notes Ian Stewart (*Does God Play Dice?* p. 53).

It is, moreover, impossible to predict, either for good or for evil, what any given individual will make of, or do with, any given quanta of information or experience: 'Information is stored in a plastic way, allowing fantastic juxtapositions and leaps of imagination.' Thus, in the development of one person's mind from childhood, 'information is clearly not just accumulated but generated – created from connections that were not there before' (Gleick, *Chaos*, p. 164).

Creative chaos

In nature, sensitive dependence on initial conditions serves not only to destroy but to create. And what it creates is a measure of individuality within physically determined forms and species. Why are all snowflakes different? As a growing snowflake falls to earth,

> the choices made by the branching tips at any instant depend sensitively on such things as the temperature, the humidity, and the presence of impurities in the atmosphere. The six tips of a single snowflake, spreading within a millimeter space, feel the same temperatures, and because the laws of growth are purely deterministic, they maintain a near-perfect symmetry. But the nature of turbulent air is such that any pair of snowflakes will experience very different paths. The final flake records the history of all the changing weather conditions it has experienced, and the combinations may as well be infinite.
>
> (Gleick, *Chaos*, p. 253)

We human beings also record the changing conditions experienced over a lifetime, and are far more complex than snowflakes in so far as we are intellectually and emotionally, as well as genetically unique individuals with a mixture of diverse traits that allow us to make radically differing connections of our own – like Milton's Adam and Eve.

For, significantly, absolutely no amount of gender-conditioning, or ideological indoctrination, or religious instruction – or even the threat of death – serves to avert Eve's decision to eat the Fruit. Or Adam's. Both were assigned their complementary gender roles and indoctrinated in them. For 'contemplation' and for 'valor' he was formed. 'For softness shee and sweet attractive Grace.' 'Hee for God only, shee for God in him.' Programmed for 'absolute rule' and 'true authority' (IV, 295–301), Adam is repeatedly reminded that he occupies the superior, dominant role in the scheme of things: 'For well I understand in the prime end/Of Nature her th' inferior.' Eve, in turn, is conditioned to accept her lower status in the hierarchy: 'What thou bid'st', she tells Adam, 'Unargu'd I obey; so God ordains: God is thy Law, thou mine:/To know no more is woman's happiest knowledge and her praise' (IV, 635–8). Moreover, she is repeatedly led to concede that her peerless beauty is inferior to Adam's wisdom: 'Thy gentle hand/Seiz'd mine, I yielded, and from that time see/How Beauty is excell'd by manly grace/And wisdom, which alone is truly fair' (IV, 490–1).

But gender lines blur, and gender roles reverse within *forty-eight hours*, when 'domestic' Adam yields to Eve's will, lets her sally forth like a valorous hero to meet their mutual adversary, and stays behind like a wife, to weave a garland to place on the brow of the returning champion (IX, 319, 893). Gender lines blur again when Eve offers to shoulder all the blame for the Fall, like a husband who takes responsibility for his wife's debts. Psychological traits prove likewise unstable when Milton's selfish Eve unselfishly and heroically offers to return to the place of judgment and importune Heaven that all God's punishment would fall on her alone: 'On me, sole cause to thee of all this woe/Mee mee only just object of his ire' (X, 935–6).

In the end, Adam and Eve leave Eden hand in hand as absolute equals in one crucial respect: that is, in their humble/heroical knowledge of their mutual frailty and mutual need for other in the chaotic world they must henceforth live in, quite unable to command. After the Fall, the first thunderclouds appear and climatic turbulence compounds: winds 'rend the woods and seas upturn'. 'Thus began/Outrage from lifeless things'. The bifurcations proceed exponentially and extend to the animal kingdom: 'Beast now with Beast 'gan war, and Fowl with Fowl':

> . . . to graze the Herb all leaving,
> Devour'd each other; nor stood much in awe
> Of Man, but fled him, or with count'nance grim
> Glar'd on him passing. (X, 710–14)

Adios Eden, and welcome to Jurassic Park.

Like the end of *Paradise Lost* (as opposed to paradigmatic determinisms exclusively based on cultural, ideological and sexual *differences*), chaos theory provides the basis for a cosmopolitan human commonality based on a common humility and mutual dependency stemming from our universal ignorance concerning what is going to happen next; or how on earth to control it when it does. It reveals 'a universe that is vaster, more complex, more fluid, less secure, and in a sense more frightening than the one that has been portrayed by reductionist science'. But it is also conducive to comradeship, to fellowship, 'because we are all in it together'.[9]

It does seem in an odd way liberating, as well as humbling, to admit that we cannot possibly control or even calculate (nor could any computer conceivably calculate) what very small effects, or what combination of complex and simple effects (time, place, persons, physical appetites, psychological proclivities) may or may not have crucial consequences. 'Meanwhile the hour of Noon drew on, and wak'd/An eager appetite rais'd by the smell/So savory of that Fruit' (*Paradise Lost* IX, 739–41) – what dire events from trivial causes spring! Influences as banal as the time of day and the mundane fact that she was *hungry* contributed to Eve's appetite for that fragrant fruit whose 'mortal taste/Brought Death into the World, and all our woe' (I, 2–3). Satan himself expresses astonishment at the mundane triviality of the source of the primal Fall when he tells his cohorts how he seduced Adam and Eve from their Creator and irrevocably disrupted their new created world of absolute perfection, 'the more to increase/Your wonder, with an Apple' (X, 486–7).

'The butterfly effect' and 'the apple effect'

What could be called 'the apple effect' in *Paradise Lost* perfectly illustrates what chaos theorists metaphorically term 'the butterfly effect': a small change in one variable can have a disproportional effect on other variables – the flapping of a single butterfly's wing today may produce a change that affects other variables so that what the global atmosphere actually does diverges from what it otherwise would have done. Eve plucks and eats an apple and subsequently the whole global atmosphere is exponentially altered:

> Earth felt the wound, and Nature from her seat
> Sighing through all her Works gave signs of woe,
> That all was lost. (IX, 782–4)

Adam in turn 'scrupl'd not to eat' and

> Earth trembl'd from her entrails, as again
> In pangs, and Nature gave a second groan,
> Sky low'r'd, and muttering Thunder, some sad drops
> Wept at completing of the mortal Sin
> Original. (IX, 1001–4)

It is as well known in life, as in science, 'that a chain of events can have a point of crisis that could magnify small changes', notes James Gleick: 'But chaos meant that such points were everywhere. They were pervasive.' Moreover, nonlinearity 'means that the act of playing the game itself' has a way of changing the goalposts as well as the rules (*Chaos*, p. 24). And so it does in the mythic context of *Paradise Lost*. A woman who is ultra-sensitive to initial conditions eats an apple and offers one to a man who is likewise sensitive to initial conditions who likewise tastes it, and their act irrevocably alters the rules by which they subsequently have to play the game, as well as permanently altering an environment that is itself sensitive to initial conditions. Thus the course of history over millennia and the psychic and genetic state of all subsequent populations of individual human beings and animals is affected. Moreover, in the panoramic history of humankind revealed to Adam in the last books of *Paradise Lost* (as in Susan Niditch's account of the onset of chaos in Genesis 1–11), the act of disobedience alienating Adam and Eve from God bifurcates exponentially as human beings become increasingly alienated from one another – 'Adam from Eve, Cain from Abel, Ham from Shem and Japheth' and finally nation from nation through the diversification of language and culture.[10]

In *Paradise Lost*, Satan's rebellion and fall provides a cosmic template for successive alienations. As a consequence of these primal alienations between God and Man, Man and Woman, humans and animals, nation and nation, the ultimate, heroic effort of morality is to bring us back together again and so, hand in hand, create a new, very hard-earned (as distinct from an unearned) and as yet unrealized harmony:

> O shame to men! Devil with devil damn'd
> Firm concord holds, men only disagree
> Of Creatures rational, though under hope
> Of heavenly Grace; and God proclaiming peace,
> Yet live in hatred, enmity, and strife
> Among themselves, and levy cruel wars,
> Wasting the Earth, each other to destroy. (II, 496–502)

It is as if the elemental components of Chaos and Hell are here (and now) conflated on political, religious and ethnic scales, with 'all these in their pregnant causes mixt/Confused'ly, and which thus must ever fight'. And they fight on individual, domestic and psychological scales as well. After the Fall, in their chaos of thought and passion all confused, Adam and Eve had 'in mutual accusation' spent (wasted) 'the fruitless hours': 'And of their vain contest appear'd no end' (IX, 1187–9). They can arduously achieve a new reconciliation, but the way back to the original harmony in Eden is forever barred by the Angel with the flaming sword. Likewise, 'chaotic systems are irreversible in a spectacular way'.[11] A new system may emerge, but the old one in its original form is irrevocably lost. Like Paradise.

Time's arrow

Various illustrations of the way in which seemingly trivial, insignificant, inconsequential or mundane events give rise to major personal or global consequences occur in sci-fi 'Back to the Future' and *Terminator* sagas as well as in historical might-have-beens. What, for example, if Cleopatra's nose had been an inch longer? And what might *not* have happened if the Viennese Academy of Art had sent a letter of acceptance, rather than twice rejecting, the eighteen-year-old Adolf Hitler, who had consequently taken over the chairmanship of an Austrian architectural firm . . . and so on.[12] As James Gleick observes, 'sensitive dependence on initial conditions' has long 'had a place in folklore' (*Chaos*, p. 23):

> For want of a nail, the shoe was lost;
> For want of a shoe, the horse was lost;
> For want of a horse, the rider was lost;
> For want of a rider, the battle was lost;
> For want of a battle, the kingdom was lost.

But although the inadvertent and unremembered dropping of Desdemona's handkerchief, through which Othello's paradise is lost, comes very close ('And when I love thee not,/Chaos is come again', III, iii, 92), there could be no better *literary* illustration of 'the butterfly effect' than the mundane circumstances, including the time of day and the appetizing fragrance of the fruit, that contribute to the compounding consequences of the Fall in *Paradise Lost*.

In the very end Adam and Eve (like us) confront a chaotic cosmos where ultimate order (eternal Providence) can be only dimly discerned, like the barely visible shape of a distant mountain. And understood only by analogy, as in modern chaos theory or in Milton's epic, where his God ordained the very freedom to disobey that Adam and Eve were warned not to manifest if they chose to inhabit an eternally stable earthly Paradise – or his Heaven of pure order.

Ever since the Fall, in art if not in life, the image of eternal stability invariably seems boring. We want chaos to ensue. Conversely, the unrelieved portrayal (or experience) of chaos creates the desire for order to assert itself. Thus the appeal of works dealing with chaotic and terrifying phenomena stems in large measure from our desire to see what happens *when* all hell breaks loose, as well as from our certain knowledge that the catastrophes involved are safely contained in the fiction. We also know which warnings given to the characters (such as Malcolm's warnings to Hammond and Raphael's warnings to Adam) had better be, but will not be heeded, so we can, simultaneously or sequentially, want them to be heeded, and thus avert disaster for the characters, and/or hope they will not be heeded, so we can witness the catastrophe. Thus, internally speaking, a combination of foreknowledge (determinism) and uncertainty within a work of art is far more engrossing and evocative of thrills and chills than pure predictability or surprise. 'Surprise,' said Alfred Hitchcock, 'is when you show a group of men playing poker in a cellar and a bomb suddenly goes off. Suspense is when you show the audience the bomb ticking away before you show the men sitting down to play poker.' 'There is no terror in a bang', he added, 'Only in the anticipation of it.'[13]

The combination of audience foreknowledge that things will go wrong – on Hammond's island as in Paradise – with the character's ignorance as to the subsequent course of events has been the prime source of dramatic irony from Greek times to the present. Indeed, deterministic chaos is the rule in art: however dire the events portrayed may be, there is on the part of the audience a clear recognition of overall, preordained order in the fictional genre: the thriller, the epic, the comedy, the tragedy or the film. And so, in contrast to the threatened characters in the fiction, Michael Crichton's readers and Steven Spielberg's audience can enjoy an absolutely safe safari expedition through the dangers of Jurassic Park.

For that matter, once the film version was in the can, Spielberg's *Jurassic Park* itself was safe from the disruptive tenets of chaos theory as expounded in Crichton's novel. Thus Crichton and Spielberg accomplished in art what John Hammond, portrayed as Spielberg's counterpart ('a combination of Walt Disney and Ross Perot') within the film could not – and triumphantly created an island inhabited by dinosaurs who behave exactly according to direction, and subsequently made a megafortune selling the re-created dinosaurs to a global audience;[14] even as a poet who was politically defeated, helplessly blind and crippled by arthritis in real life, could imperiously incorporate God, Satan, Adam, Eve – 'Heav'n, Hell, Earth, Chaos, All' – into his own epic design. Never was there a more sublimely egotistical poem, or a more self-referential film spectacular, both of which, however, refer us directly to the uncontrollable world outside their texts where chaos operates not just in theory, but in practice; and where the mundane and trivial, as well as the fearsome and destructive forces we cannot control, for which Milton's Satan and Crichton's velociraptors are appropriately mean and magnificent metaphors, are real:

'And the velociraptors –'
'Let's not start on the velociraptors,' Hammond said, 'I'm sick of hearing about the velociraptors. How they're the most vicious creatures anyone has ever seen.'

'They are.' Muldoon said, in a low voice. 'They should all be destroyed.'

'You wanted to fit them with radio collars,' Hammond said, 'And I agreed.'

'Yes. And they promptly chewed the collars off.' (p. 140)

Compare Satan's prompt escape from the confines of Hell in *Paradise Lost*.

So far as audiences are concerned, individual reactions to these works, including responses to Milton's Satan and Crichton's dinosaurs as visually re-created by Spielberg, may themselves be chaotic. Neither authors nor *auteurs* can, ultimately, control what effects their works may have. There are arguments that some children may be traumatized by seeing dinosaurs from which the parent-figures in the film cannot protect the children (Spielberg somewhere said he wouldn't want his under-eights to watch it). Others may love the dinosaurs. And, of course, Milton's readers of an epic he explicitly designed to 'justify the ways of God to men' (I, 26) have in turn taken the sides of God, Satan, Adam, and Eve, basing their arguments, pro and con, on the identical text. To give only the most famous examples: like other Romantic radicals, in his *Marriage of Heaven and Hell* and elsewhere William Blake identified Milton himself with Satan's titanic energies: 'The reason Milton wrote in fetters when he wrote of Angels & God, and at liberty when of Devils & Hell, is because he was a true Poet and of the Devil's party without knowing it.' By contrast, in his *A Preface to Paradise Lost*, C. S. Lewis saw Milton as an establishment figure, a spokesman for hierarchical order like God, while William Empson in turn saw Milton's God as the villain of the piece. But as Christopher Hill has argued, these counter-views may stem from the fact that, as a poet, Milton was at his best when he was most divided. And certainly, as Hill's book demonstrates, Milton's personal experience of a civil war may have profoundly influenced his attitudes towards both God and Satan, as well as towards 'Eternal Providence' – and Chaos:

The Fall of Man . . . was a historical event for Milton. But it also had symbolic significance, as an allegory of man's inability to live up to his own standards . . . metaphor as well as truth. The War in Heaven and the Fall of Man were not different in kind from the historical events recorded in Books XI and XII. Events which occur in time –

those revealed or related by Michael, classical legends, or modern English history – are examples of the archetypal happenings in heaven and hell before history began. England in 1659–60 re-enacted as macabre farce the tragedy of the Fall.[15]

For that matter, the first-hand experience of a failed political re-volution and/or a successful scientific revolution may be alike in so far as both upset previous, deterministic paradigms by calling atten-tion to the unpredictable, chaotic, ways of the world.

And so, as N. Katherine Hayles has persuasively argued, chaos theory confirms certain modern critical theories – most notably deconstruction[16] – even as it resurrects certain prestructuralist crit-ical dinosaurs such as time-and-text-transcending relevance. As the Nobel Laureate Ilya Prigogine and Isabelle Stengers observe, 'Our cultural environment plays an active role in the questions we ask, but beyond matters of style and social acceptance, we can identify a number of questions to which each generation returns.' Thus, al-though 'cultural context' cannot be denied, it cannot be 'the com-plete answer either'. For instance, Prigogine and Stengers find close analogies between the ways of the world envisaged in chaos theory and in the Talmud:

> We are living in a dangerous and uncertain world that inspires no blind confidence, but perhaps only the same feeling of qualified hope that some Talmudic texts appear to have attributed to the God of Genesis: 'Let's hope it works' (*Halway Sheyaamod*) exclaimed God as he created the World, and this hope, which has accompanied all the subsequent history of the world and mankind, has emphasized right from the outset that his history is branded with the mark of radical uncertainty.[17]

Chaos theory also allows a critical emphasis on similarities that transcend generic differences. Although *Paradise Lost* is a seventeenth-century 'classic' explicitly intended by its author for a 'fit audience, though few' (VII, 31), and *Jurassic Park* exemplifies late twentieth-century 'popular' entertainment designed for a mega-audience, chaos theory allows us to see significant similarities be-tween them. As Ian Stewart observes of chaos mathematics, 'A method devised to study chaos in turbulent flows works equally well on measles epidemics'; thus 'if you concentrate too closely on too limited an application of a mathematical idea, you rob the mathematician of his most important tools: analogy, generality, and simplicity' (see *Does God Play Dice?* p. 291). It could likewise be argued that an *exclusive* concentration on literature's cultural, ideological and historical roots and branches may rob the critic of comparably important tools – analogy, generality, simplicity – in surveying the multicultural, transhistorical, international, extra-curricular forests of art. For, however important the contextual and historical differences between *Jurassic Park* and *Paradise Lost* may be (that is an entirely different subject of inquiry and would afford obviously legitimate and illuminating perceptions of both texts), there is no point arguing that the differences must necessarily be so much *more* important than the similarities that the two works can-not – equally legitimately – be considered together.

And so, to my mind anyway, chaos theory in effect negates all past and present taboos against treating together, as structurally comparable (rather than historically or categorically non-comparable), ancient and modern and popular and canonical works of varying genres that show the same pattern and may, arguably, reflect the same extratextual reality. Or may raise com-parably overwhelming questions about what *kind* of reality lies outside their texts – such as the ultimate question raised, in turn, by Milton's cosmos ('Et sine fine Chaos & sine fine Deus') and by Michael Crichton's portrayal of chaos theory in action, as well as by 'real life' scientists. 'I am an old man now', said the physicist Horace Lamb at a meeting of the British Association for the Ad-vancement of Science back in 1932, 'and when I die and go to Heaven there are two matters on which I hope for enlightenment. One is quantum electrodynamics, and the other is the turbulent motion of fluids.' 'And about the former', Lamb added, 'I am really rather optimistic.' Because so many questions about turbulence re-main unresolved, and the bafflement about the second question is so ubiquitous, the same story has been associated with the quantum theorist Werner Heisenberg, who is alleged to have declared on his deathbed (in 1976) that he also would have two questions for God: 'Why relativity and why turbulence?' 'I really think He may have an answer to the first question'.[18]

Why, then, *is* there so much chaos, so much turbulence in *art* unless art reflects cognate mysteries in life? Milton's 'eternal Anarch' – Chaos personified as part of a deterministic order – and indeed his epic as a whole, with its combination of profound uncertainty and hope (*Halway Sheyaamod*!) about the positive, as well as negative, interactions between determinism and chaos, now have a new theoretical relevance as well as an enduring mythic resonance. In turn, even as it is currently being made accessible to vast audiences in *Jurassic Park* and other popular works, chaos theory has obvious literary and cultural as well as scientific relevance in so far as it challenges certain basic tenets underlying virtually all other theoretical paradigms. Certainly, in effect, it blows sky high the more extreme assumptions of cultural determinism, which tend to equate hugely important effects with hugely important causes, as well as the most extreme assumptions of cultural relativism. By contrast, chaos science insists that a minute change in one variable can generate an immense range of different results, and it also insists that various nonlinear systems have always behaved, and will always behave, in accordance with the laws of deterministic chaos. Snowflakes and fluids have behaved in the same deterministically chaotic and wildly turbulent ways since the first snowflake fell and the first water ran. Like weather systems worldwide, and from the beginning of time, dynamically comparable nonlinear systems share 'the remarkable property that even an infinite number of prior measurements cannot predict the outcome of the very next measurement'.[19] Syllogistic chains of causality ('for want of a nail') may be discernible only in retrospect, and sometimes humanly imperceptible even then.

As ubiquitously operative in nonlinear systems, 'the butterfly effect' obviously allows for individual differences that are not conceptually explicable in terms of cultural, ideological or historical determinisms. The complex interaction of butterfly effects that make one snowflake significantly different from all others in the same weather system make it impossible to predict its individual growth, development or movement, and the same holds true of individuals who differ from others in the same political system. The heart of this mystery has been most recently stressed, in historical terms, in Steven Spielberg's film, *Schindler's List*, just as it was in the original, factually based, novel by Thomas Keneally:

> At some point in any discussion about Schindler, the surviving friends of the Herr Direktor will blink and shake their heads and begin the almost mathematical business of finding the sum of his motives. For one of the most common sentiments of Schindler Jews is still, 'I don't know why he did it.' It can be said for a start that Oskar

was a gambler, was a sentimentalist who loved the transparency, the simplicity of doing good; that Oskar was by temperament an anarchist who loved to ridicule the system, and that beneath the hearty sensuality lay a capacity to be outraged by human savagery, to react to it and not be overwhelmed. But none of this, jotted down, added up, explains the doggedness with which, in the autumn of 1944, he prepared a final haven for the graduates of Emalia.[20]

There was no way to anticipate, and there is no way, whether through historical retrospect, or in terms of culture, gender, social class, religious background, or age-category (which were virtually identical) to explain why Oskar Schindler behaved towards Jewish people in a way opposite to the behaviour of Amon Goeth. As flies to wanton boys were his prisoners to Goeth, he killed them for his sport. Schindler did not hesitate to risk his life to rescue over a thousand of them.

As the case of Schindler serves to demonstrate, however powerful a political or ideological system may be, butterflies are free, and their effects, whether for good or ill, are comparably incommensurate. The disastrous potential of this phenomenon was demonstrated on a mythic scale in *Paradise Lost* as in Genesis: the whole world was catastrophically altered when Eve ate an apple. Conversely, the effect may be incommensurately positive. The Talmud concludes that 'he who saves a single life, saves the world entire' (*Schindler's List*, p. 399), and as a result of one man's inexplicably individual, death-defying efforts to save them, more Jewish people who owe their existence to Schindler are living throughout 'the world entire' than the whole Jewish population remaining in Poland. To come full circle back to a butterfly effect on an individual: 'Rightly or wrongly', the Jewish accountant, Itzak Stern always believed he had 'dropped the right stone in the well' when he quoted those crucial *words* from the Talmud to Schindler (pp. 52–3).

As opposed to more linear (historical and psychoanalytic as well as scientific) determinisms that tend to exclude them as anomalies outside the generally linear course of things, certain older determinisms incorporated chaos, incessant turbulence, sheer chance, in dynamic interactions cognate to modern chaos theory, and in ways obviously cognate to their operation in real life: 'Death . . ./Thou art slave to Fate, Chance, kings and desperate men', wrote John Donne, even as, in the domain of Milton's eternal Anarch, Chaos, the 'high Arbiter/*Chance* governs all' (II, 909–10). Both these observations proved true to the facts of life and death when Oskar Schindler played one desperately risky hand of cards, 'double or quits', with Amon Goeth for the custody of the otherwise doomed prisoner, Helen Hirsch. What determinism ruled the game? Schindler himself, Keneally concludes, 'did not seem to see . . . any parallel with God and Satan playing cards for human souls. He did not ask himself by what right he made a bid for the girl. If he lost, his chance of extracting her some other way was slim. But all chances were slim that year. Even his own.' The Deity was invoked only by Goeth: 'God in heaven!', 'I'm busted, I'm out!' he said when he drew the king that lost him the game and through which Schindler saved the girl (see *Schindler's List*, p. 303). In this case the king that death was a slave to was one randomly drawn from a deck of cards.

Chaos theory may itself provide a purely *literary*, or metaphorical, answer to the cosmic question 'why turbulence?' which may conclusively be answered only by the Deity. Perhaps God would find the contemplation of a world without the built-in challenge to His or Her order as unexciting as we would find *Paradise Lost* without Satan – or Jurassic Park if the dinosaurs had remained safely confined. And surely the Deity would not (any more than we would) wish to contemplate a concentration-camp world entire, without the possibility of an heroically anarchic Schindler. The huge importance of the greater works, and the sheer dramatic impact of the lesser ones alike depend on the fact that their overall order ordains disruption from chaotic forces of virtually equivalent power. Looked at from this wildly speculative angle, chaos theory could be said, in some measure to justify the ways of God to us artistically, if not experientially, even as it gives us an accurate, non-idealistic account of deterministic chaos as it ubiquitously operates in nature's nonlinear systems.

As Robert Markley has observed, 'the discourses of "order" before and during the Newtonian revolution', were the sites of unstable (and practically impossible) attempts both 'to describe accurately' and 'to idealize' the natural world:

> The notions of scientific 'order' advanced by Boyle, Newton, and their successors are at least in part the unstable products of the cultural, political, and theological discourses that impinge upon and

shape the two primary projects of seventeenth- and eighteenth-century natural philosophy: to observe, record, and classify phenomena and to celebrate this process as an approximation of a metaphysical revelation that justifies the works of God to man.[21]

By contrast, non-metaphysical theories of deterministic chaos allow for condemnation (see below, p. 96) alongside justification, or either, or neither or both. Interestingly, as the history of conflicting responses to it demonstrates, quite in spite of its stated intent, the same alternatives are open in *Paradise Lost*. Did he who made the Lamb make thee? asked Blake pro-and-con the force that made the Tyger; and the identical question could be answered pro-and-con the force that made Satan. Likewise, if Chaos is perceived as essentially malevolent and destructive, the same would hold true of the force that ordained it – hence the desire to dissociate God from Chaos both within, and in critical discussions of, the epic. If Chaos is seen as essentially creative and liberating, the source of all fertility and liberty as well as destruction, the determinism that ordained it could be justified in cognate terms: hence the desire to see one as an extension of the other, again both within, and in critical discussions of, the epic.

In science, deterministic chaos obviously cannot be interpreted in traditional moral terms unequivocally equating order with good, and chaos with evil: indeed it challenges them. In art, however, the components of deterministic chaos may be portrayed or perceived by the audience in moral terms as, for instance, a confrontation between a good (or evil) order/tyranny and a good (or evil) force for disorder/liberty. Or the moral coordinates themselves may be chaotically confused in the portrayal of either or both forces. Milton's God has aroused (I think justified) moral indignation, and his Satan has evoked moral support. In real life, the heroic Schindler had undeniable faults, and in *Paradise Lost* the undeniably malevolent Satan exhibits certain qualities traditionally associated with heroic virtue. It is interesting, and indeed theoretically crucial (is there a major literary exception to this rule?) that characters opposed to a deterministic order are generally attractive to audiences *whatever* vices may be associated with them, *in so far* as they are associated with freedom, with the right to challenge, to defy, to disobey orders. In spite of its structural containments, the artistic energies in literature generally ally themselves with the rebels. And so, almost invariably, does the audience.

It is equally interesting and, I believe, theoretically crucial, that in art and in very different theologies, as in history itself, the positive and negative forces of order and chaos incessantly interact in ways so strikingly cognate to the interactions chaos scientists observe in the dynamics of nature itself. Ian Stewart thus cites the primal interactions between Vishnu, the god of maintenance, and Shiva, the god of destruction, in Hindu mythology. In this case, the distinction is not 'between good and evil but represents, instead, two different ways in which divinity makes itself manifest: benevolence and wrath, harmony and discord'. 'In the same way', Stewart observes, scientists 'are beginning to view order and chaos as two distinct manifestations of an underlying determinism. And neither exists in isolation. The typical system can exist in a variety of stages, some ordered, some chaotic.' Thus, instead of two opposed polarities, there is a continuous spectrum: 'As harmony and discord combine in musical beauty, so order and chaos combine in mathematical beauty.'[22] Looked at from this angle, the range and variety, the continuous spectrum, of *interactions* between order and chaos, harmony and discord, on every conceivable scale, are what create the enduring power as well as the strangely musical, symphonic beauty of *Paradise Lost* as a whole.

Erasing chaos: critical and artistic reformations of *Paradise Lost*

In the fallen world displayed to Adam at the end of Milton's epic, the components of Heaven, Hell, Paradise and Chaos are inextricably confused and incessantly interactive on every scale within and without the human psyche. The severe Archangel Michael offers Adam and Milton's readers a distant prospect of the ultimate end of Satan and his perverted world, from which 'conflagrant mass' will arise 'New Heav'ns, new Earth, Ages of endless date/Founded in righteousness and peace and love' (XII, 545–50). But he envisages this prospect in only five lines of verse, and only after 1100 lines both prophetically and retrospectively giving Adam – and Milton's readers – a long, and unremittingly chaotic account of human history. The catalogue of catastrophic wars, diseases and disasters is mitigated only by the actions of righteous individuals such as Noah, whose virtue redeems the world entire

(XI, 817, 875). The constant message is that freedom entails awesome individual responsibilities, and that, in effect, 'the buck stops here'. The power of God may inspire great and small acts of human righteousness, but there is no suggestion that Divine Providence will ever actively intervene in earthly affairs to punish the wicked and reward the good. This sets the epic at odds with virtually all other seventeenth-century attempts to assert eternal Providence. Active intervention in earthly affairs was what the term 'Providence' generally meant.[23]

By contrast, Milton's archangel constantly insists that even the most virtuous men and women will experience the manifold ills that flesh is heir to – disappointment, bereavement, disease, injustice – in a world plagued by incessant tribal wars and familial conflicts. 'So shall the world go on,/To good malignant, to bad men benign,/Under her own weight groaning' until the Lord descends in the clouds to dissolve it (XII, 537–9). Confronted with the suffering of his progeny, Adam looks forward to the end of 'this transient World, the Race of time', but envisions nothing of the bliss beyond it: 'beyond is all abyss,/Eternity, whose end no eye can reach' (XII, 555–6). Hope abides in God's providence active through individual human efforts: 'with good/Still overcoming evil, and by small/Accomplishing great things, by things deem'd weak/Subverting worldly strong' (XII, 565–8). Adam's ultimate recognition is that 'suffering for Truth's sake/Is fortitude to highest victory/And to the faithful death the gate of life' (XII, 569–71). There is no material, earthly reward for good behaviour.

Since the most currently fashionable theological arguments of the time asserted that a sure and certain Providential order actually intervened, in practical and material ways, to reward the virtuous and punish the wicked in *this* world, as well as in the afterlife, the younger playwright Nathaniel Lee concluded that Milton 'but roughly drew, on an old-fashion'd ground/A Chaos'. 'For no perfect World was found' until John Dryden wrote a revisionary adaptation that reformed the chaotic original and with 'softest language, sweetest manners taught'.[24]

From the very outset, the chaotic components of *Paradise Lost* inspired artistic and critical attempts to erase them – to smooth out, rationalize, marginalize, and excise its irregularities – even as it immediately gave rise to popular as well as highbrow appropriations. In his poem prefacing *Paradise Lost* Andrew Marvell prophesied that, given a work 'so infinite', 'some less skillful hand' (for example, Dryden's) which 'by ill imitating would excel/Might hence presume the whole Creation's day/To change in Scenes and show it in a Play.' But Milton himself did not object to a dramatic adaptation by Dryden. For that matter, as Marvell's poem suggests, if Dryden had not attempted an adaptation/modernization/popularization of the epic, some other, possibly even 'less skillful hand' was almost inevitably bound to. Indeed, as we shall see with reference to *The Tempest*, its inspiration of successive imitations of very different kinds may be the sure and certain signature mark of a perfect literary 'fractal' (a complex nonlinear structure). It will simultaneously and continuously give rise to critical attempts to regularize it, and artistic attempts to mimic it, just as Dryden both mimics and regularizes *Paradise Lost* in his 'Opera', *The State of Innocence and the Fall of Man*. Witness the difference between the stern archangel Michael's bleak and interminably turbulent panorama of human history and the consolatory lines of Dryden's gentle archangel Raphael, who emphasizes the 'pleasure' awaiting Adam's offspring in a happy afterlife. 'Now see your race revive', proclaims Dryden's angelic cheerleader:

> How happy they in deathless pleasure live.
> For more than I can show or you can see
> Shall crown the blest with immortality. (p. 461)

Like Dryden's Adam and Eve, we may *all* live happily ever after! The assurance with which orthodox religious certainty is expressed here explains why a later commentator, having answered the question 'Was Milton a Christian?' in the negative, concluded that Dryden's poem was the more profoundly moral: 'Justly did Dryden reject and ignore aught of Milton's writing save the literary quality of his poem' (p. 409).

But although the vocabulary in certain passages is virtually identical, the literary 'quality' of Dryden's poetry could not differ more from Milton's. Nobody could conceivably assert that Milton 'with softest language, sweetest manners taught'. And his account of postlapsarian turbulence, confusion, heroism and suffering could not be more elegantly muted than it is in the soothing cadences of Raphael's concluding couplets. The weather may be bad, but so what? The state of mind is serene:

The rising winds urge the tempestious Ayr;
And on their wing, deformed Winter bear;
The beasts already feel the change; and hence,
They fly, to deeper coverts for defence;
The feebler herd, before the stronger run
For now the way of nature is begun;
But part you hence in peace, and having mourn'd your sin
For outward *Eden* lost, find *Paradise* within. (p. 462)

The State of Innocence and Fall of Man has charms of its own, although they now seem obviously antiquarian charms. By contrast, no one would describe *Paradise Lost* as possessing antiquarian *charms*. The *à la mode* smoothing out and softening up of Milton's chaotic epic that Nathaniel Lee thought its paramount virtues now make Dryden's adaptation seem far more, not less, 'old-fashioned' than the original. This too is characteristic of a complex classic: an updated, thoroughly modern (ideologically or stylistically *à la mode*) adaptation of it will in time seem a far more conventional product of its age, and will sooner go out of date with the emergence of new vogues, and new adaptations of the original.

Another mark of a classic, however, is precisely that it inspires popular, trendy and often amusing imitations, as well as highbrow variations that are likewise enjoyable in their own time, in their own right, and on their own terms. And it is a great pity that Dryden's 'Opera' was never performed because it would have made a glorious musical spectacular. Its opening scene reveals 'a *Chaos*, or a confus'd Mass of Matter'. 'The Stage is almost wholly dark. A Symphony of Warlike Music is heard for some time, then from the Heavens fall the rebellious Angels' (p. 425). Not surprisingly, a hugely popular puppet show, in turn based on Dryden's adaptation, drew crowds to Punch's Theatre in Covent Garden. For who could have resisted the Jurassic Park style advertisements hyping the 'variety of surprizing Scenes and machines', particularly the 'Scene of Paradise with its primitive Station, with Birds, Beasts and all its ancient inhabitants'? No money, the advertisement added, would be returned after the curtain went up. By comparison, however, except for its own special effects, the puppet show based on Dryden's script could not but seem a facile, albeit entertaining, imitation of the already simplified version of the complex original from which Dryden by his own admission had lifted the 'entire Foundation, part of the Design, and many of the ornaments' (p. 409).

Comparative complexities

As well as illuminating comparabilities between canonical and popular and premodern and postmodern works, chaos theory provides us with a very useful way to distinguish between works with virtually identical outlines or character types but differing scales of complexity. According to Benoit Mandelbrot, the fractal geometry of nature exhibits detailed structure over every conceivable scale. Likewise an ideal mathematical fractal has structure on an infinite range of scales (for further discussion see below, pp. 79–81). Again according to Mandelbrot, the most satisfying works of art contain their most important elements on all scales at once. This could serve as a perfect description of the complex structure of *Paradise Lost*.

In chaos science 'complex systems' are also conceptualized as comparably rich in *informational* content on every scale. Again, it is hard to think of a more accurate description of complexity in literature generally. The qualitative difference between, say, Milton's masterpiece and an operetta or a puppet show, or 'Space Seed', a *Star Trek* episode similarly based on it, resides in their greater and lesser developments of informational content and complexity of detail on every scale, while their general outline or specific character types may be obviously and enjoyably comparable. This gradation also holds true of more or less complex popular works. In its informational content – especially its simplified accounts of modern scientific theories – as well as in its comparatively bland portrayal of John Hammond, the film version of *Jurassic Park* is markedly less complex than Michael Crichton's original novel. What gives the novel its force is the mythic fable operative in combination with state-of-the-art scientific information. What gives the film its bite is its state-of-the-art visual effects. So lovingly detailed, visually graphic and individualized were Spielberg's dinosaurs that leaving the London première, the well-known broadcaster Gloria Hunniford told an interviewer that the special effects were so good she could not tell which ones were animatronic, and which ones 'were real dinosaurs'. But in contrast to the novel, the film simplifies the scientific information about DNA and chaos theory, even as it divests the fable and the characters of their mythic resonance.

The novel originally portrayed John Hammond as a megalomaniac in some ways comparable to Milton's God and otherwise comparable to various mythic figures who aspire to be as gods, such as Baron Frankenstein and Dr Moreau. Moreover, rather like Marlowe's Lucifer, Crichton's billionaire offers Faustian contracts, in the form of immense stipends as well as forbidden knowledge, to the scientists he employs on Isla Nublar, the Costa Rican island he bought for his Edenic theme park. None of these primal frames of reference is attached to the cuddly Santa Claus figure of John Hammond portrayed in the film by Richard Attenborough as a genial, wide-eyed innocent, who knows not what he has wrought. The same softening-up process that takes the symbolic components away from Hammond smooths the realistic edge off Hammond's granddaughter, Lex. In the film, she is a stereotypically adorable child of Hollywood far removed from Crichton's continually complaining (and arguably refreshingly recognizable) brat: 'This is boring', 'But I'm hungry', she whines. In the novel, the palaeontologist protagonist, Grant, is never romantically involved with his bright and pretty research colleague, Dr Ellie Sattler. His real passion is for his scientific work in Montana, and he sells his services to Hammond (thus making a Faustian bargain) in order to subsidize it. Nor is he initially hostile to children but enamoured of them by the end. In the film, family values triumph as Grant starts out reluctant to have anything to do with Hammond's grandchildren, but learns to be a father by taking care of them. By the same token, Ellie Sattler, who shows no special inclination for motherhood in the novel, stereotypically longs to bear Grant's children in the film. And as they fly away together in the final feelgood cut, we presume that Spielberg's Grant will at last find his own true paradise with Ellie and their future family.

Given the ferocity of the dinosaurs, it could be that Spielberg's film would not have been granted an Unrestricted Certificate allowing young children to see it if the source had *not* been altered in these comforting and reassuring ways. But the changes were most obviously designed to allow for a sequel, since the film does not show the destruction of the island, and John Hammond survives to return to it with Grant and Ellie and *their* children, should his directorial counterpart, Steven Spielberg, decide to film *Jurassic Park II*. According to *The Independent Magazine* (26 February 1994, p. 45) Richard Attenborough insisted to Spielberg that his character should be devoured by dinosaurs, as he was in the book: 'I was really looking forward to a marvellous death scene.' He was persuaded otherwise by the retort: 'Do you want a marvellous death scene or a marvellous sequel?'

In a further departure from the novel's primal outline, there is no comparably ominous suggestion in the film that the most vicious of Hammond's creations, the migratory velociraptors (very like Milton's devils), have irrevocably escaped from their confines to 'raise hell' on the mainland, as they clearly have in Crichton's novel (pp. 132, 399). Nor is there a hint of the ultimate isolation and exile that awaits Grant in the final chapter, when he is informed that he will never be allowed to return to Montana. His way back to that professional paradise is effectively barred by the Costa Rican authorities who are the novel's official equivalents to Milton's angel with the flaming sword. To get Hammond's money for his research, Grant in effect tasted the fruit of forbidden knowledge and inevitably has to pay the ordained price. Both the novel and the film have cardboard characters and stereotypical endings, but the novel's primally resonant conclusion is more ironic, more chaotic, more complex, than the film's ending which contains chaos in domesticity and romance.

If Crichton's novel is, in its informational detail, comparatively richer than the film spectacular (the movie's success is in its visual detail), *Paradise Lost* is *infinitely* richer than Crichton's bestseller. But even as a fabulously successful film was immediately derived from Crichton's novel, a veritable host of popular as well as canonical fictions have been based on the themes and character types in *Paradise Lost* which simultaneously, on its own terms and in its own right, has over centuries continued to communicate its incomparably complex informational content to successive generations. Like Milton's epic, the most enduringly influential plays, novels and films (frame by frame, scene by scene, character by character) are themselves invariably more complex than their successive imitations and, therefore, can more than hold their own against all their heirs-apparent. Thus, by virtue of their continuing immediate impact *as well as* their continuing influence, they are of extrahistorical artistic importance as well as of obvious historical interest. This is one obvious reason why they should remain in the curricular canon, even as their continuing influence remains directly, as well as indirectly operative in the extracurricular artistic canon.

But before discussing successive works and comparatively linear critical interpretations based on *Paradise Lost*, its nonlinear complexity on every conceivable level (language, characterization, structure and so on) can be at least perfunctorily demonstrated with specific reference to the interactive temporal scales *simultaneously* encompassing a day in Eden, the history of the world and the history of the cosmos. The epic's flashbacks, rewinds, and fast-forwards crossing the millennia from the beginning to the end of time operate in much the same way the mind sweeps back and forth across a whole lifetime that seems, in retrospect, like a single day; just as it does in chaos theory.

In *Jurassic Park*, Ian Malcolm observes that the fractal sameness of a graph of cotton prices charted for a day, a week, a year, corresponds to the sameness of outline traceable in an individual life:

> 'The graph of price fluctuations in the course of a day looks basically like the graph for a week, which looks basically like the graph for a year, or for ten years. And that's how things are. A day is like a whole life. You start out doing one thing, but end up doing something else, plan to run an errand, but never get there . . . At the end of your life, your whole existence has that same haphazard quality, too. Your whole life has the same shape as a single day.' (p. 171)

Psychologically speaking, looked at backwards and forwards in life, as in *Paradise Lost* and other works of art, this clearly corresponds to the way people and fictional characters alike view things, especially as they get closer and closer to the end of the day. For instance: 'In me thou seest the twilight of such day/As after sunset fadeth in the west' wrote Shakespeare in Sonnet 73. 'Unarm Eros, the long day's task is done,/And we must sleep', says Antony. 'Finish, good lady,' says Charmian to Cleopatra, 'the bright day is done,/And we are for the dark' (*Antony and Cleopatra*, IV, XV, 15–16; V, ii, 192–3). To bring us right up to date, the structural correspondence between the shape of a day and the shape of a lifetime as described by Michael Crichton's chaos theorist, neatly corresponds to the structure of events in Harold Ramis's recent film, *Groundhog Day*, where (in the aftermath of an unpredicted blizzard) the smug weatherman anti-hero has to learn to live out a whole lifetime – to mature, earn love and reconcile himself to the world – in a single day.

And in the far more complex context of Milton's primal epic, so do Adam and Eve. In Milton's account of the day of the Fall, our first parents begin in morning (childhood) innocence, taste the Fruit at high noon, experience guilt and shame in the afternoon/aftermath, and then face judgment in the evening before they can be offered the promise of redemption/resurrection on the following morning. The Miltonic portrayal of a day in the life of Adam and Eve replicates the cosmic graph covering world history from the creation to the last judgment, as well as cosmic history from the fall of Satan that took place before the beginning of time, to the establishment of a New Heaven and Earth and the closing off of Hell that will take place only at the end of time. And astonishingly, this highly complex macrostructure is replicated, on a microscale, in the first ten *lines* of the poem tracing the all-inclusive action from Adam's Fall to 'our' time of reading,

> Of Man's First Disobedience, and the Fruit
> Of that Forbidden Tree, whose mortal taste
> Brought Death into the World and all our woe,
> With loss of *Eden*, till one greater Man
> Restore us, and regain the blissful Seat,
> Sing Heav'nly Muse, that on the secret top
> Of *Oreb*, or of *Sinai* didst inspire
> That Shepherd, who first taught the chosen Seed,
> In the Beginning how the Heav'ns and Earth
> Rose out of *Chaos* . . . (I, 1–10)

As has long been noted, in the first three lines *alone*, every noun (Fruit/Tree/Death/woe), every adjective-and-noun combination ('First Disobedience' 'mortal taste'), every alliterative word ('First', 'Fruit', 'Forbidden'), and every possessive-and-noun combination ('our woe') could in turn be the subject of a critical essay if not a whole book describing it as *the* major concern of the epic as a whole. Likewise, the final words of the first three lines – 'Fruit', 'taste', 'woe' – enact, in miniature, the action covering millennia from the time of 'our' first parents to the time of 'our' reading of *Paradise Lost*, whenever that may be.

Since, here as elsewhere, everything in the poem interacts with everything else on psychological, mythic, verbal, structural, emotional, and intellectual scales alike, one can *simultaneously* (or in turn) read *Paradise Lost* as a poem about the whys and wherefores of 'Man's *first* disobedience', and/or about the historical and psychic consequences – the metaphorical and literal 'Fruit' – of that disobedience. And so on. For instance, like Frank Kermode, we can read it as a poem about 'all our woe', about what we 'feel we might, but know we cannot have' (delight to reason joined, immortality) as a consequence of that 'mortal' (human, lethal) taste that introduced Death and Chaos alike into our physical and psychic systems:

> Milton gives Death allegorical substance, if 'substance might be calld that shaddow seemd' . . . The only thing it resembles is Chaos . . . and it stands in relation to the order and delight of the human body as Chaos stands to Nature. So, when Satan moved out of Chaos into Nature, he not only 'into Nature brought/Miserie'(VI, 267), but into Life brought Death and into Light (which is always associated with order and organic growth) darkness.[25]

One could, without distortion, extend Kermode's arguments in terms of scientific theory generally, and say that Milton's formless forms – Death and Chaos – are perfect allegorical representations of entropy: dissolution, disorder – the second law of thermodynamics personified.

Even as Milton's poem develops individually complex themes and conflicts, it simultaneously establishes what chaos theorists term nonlinear replications, iterations, self-similarities – that is, regular irregularities, structural correspondences (symmetries) and (asymmetrical) contrasts – between characters and actions. We are invited to compare/contrast, for instance, the fall of Satan and the falls of Adam and Eve. There are similar correspondences/contrasts between the consult in Hell and the consult in Heaven; and between the Trinity in Heaven and the unholy Trinity in Hell. Between Chaos and his consort, Night, Satan, his consort Sin, and his son, Death, and Adam and his consort Eve and their son, the first murderer Cain; and between Satan's seduction of Sin and his seduction of Eve; between the way the Fallen Angels respond to their loss and the way Adam and Eve respond to theirs; and between the war in Heaven and the English civil war – and so on *ad infinitum*.

Thus what the poet will sing 'of' to successive readers depends in large measure on the individual reader's choice, even as personal readings themselves may be chaotic and change over time. Indeed, chaotic readings of *Paradise Lost* inevitably seem more richly satisfying than linear ones, since they more accurately reflect the complexity of the poem. Historically as well as psychologically speaking, dialectically opposite readings (similarly supported by direct quotations from the text) may in time turn out to be complementary as well as contradictory. As Catherine Belsey has observed, *Paradise Lost* can simultaneously be read from both poststructuralist and humanist perspectives (since it is so obviously about the ultimate glory as well as the price and burden of human freedom). Other here-conflicting, there-complementary ancient-and-modern readings can be mythic (Jungian), or psychoanalytic (Freudian), or male-supremacist (see C. S. Lewis) or feminist (Froula) or historically radical (see Christopher Hill) and radically anti-God (Empson), as well as Christian. And so, with the parodist Robert Manson Meyers, you could say that Milton's 'poetic illusions are sacred when they are not profane', or, alternatively, conclude that the poem may be most sacred when it is *most* profane.[26]

Throughout the epic, places (Paradise, Hell, Heaven and Chaos) and characters simultaneously embody states of mind: 'Myself am hell' – *l'État c'est moi'* – proclaims Satan. Before the Fall, Adam and Eve are emotionally and erotically 'Imparadis't in one another's arms/The happier *Eden*' (IV, 506–7). By comparison/contrast, in the end, the fallen Adam and Eve are offered the hope that with arduous effort, they may achieve a spiritual 'Paradise within' that could prove 'happier far' than the unearned Paradise they lost (XII, 587). Eve sums up the compound spiritual, physical, and emotional associations accumulated around the single term, 'Paradise', when on leaving Eden, she tells Adam, 'With thee to go,/Is to stay here' (XII, 615–17). 'So spake our Mother *Eve*', but Adam has no time to respond, 'for now too nigh/Th'Arch-Angel stood' and:

> In either hand the hast'ning Angel caught
> Our ling'ring Parents, and to th'Eastern Gate
> Led them direct, and down the Cliff as fast
> To the subjected Plain; then disappear'd.
> They looking back, all th'Eastern side beheld
> Of Paradise, so late thir happy seat,
> Wav'd over by that flaming Brand, the Gate
> With dreadful Faces throng'd and fiery Arms:
> Some natural tears they dropp'd, but wip'd them soon;
> The World was all before them, where to choose
> Thir place of rest, and Providence thir guide:
> They hand in hand with wand'ring steps and slow,
> Through *Eden* took thir solitary way. (XII, 637–49)

Milton's very fast, then very slow, concluding lines reiterate the entire epic action – Paradise was quickly lost, but can only very slowly be regained. And since they have the impact of the whole structure behind them, the last lines are, if possible, even more complex and structurally resonant than the opening lines (this is why they have elicited more attempts to regularize them). The last words of the last four lines (choose/guide/slow/way) encapsulate the difficulties facing the fallen Adam and Eve and their successors. They (we) can only slowly and arduously proceed forward. A nostalgic glance back at a Paradise without sin, death and chaos is all that Adam and Eve – like Milton's readers – are allowed. And, of course, any tears they/we shed on looking back are now described as 'natural'.

In terms of physical scale, the same figures who stood so tall (godlike erect) in Paradise now seem infinitesimally small in contrast to the immensity of the world before them. Like their descendants, they will now need to rest after long labour and their 'place of rest' has overtones of death, of a last resting place at the end of a life as well as the end of a day. Wandering in the wilderness of the world, they will no longer have direct access to God; only a distant, vaguely discernible, Providential order remains as their guide. And, of course, the last angel they see is the one with fiery sword. They now walk 'hand in hand' as if necessarily, for mutual support in their individual and cosmic solitude, and their 'wand'ring steps and slow' reflect the uncertainty of their/our way ahead and the slowness of their/our progress forwards. From one decision – to eat or not to eat the fruit – Adam and Eve and their progeny face infinite degrees of choices ('The World was all before them') as well as the most limited and mundane of all – 'where to choose their place of rest'.

'Choose/guide/slow/way': our bifurcating personal and historical choices ever since entail the virtually infinite degrees of freedom to choose as projected on a large scale in the unremittingly turbulent history of mankind described without undue simplification or palliation by the Archangel Michael. This is why Milton's ending has inspired so many efforts to straighten it out in a more positively linear (moralistic, theological or ideological) way. Contrast for instance, the poignant way Milton's Adam and Eve look back at what was 'so late their happy seat' with the resolutely forward-looking way Dryden's Adam says goodbye to Paradise:

> Then farewell all; I will indulgent be
> Of mine own ease, and not look back to see.
> When what we love we ne'er must meet again
> To lose the thought, is to remove the pain. (p. 461)

It should, however, be noted to his credit that in the best lines from *The State of Innocence*, Dryden came close to replicating Milton's true-to-the-real-world informational content as well as Milton's transtemporal frames of reference, when his Eve protests against a wife's postlapsarian (seventeenth-century) as well as prelapsarian lot:

> Better with Brutes my humble lot had gone;
> Of reason void, accountable for none.
> Th'unhappiest of creation is a wife,
> Made lowest, in the highest rank of life:
> Her fellow's slave; to know and not to choose;
> Curst with that reason she must never use. (p. 437)

If Dryden erases Adam's pain in the ending, he does not erase Eve's pain here.

Successive artistic, ideological, theological and critical efforts to excise the pain from *Paradise Lost* seem to reflect an enduring and passionate desire, indeed a determination amounting to a need, to impose a linear ideological and moralistic order on the chaotic components of *Paradise Lost* – which is rather like trying to put a theoretical or historical lid on a still-active volcano. Heading the list of critical efforts to control the chaotic components of Milton's ending has to be the emendation proposed by his eighteenth-century editor, Edward Bentley: 'Why', lamented the linear-minded Bentley, does Milton 'dismiss our first parents in anguish and the reader in melancholy?':

> And how can the expression be justified, *with wandring steps and slow*? Why *wandring*? Erratick steps? Very improper, when, in the line before, they were *guided by Providence*. And why *slow*? even when Eve has professed her readiness and alacrity for the journey . . . And why their *solitarie way*? All words to represent a sorrowful parting? when even their former walks in Paradise were as solitary as their way now; there being nobody besides them two both here and there. Shall I therefore, after so many prior presumptions, presume to offer a distich, as close as may be to the author's words, and *entirely agreeable to his scheme*?

> Then hand in hand with *social* steps their way
> Through Eden took, *with heavenly comfort cheer'd.*[27]

Bentley's revision of Milton's lines is far more risibly feeble than Dryden's, although Bentley explicitly set out not just syllogistically and logically to improve the chaotic original but to reinforce 'the author's' actual 'scheme'.

Perhaps the most determinedly revisionist adaptation of *Paradise Lost* occurred in the twentieth century, when C. S. Lewis wrote a science-fiction version, *Perelandra: A voyage to Venus*, wherein the 'Lady' (Lewis's Eve) thinks first of her 'Lord' (the Adam-figure) as Lewis so devoutly believed her prototype ought to have done. She thus refuses to succumb to the Satan-figure's temptation, the sexual hierarchy is triumphantly maintained, and all Heaven rejoices when the Fall does not take place, an all-time happy ending which, to my mind, comes as the all-time let-down compared to Milton's. But love them or loathe them, it is as if successive artistic and critical efforts to control Milton's chaotic effects represent a profound need to do so. Likewise, artistic and critical and efforts to disrupt order, celebrate transgression and release chaotic forces in art seem to represent a comparably profound and continuing need.

Obviously, individual reader-responses, artistic-responses and critical-responses to a complex work are themselves sensitively dependent on a whole range of initial conditions: historical, psychological, economic, ideological, generational, gender-based, class-based, professionally-based and purely personal. So a work such as *Paradise Lost* may have an enormous historical and literary influence that has nothing whatsoever to do with its own historical or ideological context or with its author's stated intent (say, to assert eternal Providence and justify the ways of God to men). By far the most obvious example of a work's incontrollable impact is *surely* the admiration and sympathy extended to Milton's Satan by Milton's Romantic imitators. Byron's rebellious Cain and Shelley's Prometheus were inspired by him. So was Blake's 'The Tyger' as well as his *Milton*. And whatever their differences in intent, it could be that Blake and Milton would answer 'yes' to the self-reflexive question Blake raised about the Creator of the original Tyger/Satan, 'And did he smile his work to see?'. Having derived so many of his poetic allusions from pagan sources, Milton might well have been pleased that his epic inspired quite different, albeit comparably sacred and profane, analogies.

For that matter, the paradox of a 'fortunate fall' resulting in a 'Paradise within' that may be far more difficult to achieve but ultimately more satisfying than the one offered without effort, has been replicated by various canonical authors as well as in several episodes of *Star Trek* (most notably 'The Apple') portraying the replacement of a rigid but secure order based on obedience with a freer, but more arduous existence, even as, in its evocation of interplanetary travel and alternative worlds, Milton's epic has obvious sci-fi aspects of its own. In fact, it could be argued that *Paradise Lost* may be *the* most historically influential of all science-fiction fantasies. In 'The Apple', for instance, the humanoid inhabitants of a computer-ordered planet do not grow old and die. They obediently worship the force that assures their security until the arrival of Captain Kirk (who compares himself to Satan) and Spock (who with his traditionally pointed ears resembles him) who destroy the controlling system, leaving the planet's inhabitants to make their own way in a world where they will bear children, and also bear the burden of freedom, and may in time achieve a paradise happier far. In the 'Space Seed' episode, Captain Kirk's arch-enemy, Khan who is forced into exile on a cosmic Devil's Island, explicitly echoes his Miltonic (non-Biblical) prototype when he insists that it is 'Better to reign in Hell than serve in Heaven'. Likewise, the rebellious Jedi knight, Darth Vader, is obviously comparable to the Miltonic archangel who started – and, for all we know, may yet win – the most crucial of all 'Star Wars'. To come full circle, in the original film version of *King Kong*, a major cinematic precedent for Spielberg's *Jurassic Park*, the hauntingly memorable, 'realistically unreal', 'dawn-of-creation' effects – the 'lighting, the jungle, the foliage' – were copied directly from Gustave Doré's engraved illustrations of Milton's Eden (see Figs 1 and 2). According to the director, Merion C. Cooper:

> The lighting, the jungle, the foliage we stole direct from Doré. But we had great difficulty getting a sense of depth on the miniature jungle. Between the two of us we devised what we called 'ariel perspective', whereby the jungle sets were built on three large tables. On those tables were a series of plate-glass panes on which [were] painted sections of the jungle and skies, all copied directly from Doré's steel engravings for *Paradise Lost*.[28]

Figure 1 *Gustave Doré's engraving of Milton's Satan surveying Paradise.*

Figure 2 *Doré's skyline and foliage as copied in* King Kong.

As subsequent works of all kinds based on it serve to demonstrate, the poem's resonating images, characters and meanings allow for a cascade of bifurcating artistic appropriations and interpretations. Again, the signature of a complex nonlinear work such as *Paradise Lost* could well be that it will inevitably prove useful to other artists, as an inexhaustible source of inspiration, since entirely different facets of its structure, imagery and characterization can be foregrounded in differing contexts.

For instance, 'the mists were rising' when Adam and Eve left Eden, and Miltonic mists likewise paradoxically rise to lend irony and impact to the scene in *Great Expectations* when Pip sets forth to London with the (fallen) world all before him, and simultaneously leaves primal innocence (Joe and Biddy) behind him. The historical impact of Miltonic imagery is so ubiquitous that far-fetched and purely fantastical comparabilities between *Paradise Lost* and subsequent texts may establish themselves in the minds of a reader familiar with both. To give a personal example, Jonathan Swift's unforgettably satirical image of our first parents in *Gulliver's Travels* – the two Yahoos first glimpsed on a mountain in Houyhnhnmland – has always suggested to me that Adam and Eve migrated there directly from Milton's Paradise (as well as Genesis), even as Crichton's velociraptors migrated from Jurassic Park, to infest the world with their congenitally vicious and violent offspring. Swift himself, of course, counters this primally mythic and essentialist interpretation of their point of origin with the new historicist suggestion that the first Yahoos sighted there may have migrated to Houyhnhnmland specifically from England.[29] But the primal reading holds a measure of validity, in so far as we Yahoos by now inhabit, and as often as not have fouled-up, virtually every place on earth. The critical point of this parodic example is that when released from (as well as within) their differing artistic and historical confines, characters, images, and so on, can migrate, mate, and mutate in the minds of individual readers, as well as in successive works of art, in entirely different and unpredictable ways cognate to the dynamics of deterministic chaos and postmodernism alike. In our minds, as in everyday life, we are all postmodernists, experiencing and fusing popular and classical and ancient and modern works in wildly eclectic and chaotic combinations.

But these, and more specific points about chaotic interactions, iterations, recursions and self-similarities, as they occur within a complex work of art itself, as well as in successive canonical and popular replications, appropriations and adaptations of a complex classic, can best be illustrated with reference to *The Tempest* and its 'fractal forgeries'.

Notes

1. See *Paradise Lost* in *John Milton: Complete poems and major prose*, ed. Merrit Y. Hughes, II, 890–1009, and Hughes' Introduction, pp. xxiii–xxv. Subsequent line references to this edition are cited parenthetically in the text. For representative critical discussions of Chaos as a governing principle in the epic, see Isabelle McCaffery, *Paradise Lost as 'Myth'*, Harvard University Press, Cambridge, Massachusetts, 1959; Harry Blamires, *Milton's Creation: A guide through 'Paradise Lost'*, Methuen, London, 1971; R. M. Adams, 'A little look into chaos', in *Illustrative Evidence*, ed. Earl Miner, University of California Press, Berkeley, 1975, p. 71–89; Regina Schwartz, 'Milton's hostile chaos', *English Literary History* 52 (1985), 339–69; and John Rumrich, *Matter of Glory*, Pittsburgh University Press, Pittsburgh, 1987 (see especially chapters 3 and 4), and 'Uninventing Milton', *Modern Philology* 87 (February 1990), 249–65. I am indebted to Professor Rumrich for letting me read, prior to publication, the typescript of his important article on 'Milton criticism and the matter of chaos'.
2. See *The Dunciad* ll. 654–6, and *The Essay on Man*, Epistle II, l. 13, in *Pope: Poetical works*, ed. Herbert Davis, Oxford University Press, Oxford, 1966, pp. 251, 584. Blake also followed Milton ('Milton fell thro Albions heart, travelling outside of Humanity beyond the Stars in Chaos') in his depiction of Chaos in various works. For detailed discussion see Christine Gallant, *Blake and the Assimilation of Chaos*, Princeton University Press, Princeton, NJ, 1973.
3. See Ian Stewart, *Does God Play Dice? The new mathematics of chaos*, Penguin, Harmondsworth, 1990, p. 303, cited parenthetically in the text as *Does God Play Dice?*
4. See Michael Crichton, *Jurassic Park*, Arrow, London, 1991, p. 305. Subsequent page references are inserted parenthetically in the text.
5. See James Gleick, *Chaos: Making a new science*, Cardinal, London, 1991 (first published in Great Britain by Heinemann, 1988), p. 267; cited hereafter as *Chaos*, with page references parenthetically inserted in the text. As Michael Crichton acknowledges (see *Jurassic Park*, p. 401) Gleick's history of chaos theory was a source for his best seller. Compare also the sudden transition from order to chaos in Crichton's film, *Westworld*.

6. See *S. B.*, M.D. IN *PARADISUM AMISSAM* SUMMI POETAE JOHANNIS MILTONI, in *Paradise Lost*, ed. Hughes (n. 1, above), p. 3.

7. See the discussions by John Rumrich (n. 1, above), and by John Briggs and James Peat in *Turbulent Mirror: An illustrated guide to chaos theory*, Harper & Row, New York, 1989, p. 20:

> Perhaps God's struggle with chaos is really an internal one, since the Biblical creator *himself* is chaos as much as he is order. God is the whirlwind, the fiery destruction, the bringer of plagues and floods. Many cultures have shared this vision. The shape that emerges out of the borderland is Dionysos, the god of random frenzy that underlies the routines of culture; it is the Indian creator god Shiva, who lives in horrible places such as battlefields and crossroads; it is the monsters of sin and death.

8. As it were to suggest their underlying intertextual reality, Milton 'integrated the alien codes of Hebraic, Christian and classical mythology' – see Philip Kuberski, *Chaosmos: Literature, science and theory*, State University of New York Press, Albany, NY, 1994, p. 180. And as an account of a reality beyond all texts, in *The Worst Journey in the World: Antarctica 1910–1913*, Chatto & Windus, London, 1951, p. 79, Apsley Cherry-Gerrard quotes blind Milton who wrote, as if prophetically, an exact geographical and geological description of Antarctica before any human being on earth had ever set foot on it:

> Beyond this flood a frozen Continent
> Lies dark and wild, beat with perpetual storms
> Of Whirlwind and dire Hail, which on firm land
> Thaws not, but gathers heap, and ruin seems
> Of ancient pile; all else deep snow and ice. (II, 587–91)

9. See Briggs and Peat (n. 7, above), p. 203.

10. See Susan Niditch, *Chaos to Cosmos: Studies in biblical patterns of creation*, Scholars Press, Chico, California, 1985, p. 67.

11. See Peter Coveney, 'Chaos, entropy and the arrow of time,' in *The 'New Scientist' Guide to Chaos*, ed. Nina Hall, Penguin, London, 1992, p. 203. See also Adam's lines shortly after Eve's fall, 'But past who can recall, or done undo?/Not God Omnipotent, nor Fate' (IX, 926–7). As the graveyard epigram puts it, 'We cannot put the clock back – not even by two seconds'.

12. See Alan Bullock, *Hitler and Stalin: Parallel lives*, Harper Collins, London, 1991, pp. 7–11. Hitler repeatedly bewailed the Academy's dual rejection of his applications for admission in turn as a student of art and of architecture, on the grounds that the world had lost a great artist (of Wagnerian stature) when he was consequently forced to turn to mundane politics. And indeed the world would have been far, far better off with a career architect, however untalented. Ira Levin stresses this irony in his thriller, *The Boys from Brazil*, where the boy-Hitler cloned decades later wants, above all, to be a film director.

13. See Hitchcock in Leslie Halliwell, *Halliwell's Filmgoers Book of Quotes*, Granada, London, 1973, p. 140.

14. Before the film was in the can, Hurricane Iniki (the worst storm to hit the islands in this century) threatened Spielberg's cast and crew on the Hawaiian island of Kauai, even as the storm threatened the inhabitants of *Jurassic Park* itself. See Don Shay and Jody Duncan, *The Making of Jurassic Park*, Boxtree, London, 1993, p. 85–6. By the same token, as Whoopi Goldberg perceptively observed at the 1994 Oscar ceremonies, the chaotic dynamics that resulted in the destruction of Jurassic Park seemed analogous to the unforeseeable economic crisis in EuroDisneyland.

15. See Christopher Hill, *Milton and the English Revolution*, Viking, New York, 1977, p. 473.

16. See Hayles's invaluable editorial introduction to *Chaos and Order: Complex dynamics in literature and science*, University of Chicago Press, Chicago and London, 1991, as well as her discussion of chaos theory and postmodernism, *Chaos Bound*, Cornell University Press, Ithaca, New York, 1989.

17. See Ilya Prigogine and Isabelle Stengers, *Order Out of Chaos*, New Science Library, Shambhala/Boulder and London, 1984 (pp. 309, 313). Extreme cultural relativism attacks extreme scientific claims to non-cultural objectivity, and insists that scientific 'progress' is no improving map of external reality, but only a derivative expression of cultural change, since 'truth has no objective meaning and can only be assessed by the variable standards of different communities and cultures'. Few serious scientists today claim that their concerns and theories are *not* influenced by their culture, but do insist that their discoveries may represent increasingly accurate approximations of external reality in so far as they are tested, and may be overthrown, by negative evidence from nature. 'The factual correction of error may be the most sublime event in intellectual life, the ultimate sign of our necessary obedience to a larger reality and our inability to construct the world according to our desires.' Only one example of a left-coiling periwinkle, 'Samsonlike', brought down a whole 'conceptual edifice' based on 'centuries of well-nurtured evidence' that there was no such thing. See Stephen Jay Gould, *Eight Little Piggies: Reflections in natural history*', Penguin, London, 1994, pp. 412, 452.

18. Horace Lamb is quoted by Tom Mullin in 'Turbulent times for fluids', *The 'New Scientist' Guide to Chaos* (n. 11, above), p. 59. For the story about Heisenberg see James Gleick, *Chaos* (n. 5. above), p. 121. On turbulence generally, as Mullin observes, 'babbling brooks and bracing breezes may please poets, but they bother physicists. These natural examples of turbulence are difficult to analyse mathematically. Turbulence is probably the most important and yet least understood

problem in classical physics. Now, theories of chaos combined with some simple laboratory experiments may provide some answers.' By the way, reviewing Spielberg's *Jurassic Park*, Sir Walter Bodmer, past president of the international Human Genome Organization, thought the watered-down version of chaos theory offered by Jeff Goldblum (miscast) as Ian Malcolm, confused theoretical and mathematical analyses of complexity and fluctuations in nature with the 'idea of chaos that encompasses the all-too-human mistakes that are *Jurassic Park's* downfall' (see *The Observer*, 18 July 1993, p. 60). But, of course, the conflation of external and internal chaos (in nature and in the human psyche) is characteristic of artistic portrayals of both: 'nor only Tears/ Rain'd at their eyes, but high Winds worse within . . . shook sore/Their inward State of Mind, calm Region once/And full of Peace, now toss't and turbulent'.

19. See Peter Coveney, 'Chaos, entropy and the arrow of time' (n. 11, above), p. 211.

20. See Thomas Keneally, *Schindler's List* (originally published in England by Hodder & Stoughton as *Schindler's Ark*), Sceptre, 1991, p. 305. The associations of Keneally's biblical title are clearly pertinent to Milton. See the lines describing Noah as a 'just man', 'fearless of reproach and scorn,/Or violence', who built a wondrous Ark 'To save himself and household from amidst/A world devote to universal rack' (XI, 809–10, 819–21).

21. See Markley's brilliant essay, 'Representing Order: Natural philosophy, mathematics, and theology in the Newtonian revolution', in *Chaos and Order*, ed. N. Katherine Hayles (n. 16, above), pp. 125–48; the quotation is from p. 126.

22. Ian Stewart, *Does God Play Dice?* (n. 3, above), p. 291.

23. For these and innumerable other examples of this dicta as constantly reiterated in the seventeenth century, see Aubrey Williams, *An Approach to Congreve*, Yale University Press, New Haven and London, 1979 (quotations are from p. 4): 'Both Virtue and Vice are generally, and for the most part, sufficiently distinguished by Rewards and Punishments in this Life', proclaimed Bishop John Wilkins. Likewise, Archbishop John Tillotson insisted that:

The providence of God many times preserves good men from those ends which happen to others, and by a particular and remarkable interposition, rescues them out of those calamities which its suffers others to fall into; and God many times blesseth good men with remarkable prosperity and success in their affairs.

Milton's reminder that the ways of the world may be 'to good malignant, to bad men benign' was radically opposed to this view.

24. See Nathaniel Lee, 'To Mr. Dryden, on his Poem of Paradise', in *The Works of John Dryden*, ed. Montague Summers, Nonesuch Press,

London, vol. 3, p. 409. Subsequent page references to this edition of Dryden's *The State of Innocence and the Fall of Man* are cited parenthetically in the text.

25. See Frank Kermode, 'Adam Unparadised', in *Renaissance Essays*, Fontana, London, 1973, pp. 291–2. As R. M. Adams observes (see 'A little look into chaos', n. 1, above) it looks as if Satan kept the promise he made to Chaos: 'Yours be th'advantage all, mine the revenge.' Neither Heaven nor Hell is the conclusive winner of the conflict enacted on earth: the advantage goes to Chaos, since the components of good and evil, order and disorder, are all mixed up, chaotically confused – like the weather – in the passions, in the history of the postlapsarian world. See also Milton's *Areopagitica* (Hughes, p. 728): 'Good and evil we know in the field of this world grow up together almost inseparably, and the knowledge of good is so involved and interwoven with the knowledge of evil, and in so many cunning resemblances hardly to be discerned, that those confused seeds which were imposed on Psyche as an incessant labor to cull out and sort asunder, were not more intermixed.'

26. See C. S. Lewis, *Preface to Paradise Lost*, Oxford University Press, 1942, William Empson, *Milton's God*, Chatto & Windus, London, 1961, Christopher Hill, *Milton and the English Revolution*, Viking, New York, 1977, Christine Froula, 'When Eve Reads Milton: Undoing the Canonical Economy', *Critical Inquiry* 10 (1983–4), Catherine Belsey, *John Milton: Language, gender, power*, Basil Blackwell, Oxford, 1988, and Robert Manson Meyers, *From Beowulf to Virginia Woolf*, University of Illinois Press, Chicago and Urbana, 1984.

27. See Bentley, as quoted and further discussed by R. M. Adams in *Milton and the Modern Critics*, Cornell University Press, Ithaca, New York, 1966, pp. 126 ff, and see also Kermode (n. 26, above), p. 277.

28. Cooper is quoted by Ronald Haver in *David O. Selznick's Hollywood*, Bonanza, New York, 1980, pp. 84–5.

29. See Jonathan Swift, *Gulliver's Travels and Other Writings*, ed. Louis A. Landa, Oxford University Press, Oxford, 1976, p. 238:

> I am ready to dispose . . . that no European did ever visit these countries before me . . . unless a dispute may arise about the two Yahoos, said to have been seen many ages ago on a mountain in Houyhnhnmland, from whence the opinion is, that the race of those brutes hath descended; and these, for anything I know, may have been English.

CHAPTER THREE

Fractals and forgeries: self-similarities in Shakespeare and popular modern genres

Clouds are not spheres, mountains are not cones, coastlines are not circles, and bark is not smooth, nor does lightning travel in a straight line. All of these natural structures have irregular shapes that are self-similar. In other words, we discovered that successively magnifying a part of the whole reveals a further structure that is nearly a copy of the original we started with.

Benoit Mandelbrot

> And, like the baseless fabric of this vision,
> The cloud-capped towers, the gorgeous palaces,
> The solemn temples, the great globe itself,
> Yea, all which it inherit, shall dissolve,
> And, like this insubstantial pageant faded,
> Leave not a rack behind. We are such stuff
> As dreams are made on, and our little life
> Is rounded with a sleep.

Prospero in *The Tempest*

'La nouvelle alliance'

Instead of seeing literature and science, high art and popular art or premodern and postmodern art as intrinsically at odds, mutually exclusive, or otherwise distinct from each other, chaos theory enables us to think of artistic and intellectual expressions as a dynamic continuum allowing for differing degrees of complexity, variation, recursions, unpredictabilities and irregularities. In *Turbulent Mirror*, their popular introduction to chaos science, John

Briggs and James Peat have thus described 'the new realization spreading across science that order is interleaved with randomness, randomness is interleaved with order, that simplicity enfolds complexity, complexity harbors simplicity, and that order and chaos can be repeated at smaller and smaller scales – a phenomenon the scientists of chaos have dubbed "fractal" '. 'At the very least', they observe, these insights seem reflections of an ancient artistic and theological tension between determinism and freedom, certainty and uncertainty, chaos and order. 'More and more', they conclude, 'we see how that tension is a creative one.'[1]

For obviously, as chaos scientists everywhere acknowledge, the principles of 'self-similarity' and 'recursive symmetry', as well as the irregularities they have found in the dynamical systems of nature, have long since been observable in art. In turbulent fluid systems, Mitchell Feigenbaum notes, 'things work on themselves again and again'. Likewise, 'with Ruysdael and Turner, if you look at the way they construct complicated water, it's clearly done in an iterative way.' Small painterly effects give rise to large effects and there are irregularities within regularities as well as an interplay between the iterated irregularities themselves.[2] The complex 'nonlinear' structure of a literary 'fractal', in contrast to more linear works (which was earlier discussed with reference to *Paradise Lost*), is described in markedly similar terms by John McVicar, who first read Vladimir Nabokov's *Pale Fire* while serving time in prison. McVicar had been used to reading novels by Harold Robbins, and the comparative complexities of Nabokov's novel struck him with the force of revelation:

> In *Pale Fire* every surface of reality throws up other often inconsistent, contradictory interpretations that make equal sense. Reading it – and it can be read non-linearly, as Nabokov's biographer, Brian Boyd, suggests . . . there is always more than there seems, but whatever levels of complexity the reader understands, each works and satisfies and, most of all delights (*Sunday Times*, 19 June 1994, p. 9).

By the same token, Briggs and Peat cite the interactive and self-similar details in Katsushika Hokusai's eighteenth-century painting, 'The Great Wave', to illustrate the way regularity (predictability) and chaos (unpredictability) combine in art as in nature. What most impresses them are the 'tensions between the momentary fluid shape of the foreground wave and the solid

Mt. Fuji in the background, between the boats which repeat the curve of the waves, but are also imperilled by them; between the faces of the boat crews and the flecks of foam' (*Turbulent Mirror*, p. 198). Clearly, the new burst of insider-trading between artists and scientists that chaos theory has recently inspired is mutually beneficial to both, as witness *La nouvelle alliance*, the Belgian title of the book by Ilya Prigogine and Isabelle Stengers (published in English as *Order Out of Chaos*), which was 'designed to express the coming together of "the two cultures" '.[3]

As Briggs and Peat go on to remind their readers, 'when the ancients said that the artist's task was to hold a mirror up to nature', what they meant was obviously misunderstood by later ages, since the 'mirror of art' has never involved other than a metaphorical (non-literal) mimesis (*Turbulent Mirror*, p. 200). They insist that it is, however, a remarkably accurate mirror of the world, in so far as the greatest works of art metaphorically reflect its turbulent as well as creative dynamics: things work on themselves in unpredictable as well as iterative ways in art, just as they do in the dynamic systems operative in nature itself. This is why the holistic dynamic of certain works of art and nature alike is never entirely subject to external, analytical control. Quite the contrary. As David Ruelle observes, what remains a mystery is 'how fractal shapes arise' in nature.[4] And the same is true in art: one expert in computer fractals said his best efforts could not rival the worst painting by Monet – they seemed comparatively lifeless and mechanical. And, as we have seen, the length of a set of instructions and information necessary to replicate a literary work like *Paradise Lost* (which is comparatively short in word count) would be interminable.

In complex works of art, as in the fractal formations of nature, there are interactive effects within interactive effects, and the whole is larger than the sum of its parts. The holistic interaction between components cannot be analytically dissected precisely because analysis requires segregation: 'I truly do want to know how to describe clouds', says Mitchell Feigenbaum. 'But to say there's a piece over here with that much density, and next to it a piece with this much density . . . I think is wrong. It's certainly not how a human being perceives those things, and it's not how an artist perceives them. It is not a description that entails your intuition of the world' (*Chaos*, p. 185). By contrast, as Feigenbaum and various other chaos scientists continually remind us, certain artistic perceptions do correspond to our own intuitions, as well as their scientific conclusions, about the dynamical processes observable and operative in the world even as, in chaos theory, the order of nature itself, very like Keats' Grecian urn (the Apollonian order of art), not only allows for, but mandates chaotic complexity. Thus the first scene Keats depicts on the urn's serene surface is Dionysian nature out of control, chaotic, rapacious: 'What maidens loth?. . . What struggle to escape?' Art's Prosperos themselves ordain, and therefore must needs acknowledge, their own Calibans. Whose are Shakespeare's things of darkness if not his?

Indeed, the fact that order ordains as well as governs chaos in nature, even as Prospero conjures up the tempest and acknowledges Caliban as his own, may account for the fact that a similar dynamic (and arguably both realistically and aesthetically pleasing) interaction between 'Apollonian', 'classic', 'Augustan' order and 'Dionysian', 'Romantic', 'irrational' disorder tends to occur in literature from ancient times to the present.[5] Likewise, character types effectively designed to embody the interaction between order and chaos within and without the human psyche in high literature reappear in popular genres: Prospero/Caliban, Milton's God/Satan, Swift's Houyhnhnms and Yahoos, Frankenstein and the Monster, the ultra-rational Mr Spock and the passionate Dr McCoy, Obiewan Kenobi and Darth Vader, John Hammond and the dinosaurs emblematic of chaos, are obvious classic and popular examples.

The remainder of this chapter will further develop previous arguments that chaos science offers new theoretical perspectives on the dynamic interaction between classic and popular art while simultaneously providing a useful way to distinguish between a complex original and its less complex look-alikes that allows for enjoyment of them all. Compare, for instance, the similarities and differences between coastlines, as described by Ian Stewart:

> The same general structure is visible in the magnificent sweep of the Gulf of Mexico, the Pandower Coves near Land's End, the gap between two rocks on the foreshore at Acapulco, and even the individual indentations of a single rock.[6]

Much the same thing could be said about *The Tempest* and successive works directly based on it, which range from *The Enchanted*

Island by Dryden and Davenant to a *Star Trek* episode, 'Requiem for Methuselah', and the rock musical, *Return to the Forbidden Planet*. However markedly they differ in magnificence, magnitude, and impact, the same general structure is observable in them all the way down the literary scale. The difference lies in their degrees of internal complexity and (as we have seen with reference to *Paradise Lost*) their extratextual relevance to the real state of sublunary nature *outside* their literary contexts. For surely the most important of all the insights chaos theory offers late twentieth-century criticism is its entirely new perspective on the creative interaction between order and chaos in the nonlinear systems of nature, and the markedly comparable dynamics governing certain complex works of art.

Natural, mechanical and artistic fractals

In nature, a complex nonlinear ('fractal') structure such as an *individual* coastline, cloud formation, or rugged mountain peak involves comparably complex irregularities repeated on all scales simultaneously. In 1975, Benoit Mandelbrot coined the word 'fractal' from the Latin *fractus*, which describes a broken stone – broken up and irregular. As Mandelbrot defines them:

> Fractals are geometrical shapes that, contrary to those of Euclid, are not regular at all. First, they are irregular all over. Secondly, they have the same degree of irregularity on all scales . . . Nature provides many examples of fractals, for example, ferns, cauliflowers and broccoli, and many other plants, because each branch and twig is very like the whole. The rules governing growth ensure that small-scale features become translated into large-scale ones.

The same, of course, holds true of the famous computer graphics derived from the mathematical equations illustrative of deterministic chaos that are known as the 'Mandelbrot set' (see Figs 3 and 4). As an ideal mathematical fractal, it reveals the same degree of complexity on an infinite number of scales.

Mandelbrot himself 'set out to find mathematical descriptions for some of the most irregular and complicated phenomena we see around us: the shapes of mountains and clouds, how galaxies are distributed in the Universe, and examples nearer home.' To do so,

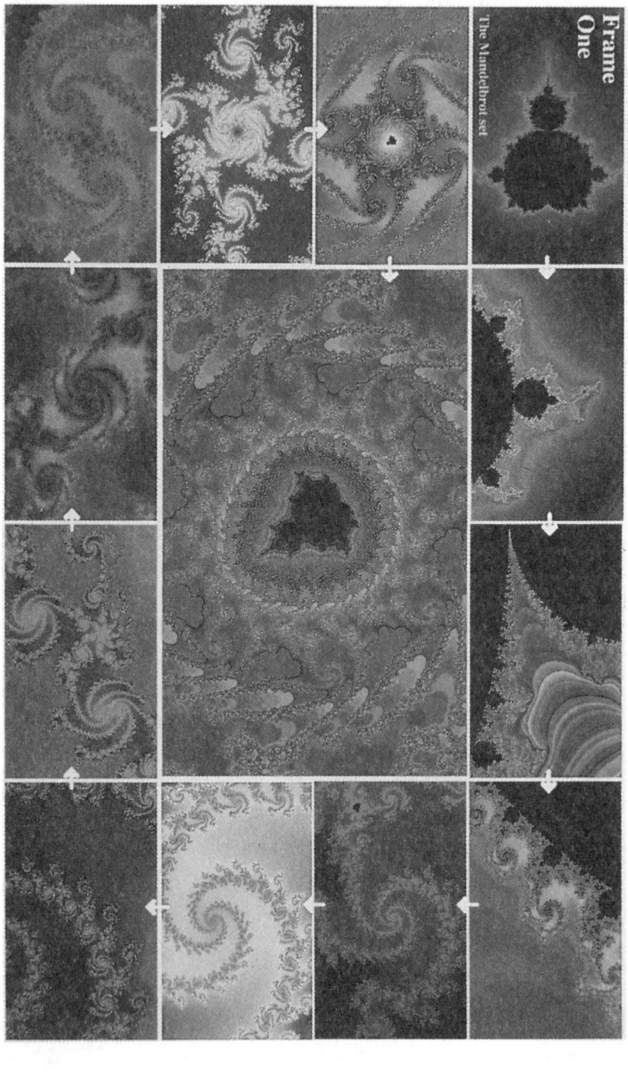

Figure 3 *The mandelbrot set. Intricate details emerge on all scales of magnification. In fact the complication increases as one zooms in. This can be seen by comparing the first and last frames in the above sequence, where the interaction between self-similarity and unpredictability goes on forever.* © 1994 Gregory Sams at Chaos Works, London.

he identified mathematical rules that 'can produce on a computer "mechanical forgeries" of some part of the reality of chaos'. Thus, through iterating a relatively simple equation, the Mandelbrot set produces the most extraordinary computer graphics, rich in complexity, with graceful seahorse swirls and curlicues containing graceful coils and curlicues in infinitely varied combinations. And thus Mandelbrot conclusively demonstrated that deterministic chaos in mathematics (as in nature) is aesthetically beautiful. By now, computerized fractals abound: 'some are representational, while others are totally unrealistic and abstract.' 'To the layman, fractal art seems to be magical', while 'it must come as a surprise to both mathematicians and artists to see this kind of cultural interaction.' A satisfying spin-off from fractal pictures, Mandelbrot concludes, 'is that their attractiveness seems to appeal to the young and is having an influence on restoring interest in science':

> Many people hope that the Mandelbrot set and other fractal pictures, now appearing on T-shirts and posters, will help to give the young a feeling for the beauty and eloquence of mathematics and its profound relationship with the real world.[7]

Obviously, it is in the ubiquitous insistence on its 'profound relationship with the real world' that chaos theory parts company with modern critical theory. Given certain tenets of poststructuralism, it would seem positively heretical to say that a play like *The Tempest* can give the young a feeling for the beauty and eloquence of poetry and *its* profound relationship with 'the real world'. But when *The Tempest* is looked at in terms of some of its major tenets, chaos theory allows us to say just that.

Coleridge tellingly described the form of Shakespeare's plays as 'organic', rather than 'mechanical'. He may now be proved right both in terms of new scientific theories and, illustratively, in actual practice. For arguably, when looked at with reference to Shakespeare's last play, chaos theory metaphorically offers a new insight into the mimetic relationship between determinism (Prospero's/ Shakespeare's artistic control and containment) and chaos (irregularity, disruption, unpredictability, dissolution) in art and in nature itself. Indeed, *The Tempest* could, without distortion, be described as an 'imaginative forgery' – as an artistic cognate to Mandelbrot's 'mechanical forgery' – of the nonlinear dynamics of

nature, in so far as comparably complex concepts, conflicts, irregularities, iterations, and interactions between governing order and
chaotic disorder can be observed in individual lines, characters and
scenes as well as in the overall structure of the play as a whole. In
Shakespearian drama, as in the fractal geometry of nature itself, it
would seem that the laws of growth assure that small-scale features
will be translated into larger ones.

To give an appropriately mathematical example: from the beginning to the end of the play, Shakespeare stresses the number
three. Prospero has around three hours in which to achieve his three
major goals: to reclaim his dukedom; to bring Ferdinand and
Miranda together; and to bring the usurpers to their knees (III, i, 21;
V, i, 136; V, i, 223).[8] Miranda was going on 'three years old' when
they arrived on the island, Ferdinand was the 'third man' that ever
she saw (I, ii, 446), and along with his daughter, Prospero says he is
giving Ferdinand 'a third part' of his life (I, ii, 41; IV, i, 3). Finally,
having accomplished his predetermined purposes, upon leaving the
enchanted island, Prospero concludes that henceforth his 'Every
third thought' will be his grave (V, i, 312). References to the number
three thus encompass the imaginary past and present of the play, as
well as the aftermath of events in the continuing play beyond the
play.

On a structural scale, the play's internal complexities compound
exponentially, as its characters are portrayed in interactive, dramatically intersecting sets of three. Prospero often appears at the apex of
the triangular configuration of differing power-relationships: for example, Prospero-Miranda-Ferdinand; Prospero-Miranda-Caliban;
Prospero-Ariel-Caliban. And the same triangular configuration is
replicated in the scenes involving Caliban, Stephano and Trinculo,
and in the power-plays involving Alonso, Sebastian and Antonio,
and so on. The upper-class villains are 'three men of sin' (III, iii, 53),
while the trio, Stephano, Caliban and Trinculo, likewise attempt to
take power (V, i, 272).

The principles of self-similarity or near self-similarity that Mandelbrot and others have observed on every scale in natural structures
is, as everyone has observed, metadramatically as well as mathematically operable here, since the playwright, Shakespeare, like the
playwright-within-the-play has about three hours to resolve the conflicts, while Shakespeare's play containing Prospero's masque will
likewise finally dissolve and leave not a rack behind – and so will we.

The inclusive principle of self-similarity operative throughout Prospero's most famous speech extends from the cosmic scale of the great globe, to the gorgeous palaces cloud-capped by nature, to the theatre that contains the play that contains the masque, and so on down to ourselves, to our own 'little lives' that will be 'rounded with a sleep'. Arguably, the recognition of self-similarities in the nonlinear structures of nature itself, from cloud formations to coastlines, gives us a new way of perceiving the same phenomena (including Shakespeare's metadramatic self-similarities) obviously observable in past and present works of art.

In his discussion of 'the new aesthetic of art, science, and nature', John Briggs observes that in some of the greatest works of art:

> whatever it is that the painter, poet, or musician depicts – whether abstract or realistic – the artist's final product implies worlds within worlds. Within art there is always something more than meets the eye, the mind or the ear. Because of this ability to intimate worlds within worlds, art has always been fractal. The science of chaos is helping to newly define an aesthetic that has always lain beneath the changing artistic ideas of different periods, cultures and schools.[9]

In art, the process operates in such a way that its relationships between forms that are 'simultaneously self-similar and self-different' are 'like' life forms. They are not literal representations, but metaphorically satisfying because they 'work like nature'.[10] It is not uncommon for art and science to reflect the same culture. What is unusual here is that chaos science so often seems to confirm dynamical processes obviously observable in premodern, as well as postmodern art.

For that matter, yet again extending Katherine Hayles's observations about the relevance of chaos theory to postmodernism (see above, p. 10), its definition of a deterministic order allowing for the replication of symmetries and asymmetries as well as unpredictabilities could serve as an exact description of the dynamics of *The Tempest*. For clearly throughout *The Tempest* (and other works by Shakespeare – see below – just as in *Paradise Lost* – or in jazz) comparable symmetries and irregularities are replicated on every conceivable scale. To give only a few examples: various characters aspire to rule; various characters (Caliban, Ferdinand, Ariel, Prospero) are held in bondage of one form or another and ask for or achieve freedom of one kind or another. There are also unpredictabilities: Prospero does not seem at all certain that 'the rarer action is/In virtue than in vengeance' until Ariel's unexpected, nonhuman pity inspires him to forgive his enemies. Prospero is not just the master of tempestuous and chaotic forces; he is himself threatened by heartless Antonios and rebellious Calibans within as well as without – as who is not? To see personal examples of uncertainty whether the rarer action is in virtue or in vengeance, most of us need only look in the mirror; to see political and historical examples, have a look at a newspaper. The internal and external orders that tenuously govern us today, our established powers-that-be, are as vulnerable to chaotic forces within and without, as Prospero was. And so are most of us, who, like Prospero on his island, exist on the edge of chaos, which is a term descriptive of a balance point, a point of inherently unstable equilibrium, where the components of a system never quite lock into place, and yet never quite dissolve into turbulence.

The seemingly organic – self-similar, self-organizing – principle inheres in the text's nonlinear complexity, in the myriad possible ways that the components of its system can dramatically interact. Its basic components may seem simple and familiar; the complexity arises when you have a great many of these components interacting simultaneously. Throughout the play, what are usually seen as stock binary oppositions converge and fuse as *simultaneously* creative and disruptive, internal and external interactions between (and conflations of) deterministic order and disorder; and art and nature, human catastrophe and providence divine, freedom and servitude, justice and mercy, 'raging tempests' and 'auspicious gales' (which are which?) occur on the play's psychic and linguistic as well as its largest and smallest structural scales of action.

'Stormy Weather': *The Tempest* and the dynamics of chaos

Climatic and psychic storms are everywhere conflated in literature, as deterministically emblematic (within the order of art) of nature *out* of control. A tempest rages, even as sexual passion is unleashed in lovers from Virgil's Dido and Aeneas through the heyday of Hollywood. So commonplace are these internal/external weather conflations in art that they were technically termed the 'pathetic fallacy'. Thus rain falls, like (sympathetic) tears, on the bereaved lover in Hemingway's *A Farewell to Arms*. And 'Since my man and I ain't together, keeps rainin' all the time' ('Stormy Weather'). 'The tempest in my mind/Doth from my senses take all feeling else/Save what beats there', says King Lear (III, iv, 12–14).

Everywhere in Shakespeare's tragedies, storms presage psychological and social chaos. Thunder and lightning introduce the witches, and an apocalyptic storm rages when the king is killed in *Macbeth*. Various characters attempt to construe the political meaning of the storm in *Julius Caesar*: 'Let not men say' such storms are only 'natural', says Casca, 'For I believe they are portentous things/Unto the climate that they point upon' (I, iii, 30–2). In *King Lear*, the great storm is in turn interpreted as a minister of divine retribution ('Crack nature's moulds, all germans spill at once/That makes ungrateful man' III, ii, 8–9); as indifferent to human suffering as well as pomp and rank; and seen by Lear, personally, as nature's reflection of the merciless ways of ungrateful daughters to old men:

> Here I stand your slave,
> A poor, infirm, weak and despised old man,
> But yet I call you servile ministers,
> That will with two pernicious daughters join
> Your high-engendered battles 'gainst a head
> So old and white as this. (III, ii, 19–24)

Yet the storm's cruelty is not comparably unnatural: 'I tax not you, you elements, with unkindness/ I never gave you kingdom, called you children./You owe me no subscription' (III, ii, 16–18). And, finally, King Lear both personally and socially interprets the storm as morally instructive to the proud and powerful:

> Poor naked wretches, wheresoe'er you are,
> That bide the pelting of his pitiless storm,
> How shall your houseless heads and unfed sides,
> Your looped and windowed raggedness, defend you
> From seasons such as these? O, I have ta'en
> Too little care of this. Take physic, pomp,
> Expose thyself to feel what wretches feel,
> That thou mayst shake the superflux to them
> And show the heavens more just. (III, iv, 28–36)

Clearly, in *King Lear* as elsewhere, however wrongly – or rightly – they may be interpreted by Shakespeare's characters, his storm scenes serve the deterministic purposes of Shakespeare's art.

Likewise, when he discovered the principle of deterministic chaos governing nature's weather systems, Edward Lorenz did not stop with an image of predictability giving way to pure randomness: 'He saw a fine geometrical structure, order *masquerading as randomness*' (*Chaos*, p. 22). And that is just *exactly* what we discover in the first two scenes of *The Tempest*. In the opening scene we have a storm that is subsequently revealed to be Prospero's order 'masquerading' as chaotic disorder. Looked at in terms of self-similarity operative on the level of metadramatic structure, the artistically staged storm that Shakespeare ostensibly portrays as a 'natural' storm turns out to be a storm staged by Prospero's 'Art'. And the way Prospero dramatically masquerades his predetermined design (to bring the court party to the island) as a tempest on the scenic scale of action is replicated on a psychic level when he dramatically masquerades his predetermined design to bring Ferdinand and Miranda together in a tempestuous (irrational, chaotic, ungovernable) temper-tantrum hostile to their union – 'lest too light winning/Make the prize light' (I, ii, 455–6).

As they deterministically serve Shakespeare's dramatic purposes in the other comedies and romances, wherein they are comparably paradoxical instruments of union, reunion and reconciliation as well as separation and loss, 'Tempests are kind, and salt waves fresh in love' (*Twelfth Night*, III, iv, 376). Out of chaos comes concord. But there cannot be more dramatic illustrations of Edward Lorenz's recognition of order masquerading as randomness in *actual* tempests, than the tempests within *The Tempest*. Nor could there be better dramatic illustrations of Mandelbrot's principles of self-similarity in fractal geometry: compare Prospero's art to Shakespeare's – deterministic chaos simultaneously rules in both. Call this just another way to see the obvious if you will, but if the obvious chaotic components in art, in nature, and possibly in human psychology are themselves self-similar, it could be called an entirely new way to see the mimetic (self-similar) relationship between all three, and (retrospectively) to explain why even those neo-classic critics who correctly categorized his nonlinear dramatic structures as 'irregular' and deplored his moral, ideological and political views as chaotic, *nevertheless* found

Shakespeare's plays unrivalled as dramatic representations of the real state of sublunary nature.

Moreover, in so far as deterministic chaos rules in certain works of art, just as it does in sublunary nature, chaos theory serves to explain why certain complex classics continually inspire markedly differing kinds of mimetic responses in art and criticism alike, even as Shakespeare's plays have inspired grand operas, ballets, musicals, novels, and science fictions, along with diametrically opposite critical and ideological interpretations. As noted earlier, the signature of a complex 'irregular' (nonlinear) work may be that its internal dynamics (order containing chaos, regular irregularities, and so on) inevitably (as it were deterministically) evoke artistic and critical responses that are themselves unpredictable, chaotic, contradictory, and uncontrollable either by the author or by the critical tradition. Thus, where past critics joined forces with Prospero, current critics join forces with Caliban; while artists in turn have foregrounded differing, but equally recognizable, components of *The Tempest* in works of differing kinds that range from 'serious' literature to kitsch. But its unique network of symmetries and asymmetries interactive on every scale assures that neither its immediate impact on individuals nor its long-term impact on the artistic tradition can ever be certainly predicted, and that its complexities can never be finally duplicated in art. Although it has served as a point of departure for innumerable works of art, 'Shakespeare's Magick could not copied be', wrote Dryden in the Prologue to the first adaptation of *The Tempest*. Nor, in certain cases, need it be. In fact, various popular works based on *The Tempest* are designed to be enjoyed by an audience on only one, clearly designated scale, while certain critical interpretations are designed to foreground only one specific aspect of the script.

By exactly the same token, the chaos mathematician, Ian Stewart, observes that:

> To store in a computer the exact data needed to reconstruct the complex surface of the Moon requires absolutely vast amounts of memory; reasonable enough for a catalogue of lunar geography, but pointless if the purpose is to produce a convincing background for a TV science fiction drama.[11]

For this purpose, Stewart concludes, the answer is a 'fractal forgery' that mimics *only* the required forms without worrying about less obvious details, even as computer-programmed fractal images were used to create the landscapes of the Genesis planet in the movie *Star Trek II: The Wrath of Khan,* and the geography of the moons of Endor and the outlines of the Death Star in *Return of the Jedi.* Likewise, *The Forbidden Planet,* a classic science-fiction film based on *The Tempest,* as well as *Return to the Forbidden Planet,* the rock musical based on both, could in turn be described as popular 'fractal forgeries' of Shakespeare's complex script – which could in turn be described as a 'fractal forgery' of dynamical processes operative in nature.

The Tempest and its fractal forgeries

Given its chaotic dynamics, complexities and beauty, it is not as surprising as it otherwise might seem that if you had to name only one work in English as *the* primary point of reference in twentieth-century 'high' art and popular culture alike, *The Tempest* would be the show to name, the show to know. 'Shakespeare meets rock 'n' roll in 50s sci-fi!' proclaimed the posters for *Return to the Forbidden Planet,* the Olivier-award-winning musical. And the advertisement is accurate. This 'long-lost rock musical by William Shakespeare' was in fact based on a sci-fi film adaptation of *The Tempest* (*The Forbidden Planet,* 1956) that *also* inspired the original *Star Trek* series. 'Requiem for Methuselah', an episode involving a genius-artist-scientist and a young girl who meets a handsome young man for the first time, might just as well have been entitled 'Captain Kirk meets Prospero on the Forbidden Planet'. Thus the wildly eclectic-chaotic artistic tradition (premodern as well as postmodern) knows no class distinctions between high and popular art (comparable to the ones made by critics); and it makes no historical distinctions (remotely comparable to the ones made by critics) between works it deems appropriate for appropriation. The dynamics operative in the artistic tradition itself could, in the case of wildly different adaptations and interpretations of complex nonlinear works, be seen as cognate to the iterations, recursions, self-similarities, symmetries and asymmetries operative in the nonlinear systems of nature, in contrast to the regularities and predictabilities of comparatively linear (generically determined) systems and fictions such as formulaic romance novels.

From a Meteor Mail Order romance, you can, with certainty, predict what the next Meteor romance you order will be like. By contrast, although they have elements in common (supernatural overseers, metadramatic frames of reference), given the nonlinear nature of Elizabethan drama, it would have been impossible to predict how components of *The Spanish Tragedy* would subsequently interact in *A Midsummer Night's Dream*, in *Hamlet*, and finally in *The Tempest*. By the same token, given the nonlinear nature of the artistic tradition, it is as impossible to predict the next artistic permutation of *The Tempest* as it is to predict the weather. For the historical fact is that from *The Enchanted Island* by Dryden and Davenant in 1674 to Marina Warner's *Indigo* in 1992, *The Tempest* has been appropriated, recycled and updated in successive works of every conceivable genre, recalling (chaotic, unpredictable) variations on a set (determined) text, as in jazz. Obvious twentieth-century appropriations include novels and short stories: for example, Aldous Huxley's *Brave New World*, Robertson Davies's *Tempest Tost*, Karen Blixen's 'Tempests', John Fowles' *The Collector* and *The Magus*, and Iris Murdoch's *The Sea, The Sea*. Its science-fiction appropriations range from *The Forbidden Planet* and 'Requiem for Methuselah' to Rachel Ingalls' 'Mrs Caliban', by way of *The Creature from the Black Lagoon*. It is hard to see how stage appropriations of the same text could differ more than Aimé Cesaire's *A Tempest* (designed as a critique that recalls Shakespeare's play to reveal its inscribed ideology and to flesh out colonial issues that the play raise) and the lighthearted rock musical, *Return to the Forbidden Planet*. Its obviously contrasting film adaptations range from Derek Jarman's version ending with a fabulous jazz rendition of 'Stormy Weather' (1979) to John Cassavetes' modernized parable, *Tempest* (1982) and Peter Greenaway's technically innovative *Prospero's Books* (1991). 'We are such stuff as dreams are made on', said Prospero (IV, i, 157), and his play is the stuff that dreams have been made on ever since.

Comparably resonant and ironic echoes of *The Tempest* occur in the most critically acclaimed, as well as the most popular modern works. In 1922 T. S. Eliot quoted the enchanted Prince Ferdinand in the disenchanted context of *The Waste Land*, ' "This music crept by me upon the waters"/And along the Strand, up Queen Victoria Street'; while in 1941 Humphrey Bogart, as Sam Spade, echoed Prospero when he answered the ultimate question asked at the end of *The Maltese Falcon*: 'It's heavy', says the police inspector, picking up the leaden version of the priceless statuette that everyone in the film has sacrificed so much for. 'What is it?' he asks. It is 'the stuff that dreams are made of', Bogart replies, in a final line that does not appear in Dashiell Hammett's original novel, but which imparts a poignant, poetic quality to John Huston's film as well as its hero. And, of course, Bogart's version of Prospero's line in turn inspired the popular song by Carly Simon.

A comparably evocative reference to *The Tempest* occurs in John Fowles' *The Magus*, when Maurice Conchis, the god-like master of what seems an enchanted island, pointedly compares himself to his Shakespearian counterpart: 'Prospero will show you his domain', says Maurice to Fowles' antihero, Nicholas Urfe. 'Prospero had a daughter', observes Nicholas hopefully. 'Prospero had many things', replies Maurice. 'And not all young and beautiful, Mr Urfe.'[12] This ambiguous allusion to the things of darkness at Prospero's command adds to Fowles' atmosphere of mystery, magic and suspense, just as Bogart's line about the stuff that dreams are made of encapsulates the romantic, albeit cynical mood and message of John Huston's movie masterpiece. In cases like these, past and present works of different kinds successfully collaborate with each other in enchanting or enlightening us, even as audiences at *Return to the Forbidden Planet* relished its various references to the original film and *The Tempest* alike. The difference is that *The Tempest* has an extratextual relevance that the self-consciously postmodern *Return to the Forbidden Planet* does not. Its single scale is *exclusively*, if enjoyably, intertextual. By contrast, in *The Tempest* the intertextual allusions, most notably to Ovid and Virgil,[13] contribute to its constant evocation of forces operative in nature, history and psychology, just as they are operative on the stage.

Yet the ultimate effect of its various fractal forgeries, in popular as well as 'serious' art, is surely one of retroactive enhancement. Because they foreground entirely different components of Shakespeare's script – the fantasy island, the pretty girl who has never seen a handsome young man, the magus who educates others, the magician who must control dangerous forces within as well as without – the various appropriations all tend to illuminate different, but equally recognizable, features of the many-faceted text and so positively encourage a return to the original. 'You can't truly appreciate Shakespeare unless you have read him in the original

Klingon', observes Chancellor Gorkon in *Star Trek VI: The Undiscovered Country* (with its title echoing *Hamlet*). You could in turn argue that you can't fully appreciate certain *Star Trek* episodes, such as 'Requiem for Methuselah', unless you have read them in the original Shakespearian versions. For that matter, Shakespeare's spirits of a gentler sort, such as Ariel and Puck, have been reincarnated as C3PO and R2D2 in *Star Wars*, just as Prospero is the prototype of Obie-wan Kenobi – 'The Force' is with them both. And Disney studios pointedly named characters Ariel and Sebastian in *The Little Mermaid*, whose heroine has an irascible father markedly comparable to Prospero.

But perhaps the most influential of all Shakespearian prototypes is the monster-son of a witch, who would have raped Miranda and peopled the isle with Calibans, but who also had dreams so beautiful that when he woke he cried to dream again. Previous monsters from the Minotaur to the swamp-creature Grendel had played important parts in literature. But Shakespeare's Caliban was the first beauty-loving, tear-shedding monster to enter the Western European *dramatic* tradition upstage centre. Representing elemental nature as opposed to Prospero's 'Art', threatening and threatened, pitiably tormented, victimized, and oppressed, the monster who was originally king of the island has, in fact, subsequently peopled the islands of art with progeny from Kong the king of all the beasts that beauty killed, to the fish-like Creature from the Black Lagoon, who evoked such sweet sympathy from Marilyn Monroe as the Girl in *The Seven Year Itch*:

> 'I just felt so sorry for the Creature at the end. He was kind of scary looking, but he wasn't really all bad. I think he just craved a little affection. You know, a sense of being loved and needed and wanted.'

Of course the same could be said of innumerable popular monsters. By the time the Girl expressed her sympathy for Caliban's creature-feature counterpart, the pitiable, beauty-loving monster had become such a dramatic cliché that Marilyn's lines seem a perfect send-up of the easy sympathy evoked by the type. By now it is comparatively hard to think of a completely *unsympathetic* beast-like monster.

The ubiquitous popularity of the Caliban prototype *as well as* the Prospero prototype seems retrospectively revelatory. For, given the spate of recent critical arguments that tend to see *The Tempest*

primarily as an ideological apologia for colonialism,[14] it is important
to note that the artistic tradition itself has as often as not joined
forces with Caliban, just as George Eliot anticipated Marilyn
Monroe's sympathy for the 'monster' in *Daniel Deronda*: 'Grand-
court held that the Jamaican negro was a beastly sort of baptist
Caliban. Deronda said he had always felt a little with Caliban, who
naturally had his own point of view':[15] compare also Browning's
'Caliban upon Setebos' and Marina Warner's *Indigo*. For that matter, the dynamic *interaction* between Prospero and Caliban, chaos
and order, in *The Tempest* itself seem far closer to the dynamic
relationship between order and chaos in nature, as described by
modern chaos theory, than to past and present criticism's more linear
and more exclusively ideological, or historical determinisms. It also
seems truer to life today, given our post-imperialist world with its
break-up of seemingly monolithic ideologies and its ubiquitous
power-plays amongst its once-oppressed and newly liberated subjects
of old imperialisms (like Caliban), *as well as* its privileged Antonios.

'This thing of darkness I acknowledge mine', says Prospero of
Caliban. And significantly, in *The Forbidden Planet* film, the forces
embodied in Caliban are finally shown to emanate from the
Prospero-figure himself. But in a far more complex network of interactions, in Shakespeare's script itself it is as if its counter-forces – art/
nature, revenge/mercy, cynicism/optimism – all contend within the
central character's soul as well as in the larger world portrayed on
the stage and in the theatre of the world itself. Through a series of
identifications Prospero acknowledges *everything* – good and evil –
in this play as his own: 'my art', 'my daughter', 'my brother', 'my
brave spirit', 'this thing of darkness'. These possessive identifications
lend a measure of textual support to the way John Gielgud, portraying a quintessential Renaissance magus, speaks the lines of all the
other characters in *Prospero's Books*. Yet the original play dramatically externalizes the other characters as well, giving them the freedom to rebel against and threaten Prospero's design, just as W. H.
Auden's villain, Antonio, defies Prospero in *The Sea and the Mirror*:

> Your all is partial, Prospero;
>   My will is all my own:
> Your need to love shall never know
> Me: I am I, Antonio,
>   By choice myself alone.[16]

Something profoundly chaotic at the heart of the original, therefore, seems lost in Peter Greenaway's technically fabulous film that divests *The Tempest* of fear and feeling. In *Prospero's Books*, Caliban seems more a ballet-dancer than Shakespeare's natural king of the island who wishes to reclaim his domain in the same way and for the same reasons Prospero wishes to reclaim his Dukedom. Conversely, the monster-movies starring a succession of Caliban-types from Kong, the comparably enslaved and humiliated king of a mythic island (Stephano and Trinculo think of taking Caliban back and displaying him as an exhibit, which is exactly what happens to Kong), and the comparably scaly and love-starved Creature from the Black Lagoon, stress fear and feeling – and leave out Ariel and Prospero. To my mind, Fowles' *The Magus* comes closest to combining the fear, feeling, literary and extra-literary impact of the original. And interestingly in *The Magus*, the black man whom the antihero identifies as the Caliban figure even as he identifies himself as the Ferdinand figure ('I was at last sanctioned as the Ferdinand to his salt-haired, clinging, warm-mouthed Miranda'), in fact, turns out to be the true lover of the Miranda figure and the true favourite of the Prospero figure himself (pp. 341, 469, 530).

The Magus is pervaded with references to Shakespearian characters and to situations in *Othello* and *Twelfth Night*, but its primary allusions are to *The Tempest*; and Maurice Conchis, Fowles' god-like master of a magical domain, is constantly compared to Prospero:

> He appeared, wished to appear, to survey, to bless, to command; *dominus* and domaine. And once again I thought of Prospero; even if he had not said it first, I should have thought of it then. I dived, but the salt [water] stung my eyes. Conchis had turned away – to talk to Ariel, who put records on; or with Caliban, who carried a bucket of rotting entrails; or perhaps with . . . but I turned on my back. (p. 136)

Very much as Prospero tells the story of his life, Maurice tells the story of his arrival on the island not 'as a man tells something that chances to occur to him: but far more as a dramatist tells an anecdote where the play requires'. 'Underlying everything he did I had come to detect an air of stage-management, of the planned and rehearsed' (p. 109) – like Prospero's stage-management in the scenes with Miranda and Ferdinand. Again like Prospero, Conchis stages beautiful and terrifying masques for the delight and instruction of the other characters – and Fowles' audience: 'I thought I could discern two elements in his 'game' – one didactic, the other aesthetic', observes Nicholas (p. 162) – but there is no knowing his true motives or predicting the course of events. Later, Nicholas fears that he has entered a much darker adventure, 'where Miranda was nothing and Caliban reigned' (p. 184). Still later, he remembers 'Conchis's fairy godfather exit. Our revels now are ended. But this was Prospero turned insane, maniacally determined never to release his Miranda' (p. 458).

Godgames: *The Magus* and *The Island of Doctor Moreau*

Prospero is associated with a 'god of power' as well as providential order in *The Tempest* (I, ii, 10), but he himself is also subject to chaotic forces, uncertainties, disruptions: 'I had forgot that foul conspiracy/Of the beast Caliban and his confederates/Against my life . . . [*To the spirits performing his masque*] Well done! Avoid; no more! *To a strange, hollow, and confused noise, the spirits in the pageant heavily vanish*' (IV, i, 139–43). Likewise, throughout Fowles' novel, along with the emphasis on Maurice's 'godgames', there is a constant stress on arbitrary, random, mundane disruptions and coincidences that make all the difference to the subsequent course of events (the chance meeting between Nicholas and an Australian air-hostess, the answer to a letter in the *Times Educational Supplement*), even as Conchis himself constantly stacks the deck, then shuffles it; and loads the dice, but finally leaves the game. In his seemingly predetermined but ever-unfolding surprises, Maurice Conchis continually insists to Nicholas that 'All is hazard' (p. 129), 'My plans are whatever happens' (p. 408). He also condemns as immoral society's pretensions to serve an overriding determinism as attempts 'to control hazard – to prevent a freedom of choice in its slaves' (p. 127); at the same time he condemns a resignation that leaves everything to hazard. 'What the lie was', Conchis tells Nicholas with reference to the way young men were pressured into fighting World War I, was our believing that we were fulfilling some end, serving some plan – that all would come out well in the end, because there was some great plan over all. Instead of the reality. There is no plan. All is hazard. And the only thing that will preserve us is ourselves (p. 129).

In its efforts 'to reproduce, however partially, something of the mysterious purposes that govern existence' (p. 627), the novel (first published in 1966 and revised in 1977) is simultaneously based on *The Tempest* and on ancient and modern theories anticipating chaos science, theories such as the Heraclitian conception of eternal flux (most notably stressed in Fowles' first version) and Heisenberg's uncertainty principle, which is cited in the second: 'The basic principle of life is hazard . . . this is no longer even a matter of debate. If one goes deep enough in atomic physics one ends with a situation of pure chance' (pp. 627–8).

In his 'Foreword' to the revised version, Fowles describes the 'haphazard' circumstances in which the first version itself was written: 'I had no coherent idea at all of where I was going, in life as in the book' (p. 5). But although 'it attempted to conceal the real state of endless flux in which it was written', its genuinely chaotic effects may in fact have helped to enhance the novel's original appeal, especially to adolescents – for whom it provided 'an experience beyond the literary' – in contrast to Fowles' critics, for whom it seemed a 'coldly calculated exercise in fantasy, a cerebral game' (p. 6). In its complex interaction between deterministic order and bifurcating chains of coincidence, chaos theory fits it perfectly, and helps to explain why, to its cult following, its fantastic situations (like those in *The Tempest*) have a continuing extra-literary, real-world relevance and resonance. Its 'living reality' seems more than a 'matter of technique, of realism gained through rehearsal' (p. 127).

In Fowles' novel, as in scientific theory, deterministic chaos allows for freedom and growth, and thus could be said in some measure to justify the ways of God to man, even as it certainly justifies the ultimately liberating ways of Maurice Conchis to Nicholas Urfe, who is portrayed within the novel as a kind of 'everyman' (as Fowles observes in the preface, his name puns on 'earth'). And significantly, Fowles' original title for *The Magus* was *The Godgame*. He intended 'Conchis to exhibit a series of masks representing human notions of God, from the supernatural to the jargon-ridden scientific; that is, a series of human illusions about something that does not exist in fact, absolute knowledge and absolute power' (p. 10). But before he absconds, Maurice Conchis' 'godgames' (again like Prospero's) clearly allow for cruelty, and there are occasional passages that inevitably bring to mind the cruellest of all godgames in popular literature, those in H. G. Wells' *The Island of Doctor Moreau*. Conchis himself mentions Wells in one of his pamphlets (p. 190), and in effect if not intent, his first name, 'Maurice' may inevitably bring to mind 'Moreau', while the maiden name of Maurice's associate (Lily Montgomery de Seitas) may echo the name of Dr Moreau's second-in-command, 'Montgomery'. Moreover, although Nicholas felt that he was being taught 'a metaphysical lesson about man's existence', Conchis' experiments themselves seemed to him 'more like gratuitous cruelty, closer to tormenting dumb animals than any true teaching' (p. 386), as if they were designed to torture, to rack him, 'to perform on me, for some incomprehensible reason, a viciously cruel vivisection' (p. 493). The experimental tormenting and vivisection of humanized animals by their god-figure is of course the primary action in Wells' fable, which also has obvious structural affinities with *Jurassic Park* as its ravening predators are likewise spectacularly unleashed.

The Island of Doctor Moreau, Wells himself observed, 'was written to give the utmost possible vividness' to the 'conception of men as hewn and confused and tormented beasts', and the same idea, he adds, appears in his later works 'as a weighed and settled conviction'. Compare his fable to the deterministically chaotic account of evolution quoted by John Briggs, 'The spectacular variability of beetles suggests that nature is infected by . . . a sheer lunatic exuberance for diversity, a manic propensity to try any damn thing'.[17] Likewise, on an isolated island, in random and arbitrary ways clearly comparable to the ways of evolution itself ('What is ten years? Man has been a hundred thousand in the making?' pp. 112–13), Doctor Moreau has shaped animals into human forms that combine components of the various creatures from which his Comus-crew of 'Beast People' were made to emerge: an 'Ape like' one is especially memorable.[18] Thus Doctor Moreau is explicitly, as well as metaphorically, associated with the God that ordained the evolutionary process, and its unremitting experiments with the 'extreme limits of plasticity in a living shape' (p. 108). He does nothing that it has not done, or might not do: 'I might just as well have worked to form sheep into llamas, and llamas into sheep', he casually tells Prendick the narrator (p. 105). And when Prendick complains that Moreau's work is abominable and the pain he inflicts is unjustifiable, Moreau responds that if so, so is God's. 'I am a religious man, Prendick,' he insists, '[and] I fancy I have seen more of the ways of this world's Maker than you – for I have sought His laws, in *my* way, all my life' (p. 107).

His wretched Beast People in turn deify their Maker for raising them above their brute origins and teaching them to speak. They try very hard to obey Moreau's commandments and prohibitions 'Not to go on all-Fours', 'Not to chase other Men', 'Not to suck up Drink' (p. 85), since they are condemned to his hellish 'House of Torture' (compare the tortures Prospero inflicts on Caliban) for disobedient behaviour, which sometimes amounts to no more than doing what comes naturally. 'None escape', says the Ape Man:

> 'See! I did a little thing, a wrong thing, once. I jabbered, jabbered, stopped talking. None could understand. I am burnt, branded in the hand. He is great, he is good!' . . . 'None escape', said the Beast People, looking askance at one another. (p. 87)

Wells' fantasy can obviously be read as an allegory of science turned monstrous, divorced from all humanity, as in the Nazi experiments. But in its dark internal theology, it can also be interpreted as a moral condemnation of the deification ('He is great, he is good!') of a process as unaccountable for, and as supremely indifferent as Doctor Moreau is to the pain he inflicts on his Creatures. Witness the litany of the 'Beast Folk', pointedly described by the narrator as 'gibberish', but ironically evocative of certain other liturgies as well:

> We ran through a long list of prohibitions, and then the chant swung round to a new formula:
>
> > '*His* is the House of Pain.'
> > '*His* is the Hand that makes.'
> > '*His* is the Hand that wounds.'
> > '*His* is the Hand that heals.'
> >
> > . . .
> >
> > *His* is the lightning-flash.
> > *His* is the deep salt sea. (pp. 85–6)

And so on for another long series, mostly quite incomprehensible
gibberish to me, about *Him*, whoever he might be. (p. 85)

A 'horrible fancy' came into the narrator's head, that Moreau had
'infected their dwarfed brains with a kind of deification of himself.
However, I was too keenly aware of white teeth and strong claws
about me to stop my chanting on that account? "*His* are the stars
in the sky" ' (p. 86). Apparently religious orthodoxy is a method of
control so powerful that it can force conformity even on those who
do not believe in it. For fear of the white teeth and the strong claws
of the chanting Beast Folk, Prendick joins in the litany. Later, in an
effort to control the Beast Folk, he actively participates in the process of deification itself.

   In the subsequent course of the action, chaos ensues on
Moreau's island in ways strikingly comparable to its onset in
Crichton's *Jurassic Park*, and similarly described by Briggs and
Peat in terms of animals loosed from a confined environment (in
Turbulent Mirror: see above, p. 8). The process begins when, as
an unanticipated consequence of a 'butterfly effect' (the introduction of rabbits as a food supply for Moreau and his human associates) one of the Beast People reverts to its status as a natural
predator and thus reacquires the old 'taste for blood' that Moreau's law was devised to prohibit. Small effects lead to big effects,
as other Beast People revert. In another unintended effect, a vivi-
sected puma that was tortured into defiance rather than the desired docility, breaks out, and kills Moreau, even as Crichton's
John Hammond is devoured by his creations in *Jurassic Park*.
Then chaotic effects compound exponentially: some of the Beast
People start preying on others, and some defiantly threaten the
narrator, who in desperation attempts to reassert Moreau's reign
of terror by warning them that 'he' lives on in a changed shape:
' "For a time you will not see him. He is . . . there" – I pointed
upward – "where he can watch you. You cannot see him. But he
can see you. Fear the Law" ', ' "The body he cast away because he
had no more need of it" ' (pp. 149–50). ' "The House of Pain . . .
will come again. The Master you cannot see. Yet even now he
listens above you" ' ' "True, true!" said the Dog Man' (p. 175).
The ultimate intent (to maintain control) of this theology-of-fear,
and the desired response (the willing acceptance of falsehood as
truth) could not be more satirically displayed.

Elsewhere in the novel, the narrator identifies himself with the Beast Folk, born under one law, to another bound:

> Poor brutes! . . . Before, they had been beasts, their instincts fitly adapted to their surroundings, and happy as living things may be. Now they stumbled in the shackles of humanity, lived in a fear that never died, fretted by a law they could not understand; their mock-human existence began in an agony, was one long internal struggle, one long dread of Moreau – and for what? It was that wantonness that stirred me.
>
> Had Moreau had an intelligible object, I could have sympathized at least a little with him . . . I could have forgiven him a little even had his motive been hate. But he was so irresponsible, so utterly careless. His mad, aimless investigations drove him on, and the things were thrown out to live a year or so, to struggle, and blunder, and suffer; at last to die painfully. They were wretched in themselves, the old animal hate moved them to trouble one another; only the Law held them back from a brief hot struggle and a decisive end to their natural animosities. (pp. 138–9)

As Moreau himself observes, 'Very much . . . of what we call moral education is . . . an artificial modification and perversion of instinct' (p. 104).

Moreau's assistant, the sympathetically portrayed Montgomery, identifies even more strongly with the Beast Folk than the comparatively privileged Prendick, and for obvious reasons. 'What a muddle it all is!' he exclaims:

> 'I haven't had any life. I wonder when it's going to begin. Sixteen years being bullied by nurses and schoolmasters at their own sweet will, five in London grinding hard at medicine – bad food, shabby lodging, shabby clothes, shabby vice – a blunder – *I* didn't know any better – and hustled off to this beastly island. Ten years here! What's it all for, Prendick? Are we bubbles blown by a baby?' (p. 153)

Here we have the negative sides of religious indoctrination and social determinisms, as well as the negative side of incessantly 'creative' evolution. On Wells' metaphysical scale, Moreau's experiments, along with the suffering of his victims, are themselves seen as products of his cosmic equivalent, a 'blind fate', a 'vast pitiless mechanism' that seemed to 'cut and shape the fabric of existence':

> And I, Moreau (by his passion for research), Montgomery (by his passion for drink), the Beast People, with their instincts and mental restrictions, were torn and crushed, ruthlessly, inevitably, amid the infinite complexity of its incessant wheels . . . I lost faith in the sanity of the world when I saw it suffering the painful disorder of this island. (p. 138)

When the narrator returns to London, although he desperately attempts to distance himself from the British counterparts of the Beast Folk that he sees everywhere on the streets, he yet again generalizes their plight, and fears that their suffering may be (has been?) 'played over again on a larger scale'. But, the narrator insists to his enlightened modern readers (in a consolatory disclaimer obviously loaded with irony):

> I know this is an illusion, that those seeming men and women about me are indeed men and women, men and women for ever, perfectly reasonable creatures, full of human desires and tender solicitude, emancipated from instinct, and the slaves of no fantastic Law – beings altogether different from the Beast Folk. (p. 190)

'Yet', he adds, 'I shrink from them' and 'long to be away from them and alone' (p. 190). He thus recoils from the Beast Folk as mirrored on the London streets, even the friendly ones that offer him assistance, exactly as Swift's Gulliver recoils from the human-Yahoos, including his own wife and children and the Good Samaritan Captain de Mendez, on his return from Houyhnhnmland. For the same ironical reasons: like Swift's loathsome Yahoos, Wells's pitiful Beast Folk are in fact a lot *more* like, than *unlike* the narrator – at their most repellent they remind us of us. The 'turbulent mirror' of art would not reflect things accurately if it did not occasionally remind us of our animal origins, to which any of us may, at any time, revert; or – as in *Gulliver's Travels* and *The Tempest* – that we ourselves are in some way far worse than, and – as in *The Island of Doctor Moreau* – in some ways worse off than animals. Who said that, when looking in his own mirror, he always saw the unloved face of Caliban? Don't we all?

A natural, animal fear of our *own* god-figures ('Fear the Law') may also explain the generally ambivalent attitude towards the god-figures in literature: 'Prospero had many things, and not all young and beautiful, Mr Urfe'; '*His* is the House of Pain'. The most obvious reasons why 'He' is the pronoun for most god-figures in fiction (both sexes appear as chaos figures) is that in monotheisms 'He' ubiquitously reigns over the house of pain, and as often as not the pains he is praised for healing are the ones he himself inflicted on his creations. Conversely, women are dissociated from its infliction and primarily associated with maternal comfort and relief of pain – if not with pure pleasure. As John Fowles observes, to envisage cruelty, hatred, spite in the face of the Virgin Mary would seem to reverse 'the entire order of nature' (p. 152). It is therefore virtually imposs-ible to imagine a feminine Doctor Moreau. Like the cruelty of a pagan (non-monotheistic) or animal goddess, the cruelty of his closest female counterpart, Rider Haggard's 'She-Who-Must-Be-Obeyed' (portrayed as Venus–Victrix),[19] is comprehensible since it is prompted by recognizably natural passions – love, hate, revenge, jealousy, possessiveness, the will to dominance – that are shared by beasts and Beast People alike. 'She' inflicts pain on her rivals and her disobedient slaves, but offers unimaginable pleasure to her chosen lover: 'No man who once had seen *She* unveiled, and heard the music of her voice, and drunk in the bitter wisdom of her words, would willingly give up the sight for a whole sea of placid joys.' 'No doubt,' Rider Haggard's narrator observes, 'she was a wicked person, and no doubt she had murdered [her rival] Ustane, when she stood in her path,' but she had been true to her lover for two thousand years, and by 'a law of nature man is apt to think but lightly of a woman's crimes', especially if 'the crimes be committed for the love of him' (p. 242). By contrast, the dispassionate cruelty of Doctor Moreau's in-cessant experiments has no intelligible motive or goal, no clearly desirable object or reward ('I could have forgiven him a little even had his motive been hate').

Originally inspired by Miss Havisham in *Great Expectations*, John Fowles initially thought of making Conchis a woman (p. 6), and he does in fact introduce a female power-figure. But the radiant Lily de Seitas is not only portrayed as far more benevolent than Miss Havisham, she is strongly associated with the goddess Ceres (compare *The Tempest*), and Conchis himself concludes that 'all profound definitions of God are essentially definitions of the mother. Of giving things. Sometimes the strangest gifts. Because the religious instinct is really the instinct to define whatever gives each situation' (p. 296). Interestingly, in a recent production of *The Tempest*, Prospero himself was portrayed as a woman; even as

Elizabeth Walsh, the living goddess garbed in gold who delivers the definitive rendition of 'Stormy Weather' at the end of Derek Jarman's film adaptation remains in the memory as the ultimate reigning deity of the entire show, lending it a newly and wonderfully feminine (loving, maternal) resonance.

Artistic recursions and the canon

Successive spin-offs, appropriations and adaptations of *The Tempest* and other classics do anything to them but, finally, render them obsolete. On the contrary: the case of *The Tempest* (as well as *Paradise Lost*) would seem to support Douglas Coupland's conclusion that 'Without High Culture, Low Culture would have no new forms to borrow from.'[20] This observation may well be true because complex irregular classics provide the most inspiring conflicts and character types for successive artists of all kinds. A recent feature on the popularity of Angela Carter's fictions with graduate students, 'Aspiring dons desert tradition for Angela Carter' (*The Independent*, 1 April 1994, p. 4), failed to note that since Carter herself did not desert tradition, quite the contrary – the title of her radio play, 'Come Unto These Yellow Sands', just about says it all – no one seriously studying her is likely to. There are, in fact, no more enjoyable modern variations on situations and themes in Shakespeare's comedies and romances than in Carter's *Wise Children*, and her work will be all the more enjoyable to readers who recognize them. The idea that there are fundamental class distinctions between – or an innate hostility between – premodern and postmodern literature is absolutely refuted by the artistic tradition itself, popular as well as classic, cinematic as well as literary.

The artistic tradition is chaotic, not linear, and it acts and reacts on itself in recursive, self-referential ways. Thus the behaviour of one function is guided by the behaviour of another. In linguistics, the term 'recursion' is applied to a grammatical feature or element which itself may be involved in the process by which that feature or element is repeatedly introduced; or applied to a grammatical rule in which part of the output serves as input to the same rule, as in 'This is the house that Jack built', 'This is the mouse that lives in the house that Jack built', and so on *ad infinitum*. In chaos theory, self-similarity implies recursion (see below). In the artistic tradition, one function or work may be internally or externally guided by the behaviour of the other in unpredictably recursive ways that have nothing to do with the temporal and class distinctions critics have traditionally imposed on works of different kinds and periods such as, say, *The Tempest* and *The Forbidden Planet*.

What the astonishing range of popular appropriations (to say nothing of the equally numerous canonical adaptations) of *The Tempest* most dramatically serves to demonstrate is that, in the long run anyway, it is neither, or certainly not *exclusively*, the schools nor the critics, nor a reigning ideological establishment, but successive artists and their fans who finally determine the trans-historical and *extracurricular* canons of art. Likewise in our own minds, the true distinction between an ephemerally enjoyed work (of whatever kind) and a work we lock into our individual memory banks as a priceless personal classic may have nothing to do with whether it was originally designed, or academically categorized as 'high' literature or popular entertainment, or whether, at any time, it was proclaimed to be (or not to be) ideologically correct.

In the long run, the survival of a complex literary 'fractal' may result from the fact that it continuously resonates, on multiple scales – imaginative, aesthetic, intellectual, orderly and disorderly – in the minds and memories of individual readers of successive generations, in very much the same way it continues to resonate in the artistic tradition. Which of art's 'Maltese Falcons' we, personally, treasure as the jewelled and genuine article, and which ones we reject as worthless or pretentious fakes, may finally depend on which ones are most enjoyed on various levels and in differing (often chaotic and contradictory) ways throughout a lifetime. Exactly as in the artistic tradition itself, they are therefore the plays, novels, and films that are most vividly remembered, most often returned to, and never finally outgrown, outmoded or replaced – not even by their most obvious heirs apparent; not by even the best of all their fractal forgeries.

Recursive symmetries in Shakespeare and modern genres

We have
A map of the universe
For microbes,

we have
a map of a microbe
for the universe.
Miroslav Holub, *Wings*

This wide and universal theatre
Presents more woeful pageants than the scene
Wherein we play in.

All the world's a stage,
And all the men and women merely players.
They have their exits and their entrances,
And one man in his time plays many parts
Shakespeare, *As You Like It* (II, vii, 137–43)

As we have seen, the fractal geometry of nature operates on every scale. Small storms behave like big ones, even as the symmetries and asymmetries of *individual* cloud formations, mountain ranges and coastlines look much the same on different scales of measurement. And the same dynamic obviously operates in certain works of art. For that matter, once fractal geometry had been discovered by Benoit Mandelbrot, creative artists of all sorts began consciously to recognize it as a feature of previous works, as well as their own. Briggs and Peat cite David Hockney, who now describes his own work as fractal: 'With a fractal, you look in and in and in and it always goes on being fractal.' They also cite Arnold Schoenberg and Leonard Bernstein on self-similar structures and effects in music. In his Harvard lectures, Bernstein pointed out self-similarity from the largest to the smallest scales of musical structure, calling such repeating variations 'musical metaphors'. And Charles Dodge, director of the Center for Computer Music at Brooklyn College, linked fractals to 'a basic self-similarity that has always existed in classical music'. Thus, Dodge observes, 'The awareness of self-similarity abounds in studies of musical structure' (*Turbulent Mirror*, pp. 198–9). Compare Elizabeth Bishop's independent recognition of primal self-similarities in nature in her poem 'North Haven' (quoted in the *London Review of Books*, 4 August 1994, p. 9):

The Goldfinches are back, or others like them,
and the White-throated Sparrow's five-note song,
pleading and pleading, brings tears to the eyes.
Nature repeats herself, or almost does:
repeat, repeat, repeat, revise, revise, revise.

The same holds true of the incessant repetitions and revisions in the artistic tradition in general.

The principle of self-similarity also occurs in cultural artefacts of very different kinds. In his book on the new mathematics of chaos, Ian Stewart illustrates the dynamic with reference to the most popular tourist attraction in the pretty Cotswold village of Bourton-on-the-Water. In a corner of that village is a miniature village designed as an exact duplicate of the village that contains it. In the identical corner of the miniature village is a yet smaller model of Bourton-on-the-Water which in turn contains its own tiny model of the model of the model.[21] Like those Russian dolls that contain smaller dolls that contain identical dolls, manufactured examples abound in high art, in popular art – and in kitsch. Some years ago, the principle of self-similarity was used for commercial purposes on those old American 'Quaker Oats' boxes depicting a smiling girl holding up a box of Quaker Oats on which appeared a picture of the same girl holding a box of Quaker Oats, showing the same girl smiling . . . and so on to infinity. By exactly the same (commercial) token, an amusingly pointed scene in Steven Spielberg's film version of *Jurassic Park* shows a display of posters, T-shirts and other memorabilia bearing the dinosaur-logo of John Hammond's theme park, which audiences in the cinema will immediately recognize as the identical dinosaur-logo that appears on the advertisements and promotional memorabilia on sale worldwide in association with Spielberg's film itself.

As (simultaneously) scientific and literary illustrations of the principle of self-similarity in nature, chaos theorists frequently quote Lewis Richardson's immediately recognizable parody –

> Big whorls have little whorls
> Which feed on their velocity
> And little whorls have lesser whorls,
> And so on to viscosity.

– of Jonathan Swift's biologically based original:

> So, Nat'ralists observe, a flea
> Hath smaller fleas that on him prey,
> And these have smaller fleas to bite 'em,
> And so proceed *ad infinitum*.

In obviously comparable ways (as we have seen with reference to *Paradise Lost* and *The Tempest*) 'big' works of art (and science and criticism) have smaller works of art (and science and criticism) that feed on them just as Lewis Richardson's lines feed on Swift's.

For very good reasons, Swift's lines are often quoted by Mandelbrot, whose name (as its deviser/discoverer) is appropriately attached to the most celebrated of all mathematical fractals. When iterated on a computer, the 'Mandelbrot set' not only shows fabulous details (see Fig 3 p. 80), it starts out by forming a shape that, as Ian Stewart observes, looks very much like 'a gingerbread man' – some scientists refer to it as a 'Mandelbrot'. And every so often, buried deep within the gingerbread man, perhaps a millionth of the size, you can find a tiny gingerbread man, complete in every detail and containing its own sub-gingerbread men and so on (*Does God Play Dice?* pp. 237–9).

Dramatic and cinematic 'gingerbread men'

Likewise, in artistic effects ranging from the infinitely complex to the immediately obvious and amusing, virtually exact self-similarities, as well as near self-similarities, are manifested in canonical and popular drama and films, from Shakespeare's time to ours. Metadramatic examples range from Thomas Kyd's *The Spanish Tragedy* (1592) to Spielberg's *Jurassic Park*. The millionaire director's film, announced with its dinosaur-logo, contains a sign welcoming his audience to the millionaire Hammond's 'Jurassic Park' with its identical dinosaur-logo, and their recreated animals are, simultaneously, intended to amaze and delight a world-wide audience and to make even more millions for both millionaires.

Another recent example of recursive, self-reflexive, self-similarity is Robert Altman's Hollywood satire, *The Player* (1992), with its title-pun on the role of Tim Robbins, the actor and the operator who performs within it. It is about the making of a film called 'Habeas Corpus', even as '*The Player*', itself is finally revealed to be a film within the film, while the operator making a film within the film turns out to be an actor in another one. Thus *The Player* contains 'The Player' and thus (metaphorically speaking) we see the ironic smile on the face of the eternally recursive gingerbread man.

To give perhaps the most unforgettable of cinematic examples, in Ingmar Bergman's *The Seventh Seal* (1957) an actor plays Death with such power and authority ('Nothing escapes me. No one escapes me.') that he terrifies twentieth-century audiences along with Skat, the actor within the film who had himself terrified fourteenth-century audiences when he played Death in the medieval morality-play performed by the itinerant players in Bergman's modern morality-play. 'Do you have no special dispensation for actors?' asks Skat. 'Not in your case', answers Death, with a superior smile. 'But I'm due to perform tonight', says Skat. 'Your performance will have to be cancelled due to the death of the player', says the player wielding the scythe, whose performance as Death in *The Seventh Seal* would itself have had to be cancelled had it been interrupted by a comparable summons. Self-similarity is likewise stressed when (like the procession of flagellants) the Dance of Death initially portrayed on a wall-painting is performed, to a solemn music, by virtually all the major characters in the end. Thus the film powerfully and poignantly reminds us that not *just* the characters they played, but the real-life actors performing in the film (including both the actors who play Death) will inevitably join each other in that dance 'to the dark lands' – as by now some members of Bergman's cast already have; and so in time will we, along with everyone else who will ever watch that unforgettable dance across the skyline at the end of Bergman's film.[22]

In the case of *The Seventh Seal*, as in Shakespeare's plays, the most powerful recognition of self-similarity is extratextual as well as intertextual. Self-similarity of Shakespearian complexity is *personally*, as well as metadramatically self-reflexive, inclusive and mutually participatory on the part of performers, characters, and audiences alike. Certainly it personally, as well as professionally, appears to have fascinated the actor–playwright Shakespeare, just as it fascinates his surrogate within *The Tempest*, Prospero, as well as so many of the other actor–characters and player-kings and queens within his plays. Witness Hamlet, who in turn contrasts a player's stage role with his own and compares Claudius, the usurping King 'of shreds and patches', to a guilty creature watching a usurper kill a player-king in a play with an outline comparable to the murder of Hamlet's father:

What would [this player] do
Had he the motive and the cue for passion
That I have? He would drown the stage with tears,
And cleave the general ear with horrid speech,
Make mad the guilty and appal the free.

. . .

About, my brains . . . I have heard
That guilty creatures sitting at a play
Have by the very cunning of the scene
Been struck so to the soul that presently
They have proclaimed their malefactions;

. . .

I'll have these players
Play something like the murder of my father
Before mine uncle.

. . .

The play's the thing
Wherein I'll catch the conscience of the King. (II, ii, 561–605)

Thus Shakespeare's self-reflexive effects simultaneously deconstruct and underscore the comparabilities between actors and roles played: 'The Players' would be a good subtitle for *Hamlet*.

Thus, in effect, it could be argued that the 'metadramatic' recursions recognized everywhere by his twentieth-century critics as perhaps the most ubiquitous, if not *the* most ubiquitous principle of Shakespeare's art, are so close to the tenets of 'self-similarity' in chaos theory as to seem theatrical analogues to them.

The world of the theatre and the theatre of the world

'We the globe can compass soon,/Swifter than the wand'ring moon', says Oberon (IV, i, 96–7) in a direct reference to the theatre in which *A Midsummer Night's Dream* was performed. 'I hold the world but as the world . . ./A stage where every man must play a part,/And mine a sad one', says Antonio in the opening scene of *The Merchant of Venice* (I, i, 77–9). The well-known idea of the *theatrum mundi*, so frequently referred to by Shakespeare and his contemporaries alike,[23] had obvious significance in terms of the physically mimetic shape of contemporary theatres, since the 'wooden O' shape of an Elizabethan theatre (*Henry V*, Prologue, 13) visually corresponded to that of the great globe itself. This simultaneously physical, metadramatic and metaphysical self-similarity is specifically stressed in a poem defending the drama in Thomas Heywood's 1613 *Apology for Actors* (sig. a4v):

> If then the world a Theater present,
> As by the roundnesse it appeares most fit,
> Built with starre-galleries of hye ascent,
> In which Jehoue does as spectator sit,
> And chiefe determiner to applaude the best,
> And their indeuvours crowne with more than merit.
> But by their evill actions doomes the rest,
> To end disgrac't while others praise inherit.
> > He that denyes then Theaters should be
> > He may as well deny a world to me.

Thus the same 'global' playhouse is replicated on several different scales (cosmic, human and theatrical) at once. A good visual illustration of this replication appears in Jean J. Boissard's *Theatrum Vitae Humanae* (Metz, 1596; see Fig. 4), which shows the deity and heavenly figures above, along with human figures of various ranks on middle levels, observing the spectacle of skeletons and a devil inflicting punishment on sinners. An Italian illustration stressing the relationship between the globe and the circular shape of an amphitheatre is noteworthy because immediately above the arena is a depiction of Atlas bearing the globe (see Fig. 5). For by exactly the same token, according to theatrical tradition the flag of Shakespeare's Globe Theatre showed a comparable figure of Hercules supporting the Globe, under which was written *Totus mundus agit histrionem* – all men are actors, all the world's a stage. The cosmic theatre contains the human tragedy/comedy that contains the theatrical level of action that contains . . . plays within plays containing cosmic, human and theatrical levels of action.

In experiencing the comedies and tragedies alike, from *Titus Andronicus, Love's Labour's Lost* and *A Midsummer Night's Dream* to *Hamlet* and *The Tempest*, Shakespeare's audiences watch audiences watch shows within shows. And some plays contain characters, such as Oberon, Iago, Hamlet, Prospero and the Duke in *Measure for Measure*, who successfully or unsuccessfully play – or try to play – playwrights and likewise oversee or instigate

Theatrum vitæ humanæ. **I**

THEATRVM VI-
TÆ HVMANÆ.

CAPVT I.

VITA HVMANA EST TANQVAM
Theatrum omnium miseriarum.

Vita hominis tanquam circus, vel grande theatrum est:
Quod tragici ostentat cuncta referta metus.
Hoc lasciva caro, peccatum, morsque, Satanque
Tristi hominem vexant, exagitantque modo.

A

Figure 4 *A Renaissance illustration of the cosmic theatre.*
The frontispiece to Jean J. Boissard's Theatrum Vitae Humanae,
Metz, 1596.

TEATRO, ANFITEATRO, ARENA.

Figure 5 *Implicit self-similarity. The illustration of an amphitheatre in Giovanni Ferro's* Theatro d'Imprese *(Vol. II), Venice, 1623, p. 127 shows Atlas carrying the Globe above and displays the motto 'Spectaculis Spectaculum'.*

or try to control the chaos within the plays. In *A Midsummer Night's Dream*, Puck sounds very much like a comic playwright when he delights in the chaos he has wrought: 'Those things do best please me/That befall preposterously.' Elsewhere, he speaks as a spectator at the comedy ('Shall we their fond pageant see?/Lord what fools these mortals be!' III, ii, 114–15) as well as an actor in it: 'I'll be an auditor;/An actor too' (III, i, 94–5). Shakespeare himself was, of course, an actor in and interested spectator at, as well as the author of, his comedies and tragedies. Looked at from this angle, he himself would have been ideally cast as Peter Quince, or the Duke in *Measure for Measure* – or as Iago (see below, pp. 144–6). For as author, he not only controls the dramatic course of chaos in his plays, he deterministically instigates it.

Throughout the plays, explicitly theatrical self-similarities and recursive symmetries are stressed with reference to the immediate situations of individual characters, as when the actor playing Macbeth self-reflexively compares life to a 'poor player' who struts and frets his hour upon the stage (v, iv, 24). Earlier, when Banquo tells the witches that

> You should be women,
> But your beards forbid me to interpret
> That you are so (I, iii, 43–5)

he in effect calls attention to the dramatic fact that on Shakespeare's stage the sexually ambiguous witches were apparently played by mature male actors with beards. Subsequently Lady Macbeth's lines calling on evil spirits to 'unsex' her simultaneously associates her with the witches and likewise directs our attention to the fact, as played by a boy actor, Lady Macbeth *was* comparably ambiguous sexually.

These internal recursions and self-similarities have long been recognized, but chaos theory allows us to see them in a newly significant way. By so frequently breaking down distinctions between on-stage and off-stage roles played, and between players and audiences, Shakespeare underscores correspondence between 'true' things (off-stage) and 'what their (on-stage) mock'ries be' (*Henry V, Prologue*, IV, 53). In *Twelfth Night* multiple puns interact on several scales simultaneously when the boy actor playing Viola, who is playing the boy Cesario, announces 'I am not what I am' (III, i, 139) – a statement equally true of the boy played by the girl, and of the girl playing the boy, and of the boy actor playing the girl playing the boy. 'If this were play'd upon a stage now, I could condemn it as an improbable fiction', says Sir Toby (III, iv, 125).

The principle of theatrical self-similarity also operates to mind-boggling comic effect in *A Midsummer Night's Dream* when 'Theseus, Duke of Athens', who is a character from a (literally) 'antique' fable performing in Shakespeare's fairy toy, says, 'I never may believe/These antique fables, nor these fairy toys' (v, i, 2–3). Theseus flatly says he does not believe in fairies, but do we really believe in Theseus? Within the comic fiction of Shakespeare's *Dream* he is no more or less real than Oberon, King of Fairies. Theseus's line deconstructs itself in a way comparable to the ultimately self-reflexive 'paradox of the liar', where Epimenides, the Cretan, says, 'All Cretans always lie'.[24] To end the list of examples with perhaps his most daring reminder of metadramatic self-similarity – since the line could disrupt the dramatic illusion altogether at the very climax of the tragedy – Shakespeare has the boy actor playing the great queen Cleopatra prophetically deplore her subsequent portrayal *by* a boy actor when in Rome (as on the Elizabethan stage itself) 'some squeaking Cleopatra' will 'boy my greatness/I'th' posture of a whore' (*Antony and Cleopatra*, v, ii, 214–17).

At best, metadramatic 'self-similarities' and 'recursive symmetries' are more than exercises in authorial ingenuity. They may reflect the patterns of similarity through which and by which we classify relationships and perceive experience generally. For that matter, as Jack Cohen and Ian Stewart observe, because 'our brains themselves evolved through complicity between their internal representations of reality and the external reality itself – between their content and their context – they can recognize features, analogies, and metaphors, and see patterns in them.' Moreover, precisely 'because of complicity between physics, chemistry, and biology' in their evolution, 'it is far more accurate to see our brains as figments of reality than to see reality as a figment of our imagination'. Our 'complicit brains' are both 'made with and aware of genuine complicities in the universe'.[25] Certainly analogy, metaphor and simile are as important in psychology as they are in poetry. We say what something is by saying what it is 'like'; we see what we are by seeing who or what we are like, or want to be like; and we say how we feel by saying what we feel like. Thus a highly self-conscious artistic method may simultaneously seem natural, because it corresponds to everyday life wherein we recognize patterns of similarity or near self-similarity everywhere in external nature – little leaves resemble big ones, small clouds resemble enormous clouds, tiny rocks resemble mighty mountains, player-kings resemble real ones, and so on).

Recursive geometry

In the fractal geometry of nature, things operate on themselves in unpredictable ways; when a dripping tap gets irregular, each drip sets up the conditions for the next, even as small features are translated into larger ones. In *Does God Play Dice?* (p. 229), Ian Stewart concludes that 'fractals and computers are a marriage made in heaven': 'One of the most powerful techniques in programming is *recursion*, whereby a procedure is broken down into a sequence of repetitions of itself . . . Fractals also break up into copies of themselves: they are recursive geometry.' You can likewise chart 'recursive symmetries' – a sameness of outline governing individual and overall graphs of seemingly unrelated, accidental and haphazard events (the smallest variation blows prediction apart) – that occur in differing contexts and on different scales of action throughout Shakespeare's plays. Even the most cursory examples of the outline of tragically 'untimely' events in *Romeo and Juliet* and of tragic misconstructions in *Julius Caesar* can serve to demonstrate that the characteristic structure of a Shakespearian play is fractal, not linear.

The action of *Romeo and Juliet* can be seen as entirely determined by fate (the lovers are 'star-cross'd'), or entirely determined by chaotic components, passion, hazard, chance. Deterministic chaos allows us to see it both ways at once. The action can be broken down into a sequence of repetitions of itself, even as seemingly haphazard accidents, encounters, incidents and actions, by old and young characters alike, occur too early or too late, and small effects are translated into larger ones. The pattern of unforeseen, untimely, haphazard events is verbally stressed from the outset. See, for instance, Juliet's shock on discovering Romeo's identity and realizing she has irrevocably fallen in love with her family's enemy:

My only love sprung from my only hate!
Too early seen unknown, and known too late! (I, v, 137–8)

And the same apparently random and arbitrary pattern of events that occur too early or too late for the various characters structurally propels the tragedy all the way to the end. Witness Friar Laurence's final recapitulation of the sequence of events whereby he arrived at the tomb too late to save Romeo, who had arrived at the tomb too early and therefore believed Juliet dead, while Juliet woke up too late to prevent Romeo's suicide, even as the Friar arrived back at the crypt too late to prevent Juliet's suicide:

But when I came, some minute ere the time
Of her awakening, here untimely lay
The noble Paris and true Romeo dead. (v, iii, 256–8)

In the end, Shakespeare's characteristic emphasis on self-similarity, as well as a recursive symmetry of events, is most dramatically underscored when the feigned death of Juliet in the fourth act is finally replicated by the 'real' death of Juliet in the fifth act. In order to avoid the marriage to Paris, Juliet had agreed to drink the friar's potion in spite of her terror that she might wake up 'before the time' that Romeo arrived to rescue her (IV, iii, 30–1). But having dreaded waking up too early, she instead wakes up too late to save him from despair and death. And where Juliet had toasted her love with the friar's sleeping potion in the fourth act ('Romeo, Romeo, Romeo! Here's drink. I drink to thee' (IV, iii, 57), Romeo toasts Juliet with the apothecary's real poison in the fifth:

Here's to my love.
He drinks the poison
O true apothecary,
Thy drugs are quick. Thus with a kiss I die.
He kisses Juliet, falls, and dies.

'*Enter Friar Laurence*' – one minute too late (v, iii, 119–22).

Thus tragically ironic (non-linear) self-similarities and near self-similarities mesh with a zig-zag sequence of mistimings to create the poignant climax of *Romeo and Juliet*.

The dynamics of deterministic chaos governing irregular structures in nature give us a new perspective on Shakespearian structures which neo-classical critics had deemed highly 'irregular' yet oddly more evocative of 'nature' than the syllogistically linear cause-and-effect, quid-pro-quo structures of more 'regular' neo-classical plays. As Coleridge subsequently observed, the plays also seem 'organic' because their form corresponds to that of nature's fractal self-similarities, bifurcations and recursions wherein a small difference in input (who is going to the Capulet party), gives rise to a huge difference in output, and everything affects everything else.

By adapting terms from chaos theory, it is possible to argue that in ways comparable to the 'fractal' forms of nature, wherein each part is a reflective image of the whole, Shakespeare's words, speeches and actions likewise display the same outline over various levels of magnitude. To give another example, like the seemingly haphazard convergence of untimely events in *Romeo and Juliet*, tragic 'misconstructions' and the destruction that results from them, govern the recursive symmetries of *Julius Caesar* on the verbal level, on the level of an individual character's fate, and in the overall pattern of the whole play. Pondering the significance of the great storm in the beginning of the play, Cicero pointedly concludes:

> Indeed it is a strange-disposed time;
> But men may construe things after their fashion,
> Clean from the purpose of the things themselves. (I, iii, 34–5)

And so indeed they do. Subsequently, Cicero's observation about misconstruction is dramatically illustrated on personal, political and military scales. Various characters misconstrue the significance of their dreams as well as the significance of the storm. Both with unpredictable and incommensurate consequences, various characters misconstrue the motives of friends and foes alike: Caesar trusts Brutus and Brutus trusts Antony. The conspirators tragically misconstrue the results of the assassination they plan. They take actions they hope will bring good consequences for themselves and for their nation. But, as an audience with foreknowledge of the historical consequences of their actions will already know, the chaos (and subsequent Empire) that ensues will ironically prove the opposite of the republic the conspirators had desired and killed for. Time after time, what in fact turns out to be

true is not what the individual characters had sincerely believed to
be true. This tragic irony is driven home like a dagger in the heart
when Cassius sends Titinius to find out whether the troops in the
distance are friends or foes, and is told that Titinius has been
surrounded by horsemen, who shout for joy. Misinterpreting the
information, Cassius concludes that Titinius was taken by the
enemy, and commits suicide in despair. Titinius returns, and finding the body of Cassius, he asks:

> Why did thou send me forth, brave Cassius?
> Did I not meet thy friends, and did not they
> Put on my brows this wreath of victory,
> And bid me give it thee? Didst thou not hear their shouts?
> Alas, thou hast misconstrued every thing! (v, iii, 79–83)

Outline the choric speeches about misconstruction by Cicero and
Titinius, or chart the misconstructions acted upon by individual
characters (Caesar, Cassius and Brutus), and you will come up
with a graph of the action of the tragedy as a whole – and vice
versa. The 'fractal' outline of misconstruction will look the same
on differing scales. Moreover, *Julius Caesar* could be used to illustrate perhaps the most crucial of all differences between the experience of historical drama, where the audience has foreknowledge
of ensuing historical events, and real life where, like the characters
portrayed, we have no idea what will or might happen next on the
great, deterministically chaotic stage of the world – or what might
happen to us, personally, as unforeseen consequences of our best
intended acts. As in chaos theory, a small uncertainty concerning
the initial or current conditions of a system may lead to very large
errors in the prediction of its subsequent states.

Nor is the impact or influence of a complex work itself ultimately determined by any single one of its interactive components, including its linguistic structures. Actors may interpret the
same lines in entirely different ways and with entirely different
effects. Thus the dynamics of a Shakespearian play extend beyond
the rhetorical level of its 'Words, words, words'. As Claudius
observes, 'Words without thoughts never to heaven go' (iii, iii,
98); and it is the dynamically interactive translation of words *into*
thoughts, and into the emotional forces which they embody and
elicit in the audience that counts – and that may inspire successful

international translation into differing cultural contexts and entirely different forms of artistic expression: operas, musicals, films, ballets.

Probably no play by Shakespeare has more complex dynamics, or has internationally communicated such richness of emotional and intellectual impact as the mirror held up to nature in *Hamlet*. Fractal and metadramatic self-similarities and recursions extend back and forth from the world of the play to the world of the audience. As James Gleick observes, comparable 'images of self-similarity are recognizable everywhere in the real world', as for instance 'in the infinitely deep reflection of a person standing between two mirrors' (*Chaos*, p. 103). And *Hamlet* is a veritable hall of mirrors. 'The Murder of Gonzago' mirrors the murder of King Hamlet. Hamlet sees his situation mirrored in that of Laertes: 'By the image of my cause I see/The portraiture of his' (v, ii, 78–9). Likewise Coleridge (among others) saw himself mirrored in Hamlet. And everyone from Cain, the first murderer, to Alexander the Great, to imperious Caesar, to past and present landowners and lawyers and painted ladies watching the play, is mirrored by the image of poor Yorick's grinning skull: to this favour we all alike must come (v, i, 75–211). The play also holds a historical and political mirror up to nature, serving new historicists as an 'abstract and brief chronicle' of the time in which it was written (iii, ii, 24) and also showing political 'forms and pressures' as recognizable to twentieth-century audiences at successive times of viewing as they were to the audience at the first performance. Berthold Brecht, for instance, saw *Hamlet* as a mirror of the 'dark and bloody period' in which he himself was writing, with its 'criminal ruling classes' and 'widespread doubt in the power of reason'. And when the director Richard Eyre was in Bucharest shortly after the overthrow of Ceaucescu, he saw a Romanian production of the play, and found that its immediate resonances 'were literally, painfully telling': 'Hamlet was seen unambiguously as a man fighting painfully against Claudius/Ceaucescu, and if he vacillated, accused himself of cowardice, cursed himself for his inaction, it only reflected the audience's awareness of their own frailty.'[26]

The play's mirror is simultaneously held up to Hamlet's individual psyche and to personal relationships in general – between parents and children, men and women. Thus *Hamlet* is as open to Freudian

and feminist interpretations as it is to political and historical interpretations. Yet one-strand, linear interpretations come as single spies
on a play simultaneously dealing, on all these scales – personal,
psychological, political, historical, metaphysical – with battalions of
chaotically interacting conflicts and boomeranging schemes.[27] In
Hamlet there is a sense of chaos unleashed before the play began –
Claudius's desire for Gertrude as well as for the crown led to the
murder that leads to multiple deaths and the takeover of Denmark by
Fortinbras of Norway who set out to fight over a patch of ground not
worth farming. Gertrude was a catalyst of chaos, a 'butterfly' who
has a strangely disproportionate (given her conciliatory nature) propensity to elicit conflict, as well a powerful attraction that determined the fates of her former husband, her son, and the calculating
Claudius, who gives his poisonous scheme away in a spontaneous
effort to warn her: 'Gertrude, do not drink' (v, ii, 243). Of course,
sexual and romantic passion are often instigators of chaos in art. As
one character tells the chaos scientist in Tom Stoppard's *Arcadia*:

> The universe is deterministic all right, just like Newton said, I mean
> it's trying to be, but the only thing going wrong is people fancying
> people who aren't supposed to be in that part of the plan.

'Ah', replies the scientist. 'The attraction that Newton left out. All
the way back to the apple in the garden.'[28] Here Stoppard is
alluding to perhaps the most artistically potent concept in chaos
theory. That is the 'strange attractor' that draws a system towards
chaos. The next chapter is concerned with literary catalysts of
chaos: those who unwittingly evoke it; those who deliberately set
out to evoke it; and those who embody the strange attractions of
chaos itself.

Notes

1. John Briggs and F. David Peat, *Turbulent Mirror: An illustrated guide
   to chaos theory*, Harper & Row, New York, 1989, pp. 43, 189; hereafter cited parenthetically as *Turbulent Mirror*. In *The Transparency of
   Evil* (trans. James Benedict, Verso, London, 1994), Jean Baudrillard
   adapts the term 'fractal' to describe a viral or radiant stage of value, a
   perpetual imitation of itself.

2. See James Gleick, *Chaos: Making a new science*, Cardinal, London, 1988, pp. 186–7; hereafter cited parenthetically as *Chaos*.

3. See Ilya Prigogine and Isabelle Stengers, *Order Out of Chaos: Man's new dialogue with nature*, New Science Library, London, 1984, p. 309. See also their defence of popularization, based on Erwin Schröd-inger's conclusions:

> A theoretical science unaware that those of its constructs considered relevant and momentous are destined eventually to be framed in concepts and words that have a grip on the educated community and become part and parcel of the general world picture – a theoretical science, I say, where this is forgotten, and where the initiated continue musing to each other in terms that are, at best, understood by a small group of close fellow travellers, will necessarily be cut off from the rest of cultural mankind; in the long run it is bound to atrophy and ossify however virulently esoteric chat may continue within its joyfully isolated groups of experts (pp. 18–19).

4. See David Ruelle, *Chance and Chaos*, Penguin, London, 1993, p. 178.

5. See the dynamic/dramatic interaction between Apollonian and Diony-sian forces of order and chaos in Greek literature as described in turn by Nietzsche in *The Birth of Tragedy* (various editions); E. R. Dodds, *The Greeks and the Irrational*, University of California Press, Berkeley, 1951; and Hugh Lloyd-Jones, *The Justice of Zeus*, University of California Press, Berkeley, 1971.

6. See Stewart, *Does God Play Dice? The new mathematics of chaos*, Penguin, London, 1990, p. 217.

7. Quotations are from Benoit Mandelbrot, 'Fractals: a geometry of nature', in *The 'New Scientist' Guide to Chaos*, Penguin, London, 1992, pp. 123–5, 127, 133, 135.

8. Line references to *The Tempest* and other works by Shakespeare are from *William Shakespeare: The complete works*, eds Stanley Wells and Gary Taylor, Clarendon Press, Oxford, 1986. My subsequent discussion of *The Tempest* is also indebted to the brilliant editions by Frank Kermode, Methuen (Arden), London, revised 1964 and Stephen Orgel, Oxford University Press (World's Classic), Oxford, 1994.

9. See John Briggs, *Fractals: The patterns of chaos*, Thames & Hudson, London, 1992, p. 2.

10. *Ibid.*, pp. 28, 30.

11. See Stewart, *Does God Play Dice?* (n. 6, above), p. 229. It should be noted here that the comparatively *exact* replication of results, which is absolutely crucial in science, is virtually impossible in art. 'In science, what X misses today Y will surely hit upon tomorrow (or maybe the day after tomorrow)': 'The discovery of the structure of DNA was logically necessary for the advancement of molecular genetics. If Watson and Crick had not discovered it, someone else would certainly have done so – almost certainly Linus Pauling, and almost certainly very

soon. It would have been that same discovery, too; nothing else could take its place.' 'Much of a scientist's pride and sense of accomplishment turns therefore on being the *first* to do something.' By contrast, 'Artists are not troubled by matters of priority, but Wagner would certainly not have spent twenty years on *The Ring* if he had thought it at all possible for someone else to nip in ahead of him with *Götterdämmerung*'. See P. B. Medawar, *Pluto's Republic*, Oxford University Press, Oxford, 1982, pp. 253, 272.

12. See John Fowles, *The Magus: A revised version*, Jonathan Cape, London, 1966, p. 83. Subsequent page references to *The Magus* are inserted parenthetically in the text. I have repeated this reference, and some of the other examples of modern allusions to and appropriations of *The Tempest* from *Classics and Trash: Traditions and taboos in high literature and popular modern genres*, Harvester/Wheatsheaf, Hemel Hempstead, 1990, because they are such important and obvious ones. And the context is different: they are perfect illustrations of the chaotic spin-offs of *The Tempest* in works of entirely different kinds and times.

13. See Donna B. Hamilton, *Virgil and The Tempest: The politics of imitation*, Ohio State University Press, Columbus, OH, 1990.

14. No one would deny that *The Tempest* does contain arguments that Caliban is a born slave, whose rapacious nature nurture will not improve (I, ii, 346–75). The long list of important essays on *The Tempest* and colonialism include: Stephen J. Greenblatt, 'Learning to curse: aspects of linguistic colonialism in the seventeenth century' in *First Images of America: The impact of the new world on the old*, ed. Fredi Chiappelli, University of California Press, Berkeley, 1976, pp. 561–80; Francis Barker and Peter Hulme, 'Nymphs and reapers heavily vanish: The discursive con-texts of *The Tempest*', in *Alternative Shakespeares*, ed. John Drakakis, Methuen, London, 1985, pp. 191–205; Richard Marienstras, *New Perspectives on the Shakespearean World*, trans. Janet Lloyd, Cambridge University Press, Cambridge 1985, pp. 160–84; Stephen Orgel, 'Shakespeare and the cannibals', in *Cannibals, Witches, and Divorce: Estranging the renaissance*, ed. Marjorie Garber, Johns Hopkins University Press, Baltimore, 1987, pp. 40–66. For further examples see Donna Hamilton (n. 13, above), pp. 158–9.

15. See George Eliot, *Daniel Deronda*, ed. Barbara Hardy, Penguin, London, 1967, p. 375.

16. See W. H. Auden, *Collected Longer Poems*, Faber & Faber, London, 1968, p. 212.

17. See Peter Kemp, *H. G. Wells and the Culminating Ape*, Macmillan, London 1982, pp. 4–5 and John Briggs, *Fractals: The patterns of chaos*, Thames & Hudson, London, 1992, p. 37. Quotations are from *The Island of Doctor Moreau* (first published in 1896), Penguin,

London, 1962; page references are hereafter cited parenthetically in the text. Compare also Dr Moreau's account of his arrival on his island: 'It is nearly eleven years since we came here, I and Montgomery and six Kanakas. I remember the green stillness of the island and the empty ocean about us as though it was yesterday. The place seemed waiting for me.' (p. 108); and Maurice Conchis's account of his arrival on his: 'There were many more trees then. One could not see the sea . . . I had immediately the sensation that I was expected. Something had been waiting there all my life. I stood there and knew who waited, who expected. It was myself.'

18. The narrator refers to the 'Comus rout' of Beast People (p. 74) in the mistaken assumption that Moreau, like Circe or her son, Comus, is transforming human beings into beasts (p. 95). The horror of the alternative proves greater. By the way, a Monkey Man 'developed in the most wonderful way the distinctive silliness of man': 'He thought nothing of what was plain and comprehensible' and coined words he called 'big thinks' to distinguish them from the 'little thinks', of the common herd: 'If ever I made a remark he did not understand, he would praise it very much, ask me to say it again, [and] learn it by heart' (p. 178).

19. See H. Rider Haggard, *She*, ed. Daniel Karlin, Oxford University Press, Oxford, 1991, p. 157; further page references are cited parenthetically in the text. First published in serial form in October 1886, *She* is an orchidaceous compendium of purple passages: 'For man can be bought with woman's beauty, if it be but beautiful enough; and woman's beauty can be ever bought with gold, if only there be gold enough. So was it in my day, and so it will be to the end of time' (p. 201). It is also virulently racist. But it is satisfying (turnabout is fair play) to have one book wherein a woman is the power-figure-who-must-be-obeyed and whose chosen favourite, Leo the lion-man, is 'represented with relentless consistency as a dumb blond' (see Karlin's introduction, p. xxvi). An enjoyable movie version starring the gorgeous Ursula Andress (possibly the only actress credible as *She*), was made by Hammer Films in 1965. A film version of *The Island of Doctor Moreau* starred Burt Lancaster in 1977, and a version starring Charles Laughton, *The Island of Lost Souls*, was filmed in 1933. Nobody was satisfied with the 1968 film version of *The Magus*.

20. See Coupland's letter to the *Modern Review* 1, 11 (October–November 1993), 5. See also the question raised on the cover of 'The Culture' section of the *Sunday Times* (24 November 1993), 'Can High Art and Popular Culture ever live together?' The answer is that they obviously can – and in fact always have inspired each other. It is true that film versions of, say, complex novels may water them down, but it is also true that lesser novels and short stories may be turned into film

classics more detailed and exciting than the original printed text, even as *Othello* is more complex than Cinthio's version of the story. The anxiety of influence – one way or the other – is most notable by its absence in the best and most popular works alike.

21. See *Does God Play Dice?* (n. 6, above), p. 165.

22. The image of Death in *The Seventh Seal* proved unforgettable to Roger Corman and Woody Allen. See their copies of it in Corman's horror film based on Edgar Allan Poe's *The Masque of the Red Death* (1964) and in Allen's spoof of Bergman at the end of *Love and Death* (1975).

23. The idea is developed dramatically by (among others) Thomas Kyd in *The Spanish Tragedy*, Ben Jonson in *The New Inn* and, most notably, Shakespeare. For further discussion, see Anne Righter (Anne Barton), *Shakespeare and the Idea of the Play*, Chatto & Windus, London, 1962; Richard Bernheimer, 'Theatrum Mundi', *Art Bulletin* 38 (1956), 225–47; Frances Yates, *Theatre of the World*, Routledge, London, 1969; and James Calderwood's successive discussions of Shakespearian metadrama.

24. On the paradox of the liar and chaos theory see Briggs and Peat (n. 1, above), pp. 75–6: In the 1930s Kurt Gödel stunned the mathematics community by showing that important logical systems like arithmetic and algebra will alway contain statements that are true but which cannot be derived from a fixed set of axioms. His proof of the incompleteness theorem was based on the paradox of the liar. Instead of the Cretan saying 'All Cretans are liars', Gödel proved a mathematical statement that said 'This statement is unprovable'. Internally defending poetry throughout his plays, Shakespeare exploits this paradox when to the Platonic charge that all poets always lie, he in effect adds: 'This statement is made within a poem by a poet' (see *Timon of Athens*, I, i, 217–24). For further discussion see Harriett Hawkins, *The Devil's Party: Critical counter-interpretations of Shakespearian drama*, Clarendon Press, Oxford, 1985, pp. 16–19.

25. See Jack Cohen and Ian Stewart, *The Collapse of Chaos: Discovering simplicity in a complex world*, Viking, London, 1994, p. 435. As the work of Richard Levin has wittily demonstrated, finding correspondences, similarities and self-similarities of various kinds, very much as Fluellen does (see below, p. 162), is *the* primary characteristic of Shakespeare criticism. Even as this book finds comparable 'salmons' in both chaos theory and literature, Levin has found comparable salmons swimming around in altogether different critical approaches to Shakespeare. See, for instance, his pioneering discussion of 'The figures of Fluellen' in *New Readings vs. Old Plays*, The University of Chicago Press, Chicago, 1979, pp. 209–29.

26. Quoted by the Assistant Director, Jane Montgomery, in the programme notes to the English Touring Theatre production of *Hamlet* as

performed at the Oxford Playhouse, in September 1993. By the way, the nonlinear structure of *Hamlet* was well described in a dialogue by Brecht. 'Hamlet's experiments lead straight to disaster'. 'Not straight, zigzag. In a sense, the play has the permanence of something makeshift.' 'Shakespeare', Brecht concluded, 'doesn't need construction'. 'With him everything develops naturally.' 'He wouldn't dream of giving a suitable twist to a human life in Act 2 merely to prepare the way for Act 5'. See Brecht as quoted in the *Times Literary Supplement*, 29 April 1964, p. 333.

27. As Hereward Price observed in 'Construction in Shakespeare' (University of Michigan pamphlet, 1951), self-similar patterns of 'purposes mistook' and characters 'hoist with their own petard' are obvious throughout the play. And from the opening line ('Who's there?') to the most famous soliloquy ('That is the question') *Hamlet* is pervaded by unanswered questions. As Maynard Mack originally observed ('The world of *Hamlet*', *Yale Review* 41, 502–23) *Hamlet* is a text 'preeminently in the interrogative mood'; and as such it is interesting to contrast the imperative command-mode, the imperially reflexive mood ('I myself *will* be myself', 'he himself *will* be himself') of *Antony and Cleopatra*: for example, 'He words me girls, he words me, that I should not be noble to myself'; 'a Roman, by a Roman/Valiantly vanquished', and so on.

28. See Tom Stoppard, *Arcadia*, Faber & Faber, London, 1993, pp. 73–4.

CHAPTER FOUR

'Like to a chaos': strange attractors in Shakespeare, Milton, and popular modern fictions

> Why, then, O brawling love, O loving hate,
> O anything of nothing first create;
> O heavy lightness, serious vanity,
> Misshapen chaos of well-seeming forms
>
> Shakespeare, *Romeo and Juliet*

> 'I hate Cleopatra! . . . Everything is turned to love with her. New love, absent love, lost love . . . It only needs a Roman general to drop anchor outside the window and away goes the empire.'
>
> Thomasina in Tom Stoppard's *Arcadia*, 1992

> 'Can people be strange attractors? . . . Does that mean they have some kind of unusual influence on other people?' 'That's what I've been suspecting. And as strange attractors, they are also a magnetic basin of instability.'
>
> William Sleator, *The Strange Attractors*

Discussing the appeal of fractal images, Richard Voss (who pioneered the use of fractals in the cinema) said he got 'many, many letters' from people who 'couldn't care less' how the images were created, but thought they were remarkably 'beautiful or scary or attractive or repulsive'. This sounds like a good account of the mixed responses to Shakespeare's 'dark lady' in the sonnets, or to his beautiful, scary, repellent and alluring Cleopatra. For obviously comparable reasons, the source of these 'strange and disquieting proliferations', the generator of chaos which David Ruelle and Floris Takens originally described as 'the strange attractor', has itself proved irresistibly attractive to modern artists.[1]

125

In *Arcadia* Tom Stoppard metaphorically associates the concept with Cleopatra, who paradoxically arouses Thomasina's 'hate' because she turns everything to 'love', and 'away goes the empire'. And along with their titles, the strange attractor has provided the structural basis for works as different as an experimental play by Kevin Fegan, a fantasy for adolescents by William Sleator, and a detective novel by Desmond Cory, whose fictional chaos scientist thus defines it for his readers:

> 'Maybe for a while things can go round and round in a nice smooth orbit . . . But then some unknown factor interferes and attracts the particles – pulls them out of the pattern. And it all goes haywire. We call that factor a strange attractor. It's *strange* in the sense of *alien*, something that can't be included in the original equation.'[2]

Even as the dark lady in the sonnets is the attractor of the young man and the speaker alike, and thus the instigator of chaotic interactions between them, the strange attractor can also be seen as an outside force. Although strange attractors are not unusual, they are mysterious. Nobody can predict their effects.

Other attractors are not so strange. The term 'attractor' is associated with how a system behaves after it has been set in motion. A useful example is the behaviour of water in a glass. However hard the glass is shaken, once the shaking is stopped the end will always be the same. The water eventually comes to rest and just sits there because the system of moving water has an attractor – in this case a very simple one called a fixed point. Likewise, a particle moving in a confined region of space may be attracted to a final resting position, even as the bob on a pendulum gradually settles down to rest.[3] The literary equivalent of a fixed point attractor is well described in Donne's poem famously comparing the stability of his love to the fixed point of a compass ('Thy firmness makes my circle just,/And makes me end where I begun').

Alternatively, a particle may settle down in a periodic cycle, going back and forth like the pendulum of a clock, and thus its motions can be predicted with astonishing accuracy. There is also a quasi-periodic cycle that almost repeats itself, but never gets back to exactly the same starting state. The phenomenon that signals chaos, albeit ubiquitous in the dynamics of nature, is conceptually far stranger: while remaining in some bounded region of space, the particle will continue to move wildly and erratically. Thus, although the motion is specified by precise laws, the particle behaves as if it were moving randomly, and there is no way to predict its future path. The regions of space traced out by such motions are called strange attractors and the space they occupy is termed 'phase space': 'Once a particle is attracted to a strange attractor there is no escaping.'[4] Edward Lorenz, the discoverer of deterministic chaos in weather systems, produced the first computer image of a strange attractor (see the cover of this book) and, appropriately, it looks something like a butterfly, something like a cat's eyes, something like a mask, and always like an enigma.

The 'real-world' relevance of this metaphor will be immediately obvious to anyone who feels the strange attraction of cats: once under their influence human beings will have to (as it were deterministically) behave in erratic and humanly unpredictable ways (get up from a sickbed in the middle of the night to feed them, for instance). You can never predict what your cat is going to do next, or what it is going to make you do next. And once attached to one, there is no escaping. Cats are naturally strange attractors.[5]

Shakespeare's cat-like Cleopatra herself could be described as a strange attractor who cannot be included in the equations of a man-made (Roman) system. In the absence of her influence, Antony might have settled down to a fixed point in the Empire, as the husband of the stable Octavia. Or he might have contended with Octavius in some periodic, or quasi-periodic cycle. But Cleopatra, with her 'brawling love', 'serious lightness', 'heavy vanity' (previously associated with the chaos of erotic and romantic love in *Romeo and Juliet*) constitutes a 'magnetic basin of instability'. Compare Tom Stoppard's account (see above, p. 119) of 'people fancying people' that extends 'the attraction Newton left out' all the way back to the garden of Eden.

In Shakespearian drama other *very* strange attractors who disrupt an initially stable or quasi-stable system are associated with the primal disruptor, the serpent in the garden. Obvious examples are Richard III, the witches in *Macbeth*, and Iago, who turns everything to brawling conflict, discord, jealousy and hate so that 'chaos is come again' in *Othello* (III, iii, 94). Like Cleopatra, these characters in turn are contained within the overall determinism of the individual plays; but they also give the drama a strong sense of unpredictability, of the incalculable component in our own equations of order. For the obvious reason that, in the absence of their incommensurate and unpredicted influence, things might not have gone haywire. Independently of the influence of the witches, Macbeth might have remained a stalwart defender of the realm. In the absence of Iago's influence, the behaviour of Othello could have remained as stable as it was portrayed in the opening scenes. But while acting under the influence, the last man on earth one might have expected to do so kills a defenceless woman he loves, and other characters could likewise be described as 'acting under the influence': Cassio uncharacteristically (emblematically) gets drunk, Emilia gives the handkerchief to Iago instead of returning it to Desdemona, and poor Roderigo is incited to murder.

In *Othello* and *Macbeth*, storm scenes presage and reflect psychic, domestic and cosmic chaos and in effect transport the audience as well as the characters out of a comparatively ordered system into a tempestuous domain. The structure of *Othello* could be outlined in terms of social, psychic and climatic storms followed by calm – from the tempestuous brawl initiated by Iago in the opening scene to Othello's calming speech in the Senate scene; from the real storm that threatens the reunion of Othello and Desdemona to the calm following it ('If after every tempest come such calms' (II, i, 186)); and from the ultimate chaos in Othello's mind to the final, tragic calm and union on Desdemona's deathbed. Macbeth meets the witches in thunder, lightning and rain, and the psychic storm in his mind that follows exponentially extends to political and cosmic scales, as symbolized by an apocalyptic storm. In *King Lear* 'butterfly effects' (Lear's not unreasonable desire to divide the kingdom and retire, then his petty but not incomprehensible desire to favour the daughter who says she loves him most, and so on) in turn give rise to other effects (Cordelia's refusal to play rhetorical games) so that everything acts on everything else in uncontrollable ways, as it does in Lear's lines about the storm. In *Julius Caesar*, *King Lear*, and *Macbeth* storm scenes signify civil war on psychic, domestic, and social scales alike.

Interestingly, however, there are no comparable storm scenes in *Antony and Cleopatra*. They are not necessary, since Cleopatra herself is an entire weather system:

> *Antony.* She is cunning past man's thought.
> *Enobarbus.* Alack, sir, no; her passions are made of nothing but the finest part of pure love. We cannot call her winds and waters sighs

and tears; they are greater storms and tempests than almanacs can
report. This cannot be cunning in her; if it be, she makes a show'r
of rain as well as Jove.

Antony. Would I had never seen her!

Enobarbus. O, sir, you had then left unseen a wonderful piece of
work, which not to have been blest withal would have discredited
your travel. (I, ii, 138–49)

Within the imperial context of Shakespeare's play, Cleopatra herself can be seen as deterministic chaos personified, since she instigates and orders her own forms of chaos. She thus defies and
eludes Caesar's efforts to control and subordinate her within the
confines of a man-made, social, sexual and political system. She
cannot be caged or domesticated. She will not march in Caesar's
triumph.

Paradoxically, her chaotic components are as poetically positive as they are politically disruptive. For instance, in Enobarbus's
description of her barge, Shakespeare activates Plutarch's splendid
prose description by making fire, air, earth, and water interact with
animal, vegetable ('flower-like hands') and mineral (silver, gold)
nature both in evoking and in serving her. Like a knot intrinsicate,
the poetry describing Cleopatra further identifies her with myth –
the goddess Venus and her child, Eros – and with the delights of
fantasy and artifice as well as sensual taste (she was a morsel for a
monarch), touch, scent, sight and sound:

> *Enobarbus.* The barge she sat in, like a burnished throne
> Burned on the water. The poop was beaten gold.
> Purple the sails, and so perfumed that
> The winds were love-sick with them. The oars were silver,
> Which to the tune of flutes kept stroke, and made
> The water which they beat to follow faster,
> As amorous of their strokes. For her own person,
> It beggared all description. She did lie
> In her pavilion – cloth of gold, of tissue –
> O'er-picturing that Venus where we see
> The fancy outwork nature. On each side her
> Stood pretty dimpled boys, like smiling Cupids,
> With divers-coloured fans whose wind did seem
> To glow the delicate cheeks which they did cool
> And what they undid did.
> *Agrippa.*   O, rare for Antony!

> *Enobarbus.* Her gentlewomen, like the Nereides,
>   So many mermaids, tended her i'th'eyes,
>   And made their bends adornings. At the helm
>   A seeming mermaid steers. The silken tackle
>   Swell with the touches of those flower-soft hands
>   That yarely frame the office. From the barge
>   A strange invisible perfume hits the sense
>   Of the adjacent wharfs. The city cast
>   Her people out upon her, and Antony,
>   Enthroned i'th'market place, did sit alone,
>   Whistling to th'air, which but for vacancy
>   Had gone to gaze on Cleopatra too,
>   And made a gap in nature.
> *Agrippa.*   Rare Egyptian! (II, ii, 197–225)

For the purposes of further discussion, it should initially be noted here that it is not outside the realm of historical possibility that Shakespeare himself may have played Enobarbus. If he did, and even if he did not, throughout the otherwise sturdy and prosaic Roman's magically poetical speeches (as well as in Agrippa's admiring interjections), Shakespeare seems – in effect if not intent – to be metadramatically celebrating his own dramatic creation. Cleopatra is not only associated with poetry (she never speaks prose), she is also the cause of poetry in other characters. Indeed, most potently through Enobarbus, Shakespeare himself suggests that Antony and his strange attractor were well met on Cydnus. If Antony had never seen her, or Shakespeare's audience had not seen his play about her, they would likewise have missed 'a wonderful piece of work', and 'not to have been blessed withal' would have discredited their travels into the Alexandrias of sensuality, imagination, art.

Leaving aside the question whether he might have played Enobarbus, Shakespeare certainly had just cause to congratulate himself on the creation of a 'lass unparalleled'. Cleopatra's infinite variety was dramatically unprecedented and is still unequalled in its fusion of the intermittently hostile and cooperative, and intrinsically and unremittingly interactive forces which, as we have seen, Shakespeare later split apart and separately embodied in Caliban (animal physicality, lust, earth, water – in Cleopatra's case associated with slime, ooze, scaled snakes, the overflowing Nile, and so on); in Ariel (fantasy/etheriality/changeability/fire/air); and in Prospero, an artist-figure in temporary control of, yet simultaneously subject to all these elements within and without. At the end of *The Tempest*, these various characters/components are dramatically released to go their separate ways independently of the playwright–surrogate's 'art': 'Be free and fare thou well', Prospero tells Ariel, while Caliban is left to 'seek for grace' on an island all his own (v, i, 298–9) and the ageing magus himself in turn seeks grace from Shakespeare's audience before returning to Milan to contemplate the grave. But so enduring is their dramatic and extra-literary potency that, long after the stage is left empty, the prototypes portrayed in *The Tempest* continue to contend in our memory and imagination and to interact (migrate, mate and mutate) or independently go their own ways in successive works of art.

Describing chaos theory's most potent symbols in markedly similar ways, the scientist in Desmond Cory's detective novel observes that the strange attractor and the butterfly effect are 'something like characters in a drama':

> 'They don't stay put, you see. They move from place to place.' 'Until', Dobie said as flatly as before, 'they're terminated. And even then they go on affecting the pattern, although they're not there'.
> 'The butterfly effect?'
> 'On a magnified scale.'
>
> (Cory, p. 45)

Only a termination determined and artistically staged within the play by Cleopatra herself breaks Shakespeare's knot intrinsicate that united art and nature in her person. But even then she continues to affect the imagination and memory of her audience on stage as off, even as she leaves Shakespeare's stage-play world behind to join her Antony in that Elysium where souls do couch on flowers, where they will henceforth reign as superstar lovers in the afterlife of art.

Yet within the play there is a poignant sense of irreversible processes, of the unrelenting march of time. Chaotic systems are likewise irreversible in a spectacular way: 'Cups of tea cool, snowmen melt and bulls wreak havoc in china shops', but 'we never see the reverse process'. The two universal features of the systems described in chaos science are their nonlinearity and their irreversibility.[6] In the case of Cleopatra we witness the emergence of an exquisitely dynamic structure which exists only as long as the flow of matter and energy is maintained. Thus there is a strong sense that

a gap is left in nature when she goes; that some profound energy is
irretrievably lost when her components of fire and air (associated
with the domain of art) split apart from the baser elements of earth
and water (associated with the domain of nature):

> Cleopatra.   I have
>   Immortal longings in me. Now no more
>   The juice of Egypt's grape shall moist this lip . . .
>   I am fire and air; my other elements
>   I give to baser life.
>   [*To the asp*] . . . Come, thou mortal wretch,
>   With thy sharp teeth this knot intrinsicate
>   Of life at once untie . . .
> Charmian. . . . . Now boast thee death, in thy possession lies
>   A lass unparalleled. (v, ii, 275–310)[7]

Here again through Charmian's choric elegy, as earlier through
Enobarbus, Shakespeare seems to be metadramatically congratulat-
ing himself for an artistic re-creation of nature's own Cleopatra,
who, while living, was more beautiful than the Venus where we see
the fancy outwork nature, even as she described her own Antony as
'nature's piece 'gainst fancy,/Condemning shadows quite' (III, ii,
98–9). Throughout the play, the ageing Cleopatra is simultaneously
associated with the artifice of eternity inhabited by pagan gods and
goddesses and classic lovers such as Dido and Aeneas, and with a
highly subjective view of the world (she sees Antony in epic and
romantic terms beyond the range of others), as well as with natural
forces and physical laws.

In his interestingly comparable description of the three dimensions or domains of experience – he calls them the 'three worlds' –
we all simultaneously inhabit, the philosopher of science, Karl Popper, gives us a useful set of coordinates with which to describe
components that incessantly interact in everyday life, yet for the
purposes of theoretical analysis are usually deemed separate, if not
mutually exclusive determinisms. Everyone, for instance, inhabits
Popper's 'world one' which is ruled by physical laws such as the
second law of thermodynamics, and everyone will end the same
way: death, one chaos scientist observed, is *everybody*'s strange
attractor. Yet how we perceive death is another matter. Just as
Shakespeare's individual characters confront death in altogether
different ways, as individuals we see and interpret everything

including death in terms of our individual 'world two', our subjective consciousness, made up of personal desires, memories, and so on, which in turn is inextricably interactive with 'world three', the supply of scientific, religious, cultural, philosophical, political ideas and ideologies, as well as past and present works of art, that are stored in and accessible to us (for subjective interpretation and development) in libraries, museums, newspapers, video shops, and so on. As Popper has pointed out, the incessant interactions – the chaotic, nonlinear cascade – of input and output, of positive and negative feedback and biteback between all these 'worlds' is historically and individually unpredictable and incalculable, allowing (so to speak) for an infinite number of butterfly effects.[8] A political idea or a scientific equation from 'world three' can result in a revolution, or might result in the blowing up of the physical and material 'world one' as we know it. Likewise, our subjective consciousness may be permanently influenced by an idea or work of art from 'world three', or terminated by the physical laws of 'world one' that govern, say, an earthquake, or Alzheimer's or AIDS. As Richard Dawkins observes, cultural relativism stops for all passengers on a plane struck by lightning.[9]

Traditionally, conventionally, the drama (the same holds true for philosophy, literary criticism and ideology) tends to foreground one of Popper's interactive domains, and to marginalize the others. A disaster movie tends to emphasize the impact of a force from 'world one' – say a comet or a virus that will wipe out human life. A psychoanalytic drama will focus on 'world two', on the subjective consciousness, memory, and desire of the protagonist. And the exclusive frame of reference of a formulaic romance novel or a postmodern musical may be to 'world three' – to previous works of the identical genre in the case of the romance fiction, and to other artistic works of various times and genres in the case of the postmodern musical. In Shakespeare criticism, successive generations foreground differing components and marginalize others: neoclassical critics often concentrated on the way the plays violated Aristotelian (world three) theories about structure; or, conversely, defended them on the grounds of their experiential relevance to the dynamics of 'nature'. Romantic critics concentrated on the subjective consciousness of the characters and the Protean imagination of the author. Current critics emphasize the cultural and historical determinism that produced the texts. But all these forces, like

Popper's three 'worlds' – the physically determined, the subjective, and the intertextually cultural/mythic/artistic – are inextricably and chaotically interactive in Shakespearian drama generally (witness *The Tempest*) and all are spectacularly interactive in the portrayal of Cleopatra in particular.

Order in the chaos of love and chaos in political order

A general goal in much of Shakespeare criticism, past and present, has been to impose linear (psychological, moralistic or structural) order on Shakespearian chaos, and often, by extension, to see the author as a conscious or unconscious spokesman for the reigning political, domestic, moralistic or ideological order of his time. But, as witness the history plays, within the scripts themselves political order itself is far more often than not portrayed as all mixed up, precarious, itself irrational, ever on the edge of chaos. The processes of history portrayed are nonlinear: if the Welsh troops had not dispersed as a result of mistiming and misinformation, things might have gone differently for Richard II. They are, of course, dramatically irreversible: 'Oh, call back yesterday, bid time return,/ And thou shalt have twelve thousand fighting men!/Today, today, unhappy day too late' (III, ii, 69–70). Richard landed in England one day too late and that made all the difference. Views about the deposition and the succession of various monarchs change from scene to scene and play to play. The most *consistent* feature of the history plays is a state of *war*.

In the romantic tragedies, the chaos of love is set against a comparably chaotic order. Although it is easy to overlook this fact, Shakespeare's most romantic lovers are *invariably* portrayed in opposition to what might seem comparatively stable tenets of domestic, social and political order. But that order itself is portrayed in terms of tribal warfare: of feuds, political back-stabbing, and ancient grudges and hatreds that are far more lethal, irrational, and certainly more profoundly immoral than the erotic and romantic unions between Romeo and Juliet, Othello and Desdemona, Antony and Cleopatra – or Troilus and Cressida and Jessica and Lorenzo – that dramatically unite Capulet and Montague, Greek and Trojan, black and white, east and west, Jew and Gentile.[10]

'And thou – what needest with thy tribe's black tents,/Who hast the red pavilions of my heart?' goes the Arab love song.

The fact is that, however flawed or feckless and however physically passionate or romantically unrealistic Shakespeare's lovers may be, their subjective determination to 'make love not war', is invariably portrayed as infinitely preferable to its opposite: unrelenting tribal warfare. 'Which form of chaos would you prefer?' is the main question raised by *Romeo and Juliet*. 'Let Helen go; don't use her as an excuse to fight forever' is the message to both sides in *Troilus and Cressida*. *Nothing* any of Shakespeare's lovers do is as criminal or as irrational[11] as the pointless dynastic feud between the Capulets and Montagues; or the interminable war between the Greeks and the Trojans; or the back-stabbing and treachery that goes on in seemingly orderly Rome in *Antony and Cleopatra*; or the ancient tribal grudge between and fed by both Antonio and Shylock; or the hatred emblematic of the cultural (racial, sexual, and tribal) forces opposed to the love between Othello and Desdemona, that are so dramatically embodied in Iago. It is also noteworthy that in the Romantic tragedies the male and female characters are portrayed in terms of a mutuality, a parity of passion and heroism unprecedented in the dramatic tradition.[12]

The one force powerful enough to defy considerations of race, class, and gender-rules is romantic/erotic love as opposed to militant (national, religious) tribalism, which may also override those considerations but tends to unify its adherents *against* the adherents of other tribalisms, and thus has caused, and continues to cause, as much if not more unnecessary suffering than anything else on earth. Yet critical arguments based on the implicit cultural assumptions that identify tribal priorities with order, and assume that the primary duty of a man or a woman is to the tribe (the dynasty, the empire, the nation, or to their race, class, ideology or religion), imply that the love was the negative source of chaos, as opposed to a comparatively *positive* source of chaos in the plays.[13] This is possibly because the romantic heroes are *not* portrayed as *tribal* heroes (like Aeneas) who are superior to their love for women, and are occasionally proved tragically wrong when they try to be. Othello would have done better to make love to Desdemona, as his senses dictated, than to kill her lest she 'betray more men' (v, ii, 6).

In *Antony and Cleopatra*, 'Rome', as embodied in Octavius, seems to exemplify 'masculine' order, law and discipline while

Cleopatra is a 'feminine' force of disruption. But any ideal of Roman order is contradicted by the internal conflicts going on back there, and there is also a strong sense in which the play itself irresistibly pulls us towards its strange attractor, even as it dramatically joins forces with the combination of poetry/romance/sensuality/pleasure/disruption/excitement and the uncertainty principle embodied in Cleopatra. Looked at from a dramatic angle, the play's purely political power-figure exemplifying Roman 'order' is consistently put down as comparatively *un*dramatic and in the end, he is ironically described as an 'ass/Unpolicied' in contrast to Shakespeare's 'lass unparalleled' (v, ii, 302–3, 310). Even as butterfly effects are not just disruptive of order, but necessary to the glorious range and variety of systems (gorgeous as well as catastrophic), Cleopatra could be described as the 'butterfly' in the ointment of Roman hegemony:

'You mean the butterfly is the fly in the ointment.'
'In so far as you'd *like* things to be predictable, yes. [And some people certainly do.] But if everything's predictable, life's bound to get a bit damned dull.'

(Cory, pp. 45–6)

Elsewhere, Shakespeare portrays far darker forms of chaos, but in the context of his most festive tragedy, a Roman world from which Cleopatra's chaotic components are irrevocably banished is felt to be a bit damned dull. Banish chaos, banish butterflies, banish Cleopatra (or banish Falstaff, the comic personification of a 'strange attractor' in *1 Henry IV*) if you will – or if you must – but along with them you have to banish excitement, adventure, along with all risk and temptation from your world, and you will miss them when they are gone. Everybody urged Shakespeare to keep on writing plays with Falstaff in them – witness *The Merry Wives of Windsor*. No one insisted he keep on writing plays about the Lord Chief Justice – or about Octavius as portrayed as the embodiment of Roman order and equilibrium in *Antony and Cleopatra*.

The chaotic components embodied in Cleopatra – her power to entertain, her earthy humour and beguiling deviousness – are, dramatically speaking, perhaps most comparable to the chaotic components and beguiling deviousness earlier involved in the comic portrayal of Falstaff. But her portrayal is absolutely unique in

Shakespearian tragedy in its fusion of art with nature. References to 'art', which occur everywhere in romances such as *The Winter's Tale* and *The Tempest*, are virtually absent from the other tragedies, perhaps by necessity. Art involves an attempt to perfect and control nature, while tragedy generally represents forces in nature and psychology that are beyond any character's art to control: 'To this favour' we must all come, says Hamlet contemplating the skull, and he elsewhere suggests mysteries (things in heaven and earth) whose heart cannot be plucked out, controlled or even fathomed by reason or philosophy. 'There's no art/To find the mind's construction in the face', says Duncan in *Macbeth* (I, iv, 12–13), and Othello could have said the same about Iago. Later in *The Tempest*, even with his godlike 'art' (indeed the tragicomedy may suggest the limits of all forms of power including the power of art), Prospero cannot finally control human emotions or reactions. He can bring Ferdinand and Miranda together, but cannot mandate their falling in love (they do it independently). Nor can he mandate a heartfelt repentance in Antonio, who defiantly maintains the right to remain silent in the end.[14] And Prospero himself finally abandons his art: 'Now my charms are all o'erthrown' (*Epilogue*, 1); his ending will be despair unless he be relieved by prayers voluntarily made by Shakespeare's offstage audience to the God beyond his godgames.

By contrast, Cleopatra never abandons her art, and makes certain, even in her death, that her charms are never overthrown. It is as if she is an uncontrollable force that never loses control. Her 'storms and tempests' are *both* perfectly natural and artistically contrived. To hold the man she truly loves, she artfully deceives him: 'If you find him sad,/Say I am dancing; if in mirth, report/That I am sudden sick' (I, iii, 4–5). Like a professional entertainer, she always keeps her audience guessing, and leaves them wanting more: 'Other women cloy/The appetites they feed, but she makes hungry/Where most she satisfies' (II, ii, 236–8). Thus, as Catherine Belsey has observed in words that could be used to describe Cleopatra's enduring impact as a strange attractor, 'she personifies the elusiveness and mystery that generate desire: she is never pinned down, and so remains an object of desire, not only for Antony, but for the audience'.[15] For in marked contrast to, say Macbeth, or Hamlet, or the actor-manipulators Richard III and Iago, Cleopatra never reveals her inner thoughts or schemes to us in soliloquy, and she is never without an audience to play to on the stage. There are, in fact, several scenes where no one onstage or off can tell for certain whether she is acting or sincere.

One usually thinks of acting, whether in comedy or in tragedy, as behaving in opposition to nature: 'I am not what I play', says Viola (*Twelfth Night*, I, v, 177), even as Macbeth and his lady make their faces vizards to their hearts, disguising what they are. By contrast, the varied roles Cleopatra plays – goddess, queen, virago, the mature woman in love like a teenager – reflect differing facets of herself. Most female characters who play-act in Shakespeare at some point regret they had to do so, but Cleopatra positively enjoys making scenes. In the end, she stages her own death-scene with a prima donna's relish, calling for the right costumes and props (her robes, her crown) so as to leave an applauding world behind her. Even in death she looks like a work of art of her own devising, so beautiful that, in the words of her arch-enemy, she would catch another Antony in her strong toil of grace. But although it is clear that Caesar's show will go on without her, 'why should one stay' to see it, asks Charmian as well as Shakespeare. Don't most of us, on leaving the theatre, regret leaving Egypt to return to our duties in prosaic, grey-suited Rome? In *Antony and Cleopatra*, as elsewhere in Shakespearian drama, the same conflicts and complexities that are observable on every scale within the drama extend to contend in the subjective consciousness of the audience itself.

Thus, the big central conflict between Caesar's Rome, with its priorities of order, power and politics (even its drinking-scenes are politically charged), and Cleopatra's Egypt (with its hedonistic priorities of passion, self-indulgence and sensuality) are enacted in a single line, a single speech, an individual scene, and in the portrayal of individual characters as well as in the outline of the play as a whole. On a structural scale, the conflict is replicated in contrasting scenes set in Egypt and Rome, which are not only geographical places, but embodied in persons and portrayed as states of mind. 'I am dying, Egypt, dying' (IV, xv, 18), says Antony, addressing Cleopatra not just as head of state, but as the physical and symbolic embodiment of all that Egypt represents. On a psychic scale, the conflict is enacted both imperially and internally as Egypt and Rome contend for Mark Antony's loyalty. And after he dies, the conflict dramatically culminates when the mighty opposites, Octavius embodying 'Rome' and Cleopatra embodying 'Egypt', directly confront and contend with eath other in the last scenes. Moreover, even after the play ends, in effect leaving us free to decide whose side we are on, the opposed yet interactive forces portrayed on the stage continue to contend in the minds of the audience itself in the same way they contended in the mind of Antony.

It is interesting that Shakespeare leaves the historically valid persona of the mother out of his complex characterization of Cleopatra so that, in her affair with Antony, Cleopatra is not torn towards a competing force, or attractor. Karen Blixen noted, and said she adapted from Shakespeare, the structural practice of limiting the major characters in correspondence with the forces that contend on the psychological level of action,[16] and this interesting structural perception would suggest that Shakespeare clearly did not want motherhood – a force traditionally associated with stability, not wild sexuality or romantic passion – contending with Antony for *Cleopatra's* allegiance, any more than he shows any force of comparable power competing with Octavius's desire for empire. Antony is torn between counter needs and desires. Cleopatra and Octavius are not, since they personify the forces Antony is torn between.

The coexisting and conflicting desires for order and chaos are obviously not gender-specific either in art or in life. Female sexuality is often associated with chaos in art, but non-sexual women often represent domestic order as opposed to male desires for adventure and freedom. In *Out of Africa*, Karen Blixen portrays the archetypal Madam Knudsen, who 'washed the faces of boys, and snatched away the man's glass of gin from the table before him'. She was 'law and order embodied . . . she did not dream of enslaving by love, she ruled by reasoning and righteousness . . . In his wild heart, under his white-red hair, Old Knudsen feared her more than he feared any man, and suspected all women of being in reality Madam Knudsen in disguise.'[17] Likewise, women who make the law (Aunt Polly and the Widow Douglas) and men who make trouble (Tom Sawyer and Huckleberry Finn) are clichés in American literature, while women may fear the anarchic forces embodied in Falstaff, that attract men to taverns and lead sons astray. But for (and in) most people, the competing forces are all mixed up, as they are in the case of Mark Antony. For instance: in real life, when (metaphorically speaking) in Rome, do not most people at least sometimes feel that they are missing or have missed life's party?[18] And conversely, when revelling too long in Egypt, do not most people feel the stern summons back to Rome? It is interesting that these are exactly the same processes enacted in *The Strange Attractors*, a science fiction fantasy for adolescents by William Sleator.

In Sleator's fantasy, both men (a father) and women (a daughter who is his female counterpart) personify both chaos and order. A teenager interested in chaos mathematics meets a temptingly brilliant and uninhibited, but scheming and artificial girl of his own age, Eve Sylvan, and her comparably interesting (magus-like) father who turn out to occupy a chaotic alternative timeline. In the 'real world' there is a stable version of both the father and daughter, and the 'real', the natural, Eve Sylvan has none of the wild vices of her temptress counterpart. When with one set of Sylvans, the young man is immediately pulled towards the other. At one point, the allure of the chaotic Eve causes him to betray the true, the stable Eve, and he feels irrevocably tainted, like Adam after the Fall: 'Guilt of this magnitude was a new emotion, changing everything, like a layer of grime over the world. It made me strangely exposed, as in a dream where you are naked but no one else has noticed it.'[19] But once he gets back to the non-chaotic (so to speak unfallen) Eve, he 'still wanted to see the other Eve again, even knowing that she had lied to me, and I could never see her again because it was too dangerous.' Still, 'the possibility of a life of adventures with her blossomed in my mind like a jungle of exotic foliage' (p. 144). So he uses a phaser to transport him to her chaotic domain. Once there, he immediately feels the counter-pull towards stability:

> I had wanted so much to be with her again. I had regretted the life of adventure I was giving up. Now we were standing together in the winds under the dramatic sky, with all the time in the world. And what was I thinking about? The real Eve. (pp. 178–9)

In the end he goes back to the stable Eve and destroys the phaser that enables him to cross the timeline to her chaotic counterpart. But the tension never lets up (the behaviour of particles under the influence of a strange attractor remains chaotic), so life with the stable Eve seems unremittingly dull: 'My scientific career is assured . . . Eve and I spend a lot of time working in the lab'. But, he adds, 'it is so boring and ordinary in this timeline.' 'If I had never met the other Eve, and had that taste of adventure, I wouldn't have compared things in this way':

She [the real Eve] would tell me that the only reason I want to go
back is that the other Eve is a strange attractor, pulling the timeline
towards chaos. But that isn't it. I just need to talk to her, to explain,
to see her one more time. It wouldn't be enough of a change to bring
on chaos. I know I'm right about that. I *have* to be. Because I'm
building a phaser now. (p. 182)

Sleator's fiction is based on chaos theory, but it could just as
well have been based on Shakespeare's portrayal of the conflicting
forces operative on Mark Antony (and by extension operative on
the audience, on us). When the play begins in Egypt, a 'Roman'
thought strikes Antony, who resolves to break off from his enchanting queen for fear that he will not only forfeit his share of the
Empire, but will lose the Roman side of himself 'in dotage'. And we
might well agree. By contrast, when in purely political Rome, Antony decides he must to his Egyptian queen return, for in the East
his pleasure lies – and we might well agree that ours does too.

The emotional and imperial triumphs and defeats that culmi-
nate in the final scenes are likewise two-sided, parodixical, themselves at odds. Who, we are left to wonder, really wins and who
finally loses in *Antony and Cleopatra*? When Antony dies in Egypt,
he feels he wins in love although he lost imperial power. Caesar
wins the Empire and exacts tribute from Cleopatra, but instead of
making her march in his Roman triumph, as he so desired to do, he
has to march in her funeral triumph paying due tribute to her and
her Antony. Comparable paradoxes are enacted in extended descriptions of the various characters: Antony is noble, valiant, brave
and loved by his soldiers, as Caesar is not. But still he can no more
win against Caesar in Rome with its politically motivated marriages
and power-plays than he could lose against Caesar in man-to-man
combat. Conversely, Caesar behaves in a conventionally mature,
rational and calculating way, but compared to Antony he seems a
boy, not a man. A walking paradox, Cleopatra is a 'royal wench',
who breathless, power breathes forth. On every conceivable scale,
the play contains its own contradictions, its own forms of chaos –
and in this it is remarkably like Cleopatra herself.

This complexity makes comparatively linear, moralistic and
ideological interpretations of the play and its major characters alike
seem oversimplified. Successive critics of Mark Antony, both within
the play and in commentaries on it, have argued that Antony would

have been better off if he had broken with Cleopatra. Yet Shake-speare suggests that he would have had no more chance against Caesar than Lepidus did. Moreover, there is a strong suggestion that, as Octavius himself apparently anticipated, Antony could *never* have made it with the ladylike Octavia. Octavia would indeed be a perfect wife for another Roman general, and she is portrayed very sympa-thetically by Shakespeare as a pawn in a political game. She is also portrayed as an embodiment of domestic order and stability (com-pare Sleator's stable Eve) in contrast to Cleopatra who personifies erotic and romantic chaos and instability. But because Antony him-self was not of a holy, cold and still disposition, Octavia's conven-tional virtues work against her, even as Cleopatra makes defect perfection. But Antony's return to Cleopatra is not Octavia's fault any more than it is his, or Cleopatra's, in so far as all three of them did what came naturally. So does Octavius. It is interesting that this play consistently discourages moralistic blame. Even if you do not like Octavius much, you cannot possibly categorize him as evil in anything like the same way you can categorize Iago, any more than you can condemn Cleopatra as a villainess. One reason we may be unable to cast moral stones at this play's characters is that we all contain components of Egypt and Rome, and experience comparable conflicts between them. Offstage as on, an acute psychic desire for Egypt (for passion, adventure, chaos, Cleopatra) simultaneously competes and coexists with a need for control, discipline, order, with the sense that Rome finally had to win.

This is the reason why, in contrast to the end of, say, *Othello*, there is nothing horrifying or terrible or wrenchingly pathetic about the end of *Antony and Cleopatra*. One has not glimpsed the void, as in *Macbeth*. It is only that 'The odds is gone', 'young boys and girls/ Are level now with men', and 'there is nothing left remarkable/ Beneath the visiting moon' (IV, xv, 67–70). Having witnessed the end of Cleopatra and her world, one does not walk out of the playhouse feeling pity, terror or purgation so much as acute nos-talgia, as it were for a vanished, irretrievably lost domain of exotic experience. For whatever its faults, and indeed because of its fabu-lously hedonistic excesses and eroticism, it was in Egypt where our dramatic and poetic pleasure lay. But aesthetic and emotional nostalgia seems a very odd effect for a major *tragedy* to evoke. And in so far as the world left behind seems diminished by their absence, the loss seems the world's more than Antony's or Cleopatra's – they had what they wanted from life. Octavius likewise gets what he wanted, but to Cleopatra 'Tis paltry to be Caesar'; not being fortune, he's but fortune's temporary minister, who will in turn be replaced (v, ii, 2–4). Indeed Caesar's order is only temporary: the Christian dispensation that will replace Imperial Rome is hinted at in lines referring to Herod of Jewry and the time of universal peace. And at some point 'Imperious Caesar, dead and turned to clay,/ Might stop a hole to keep the wind away.' Thus historical time marches on. By contrast, Antony and Cleopatra will triumphantly steal the show from Dido and Aeneas in the time-transcending Elysium of art.

But if the play's hero and heroine had what they wanted, which was the other, and found the world without the other too dull to be worth staying in, then what, if anything, is tragic about their fates? *Antony and Cleopatra* is as far outside the realm of conventional tragedy as it is outside the realm of Roman morality as determined by the priorities of order, domesticity, politics, power. On whatever scale you look at it – language, characterization, victories and defeats – *Antony and Cleopatra* is ideologically, morally, and structurally paradoxical, irregular, unconventional, chaotic, like Cleopatra herself. She remains an enigma, a butterfly, a mask, a strange attractor that generates desire, and the only phaser that can transport us to her timeline is the script. Onstage, there is no art to find her mind's construction in the physical persona of any given actor who plays her, no way to tell the dancer from the dance.

Many of these points about *Antony and Cleopatra* are obvious, but it seemed necessary to show that the drama itself is based on a comparable enigma: while the show is going on, there is no way to know what the actor playing Cleopatra, or Octavia, or Enobarbus is really like behind or beyond the role being played – or to know what Shakespeare himself was like independently of the lines he wrote for players to speak and others to read.

Possible theatrical contributions to chaos in Shakespeare's scripts

To my mind, it would be far more fascinating to know what parts Shakespeare played in his own plays than to know the identity of the 'real' dark lady, or Mr W. H. For all we know, he may have played important roles. Although he compares himself to an 'imperfect' actor stricken with stagefright in Sonnet 23, he is very conspicuously cited alongside the star actor Richard Burbage in the cast lists of 'Principal' players appended to two plays by Ben Jonson, the comedy *Every Man in his Humour* and the Roman tragedy, *Sejanus*. The lists are not in alphabetical order (which at least suggests billing) and in both of them Richard Burbage is at the top of one column and William Shakespeare appears at the top of the other. And of course Shakespeare is listed first amongst the 'principal actors' cited in the First Folio edition of his own plays, which would seem odd if everyone knew he had only played minor parts in them. The billing here, like the billings alongside Burbage in the Jonson cast lists, suggests that Shakespeare may have sometimes played second-leads, or major character parts. As Jonson's editors, Herford and Simpson suggest, he might have played the enigmatic, manipulative Emperor Tiberius who sets up the protagonist's fall in *Sejanus*, which in turn at least raises the possibility that a year later he might have played the enigmatic Duke who sets up Angelo for his fall in *Measure for Measure*. A contemporary reference associates him with 'royal parts' and theatrical legend has it that he played the Ghost in *Hamlet*,[20] in which case he could have doubled as the Player King himself, as actors often do today.

Obviously all this is a matter of sheer speculation, but surely the assumption that Shakespeare may have written great lines and parts for himself (as well as for Burbage and other members of the company) is at least as tenable as the assumption that he did not. It certainly has at least as much, if not more, historical back-up than most biographical speculations about Shakespeare.

It would be especially interesting if he played major second-leads and supporting roles such as the Duke, Enobarbus, and Iago, who likewise have lines metadramatically associating them with the playwright. Enobarbus in effect commends Shakespeare's 'wonderful piece of work' to his audience. I will 'make the net/That shall enmesh them all' (II, iii, 350–1), says Iago, who acts like a demonic surrogate for the playwright, turning everything (including accidental effects) to his deterministic purposes. And the old fantastical Duke of dark corners is responsible, in turn, for the situations that get the other characters into and then out of trouble, like a playwright who wrenches the course of action from potential tragedy to a technically comic resolution.

Throughout *Measure for Measure*, the Duke and the playwright alike seem to be making things up as they go along. They likewise conjure up new characters – Mariana, Ragozine – from nowhere when the plot needs substitutes for the main ones; they arbitrarily decide what they and the other characters are going to do next (for example, substitute Mariana for Isabella in the bed-trick); and they perfunctorily pair off the other characters in the end. The Duke's line describing a dramatically convenient coincidence (the death of a pirate, Ragozine, who looks like Claudio) – 'tis an accident that heaven provides' (IV, iii, 74) – would take on special meaning if it came from the author who provided it perhaps as a result of a decision, *made in the course of writing the play*, to spare the engaging reprobate, Barnardine, Claudio's original substitute: '*That* would solve the problem, but it is so improbable I had better call attention to its improbability.' A heaven-sent accident, chance, the turns of fortune's wheel, become part of an overall dramatic determinism when, but not before, their interventions are firmly fixed in the text.

Chance certainly serves the deterministic purposes of the demonic playwright-surrogate, Iago. It is hard to find a discussion of Shakespeare that takes into account the force of sheer chance in his plays as a determinism independent of the psychology or morality of the characters it operates on. Yet the words 'chance', 'mischance', 'accident', 'accidental', appear at crucial points, and are stressed as major coordinates in many of the tragic as well as comic scripts. A storm that has nothing to do with the morality of any character averts the Turkish attack on Cyprus – had it not occurred there would have been no time for the garrison intrigues in *Othello*. Chaos theory, with its stress on butterfly effects which have nothing to do with individual morality, but everything to do with the subsequent course of events, has affinities with the drama as well as with real life where a chance encounter, an accidental convergence, the state of the weather at a given time, can irrevocably (as it were deterministically) alter what happens next.[21] Butterfly effects operative on the playwright (something he had just read, a conversation overheard while writing them) may have shaped the scripts of Shakespeare's plays, and chance effects on the performers in or out of rehearsal may have contributed to their impact in performance. Too many coincidences, as there are in *Measure for Measure* (or in certain works by Thomas Hardy) make the action seem incredible, so Shakespeare calls attention to their improbability. In comedy, manifestly improbable multiple coincidences are traditionally part of the fun. In the right balance, accident in tragedy can be fearsome. As in the case of a butterfly effect, a small chance effect can result in catastrophic consequences. In the source of *Othello*, Giraldi Cinthio's *Hecatommithi*, the Ensign (Iago) dexterously steals the crucial handkerchief from Disdemona [*sic*], then plants it in the bed of the Captain (Cassio), who, not knowing how it got there, but knowing how much Disdemona treasures it, attempts to return it to her when the Moor is away. But just at that time, the Moor returned and the Captain fled away, making the circumstances look suspicious. Thus, Cinthio concludes, 'It seemed as if fate conspired with the Ensign to work the death of the unhappy Disdemona.'[22] Shakespeare's script compounds the irony to make the chance dropping of the handkerchief (it is not entirely clear whether Othello or Desdemona drops it) far more dramatically conspire with Iago in determining the course of events.

In an obituary describing the cinematic ringmaster, Federico Fellini, Richard Corliss suggests that for him (as for Guido in 8½) what separated life from art was the recognition that on celluloid he can do *anything*: 'reunite lovers, reconcile families, turn dream into drama and lead the players in a dance around the center ring'.[23] Shakespeare also does all these things and dramatically displays the same sorcerer's power to do just the opposite – to disrupt harmony totally and recklessly – in the person of Iago.

Romantic critics thought it had nothing to do with crass theatrical reality, and was a kind of miracle that Shakespeare could as easily imagine an Iago as an Imogen, that he had a capacity to engage himself with all his characters yet also stand apart from them. But the identical terms they used to describe the most divine, the most difficult, most miraculous, most awesome achievements of Shakespeare-the-Poet might appear in any job description outlining the basic requirements for employment as a principal player in a repertory company such as the King's Men. For example: 'Must be able to enter into the thoughts and sentiments of beings in circumstances wholly and strangely different from your own; must be able to adopt the passions and rise to the functions and feelings of (say) an Enobarbus one night, a Kent on another and an Iago on the next, yet must also (of course) stand emotionally apart from the role, so as not *really* to kill the person playing Emilia when playing Iago.'

The generally unchallenged assumption that 'one of the ways in which Shakespeare served his company was certainly as an actor, though the evidence, sketchy though it is, suggests that this was the least of his professional capacities'[24] may stem from romantic canonizations of the pure poet. The evidence, sketchy though it is indeed, suggests that Shakespeare was a *'principal'* actor. But be that as it may. The fact is that whoever Shakespeare may have had in mind to play them, he wrote successive roles for *some* mature actor who was good at playing a mature star-actor/hero's loyal – or apparently loyal – long-standing, blunt-spoken and honest second-in-command: Kent, Enobarbus, Iago. So close was the identification between characters and actors in Shakespeare's company that the name of Kemp, the star clown who played him, appears in the place of the character Dogberry in the text of *Much Ado About Nothing*. Certainly – indeed, as a matter of dramatic record without any qualifications – perhaps in order to assure that the company's comedian would have roles in them, clown parts are introduced in tragic contexts of various kinds: the porter of the darkly comic hell-gate has a big scene in *Macbeth*. So does the grave-digger in *Hamlet* and the fellow who brings the asp to Cleopatra.

By the same token, with obvious consistency, the tragedies and comedies alike provide good parts for an actor who specialized in foppish gulls, such as Sir Andrew Aguecheek or Roderigo, and this may account for the appearance of Osric, the last type one would otherwise expect to encounter in the dark and devious world of *Hamlet*. Neo-classic theorists found them incongruous intrusions on tragic solemnity, but the introduction of parts designed for clowns and lightweights in the tragedies, perhaps determined by theatrical necessity, contributes to the chaotic sense of the mingled yarn of life emergent from them.

Moreover, actors generally enjoy playing Shakespeare's minor as well as major characters of all types and ages because they allow for individually bifurcating, chaotic developments of the various roles with altogether different tonalities and effects (sympathetic, moving, amusing, ironic, heroic, anti-heroic). Actors like transforming differing, perhaps otherwise imperceptibly small effects only suggested by the playwright into large, scene-stealing ones. As Robert Clare, an actor–director, once told me, chaos theory fits theatrical practice in general, as well as Shakespearian drama in particular, because within a predetermined dramatic context, unpredicted effects may unfold in rehearsals as well as occur spontaneously on stage and thus contribute to the play's total effect in performance. The various opportunities afforded a supporting actor who specialized in playing wise and not-so-wise old men is another case in point. Superb parts for old men (playable with differing degrees of sympathy) appear in the comedies, histories and tragedies alike and range from Julius Caesar to Polonius. The odds are very good that the same actor played both. When the actor playing Polonius says that he himself once acted Julius Caesar and was stabbed by Brutus in the Capitol (*Hamlet*, III, ii, 99), he may well be referring to his own performance in Shakespeare's previous tragedy, and metadramatically anticipating that Burbage (who almost certainly played Brutus and was then playing Hamlet) would in turn stab the actor playing Polonius in the present play even as he had stabbed him as Caesar in the earlier one.[25]

And certainly by the time Shakespeare wrote *Antony and Cleopatra* there must have been a boy actor in the company whom Shakespeare believed capable of playing what is certainly the most difficult of all parts for a young person (of either sex) to play. It would be comparatively easy for a boy actor to play a young heroine (Juliet, Desdemona) credibly, but to portray a mature woman with the sexual potency, glamour, and lusty (Mae West style) humour of Cleopatra would require genius. Indeed it is hard to think of a modern performance of the role wherein even the most famous and experienced actresses of our time have achieved very much more than partial success. But there *must* have been some boy actor or actors for whom Shakespeare wrote mature female parts like Gertrude, Lady Macbeth, Emilia, and Cleopatra. Certainly the injoke where Shakespeare's 'royal wench' pointedly complains how some 'squeaking Cleopatra' will 'boy' her greatness in the posture of a whore (V, ii, 216–17) suggests that the author was certain the boy actor could simultaneously maintain and completely fracture the dramatic illusion. The young actor's artful role-playing must have been cognate to Cleopatra's own.

Certain other chaotic components, including the dramatic disruption of sexual gender in his portrayal of Cleopatra, may have had to do with that fact that she *was* played by a boy. In the comedies, some of Shakespeare's other attractive heroines anticipated her disruption of gender-based decorums, yet nevertheless remain comparatively ladylike, even in doublet and hose.[26] But his most glamorous *femme fatale* is by all odds the least ladylike heroine in the annals of tragic drama. Such a chaotic disruption of gender-decorums along with neo-classical tragic decorums explains why Dryden altered the source in his adaptation to make Cleopatra far more genteel – and thus presumably more sympathetic as a heroine – and conversely made Octavia a more conventionally shrewish wife and thus less sympathetic than Shakespeare's portrayal of her as a 'feminine' ideal as opposed to his fabulous anti-ideal heroine. Not only does Shakespeare's Cleopatra play the termagant, she wears Antony's armour, goes fishing with him, laughs him into humour and drinks him to his bed. And her gender-bending is part of her strange attraction. By contrast, it is impossible to imagine her rival, the gentle Octavia (who represents domestic order) getting drunk, playing billiards or telling dirty jokes with her 'man of men'. As the portrayal of Cleopatra suggests, one signature of a 'strange attractor' in literature is that he or she combines qualities usually deemed wildly incongruous, unconventional, odd, queer, alien, outside the 'norm':

> Wendy had been more than a match for him in every sense. With that lean, pliant body and all that dynamic – well – *virility*.
>
> (Cory, p. 183)

In Desmond Cory's detective fiction the 'strange attractor' (it had to happen somewhere) turns out to be a lesbian.

Chaos and gender

Art bends both ways, but religion and its ideological derivatives tend to impose *gender* on chaos and order. In religious mythology, order is generally personified in male figures and disrupted by chaos embodied in women (Pandora, Eve, Kali and so on). As Susan Niditch observes, in her account of chaos and cosmos throughout the Bible, there is a consistent unease with a woman not under a man's control precisely because she 'has the power to disrupt safe categories'.[27] Attempts to control Eve amount to efforts to control chaos. Thus the post-Edenic insistence on the submission of Eve and her daughters – 'Thy desire shall be to thy husband, and he shall rule over thee' (Genesis 3: 16; see also 1 Timothy 2: 11–15) – was issued as a deterministic necessity by the God of our fathers as it were for all eternity. In a feature captioned 'Things go better if a man is in charge' (*The Independent*, 15 April 1994, p. 20), an Afrikaner, Frank Brummer, said 'his dad always made the decisions and his grandfather always said a man makes law and a woman makes trouble.' But it cannot go without saying here that (thanks to the determinism that ordained butterfly effects?) although he himself 'inherited these ways', Brummer notes that his brother ('Can you believe it – he got provincial colours for netball!') unaccountably turned out 'soft on the chicks, not hard like me.' So shall the deterministically chaotic world go on. As Julie Burchill has observed, efforts to impose linear determinisms on sexuality (in life or in theory) amount to efforts to impose order on, or to seek blind order in, a sphere of unremitting chaos (*The Sunday Times*, 14 February 1993, section 6, p. 3).

As Catherine Belsey has observed, in *Paradise Lost* the beautiful, innocent Eve's unfallen sexuality is, so to speak, deterministically chaotic – 'at once God-given' (determined) and 'dangerous' (chaotic):

> The instability is not individual but representative: this is what men, to be masters, must subdue, and it is precisely their ability to dominate such a powerful force that legitimates patriarchal control. The achievement of mastery is, we are to understand, a perpetual struggle . . . This is the relationship between men and women ordained by a patriarchal God. The consequence, of course, is the Fall. Adam submits to his own susceptibility; he subjects his wisdom to female charm and his will to Eve's.

But given Milton's unalterable source (Genesis), after the Fall God, 'who seems to have learned nothing' from the events that led to it, 'simply reinstates the same patriarchal relations which brought it about (X, 195–6), and the whole cycle is repeated throughout history.'[28]

Belsey's paradox explains why female gender itself is associated with chaos. It is interesting that when Eve debates about offering the fruit to Adam, it never occurs to her that he might refuse it. And it need not have: he is 'against his better knowledge, not deceiv'd' (IX, 998), but from the instant he sees what she has done, he resolves to die with her rather than be severed from her. Hers was, from the beginning, the strange attraction not deterministically – *or* deterministically? – included in the original equation.

Female sexuality is associated with chaos because it arouses chaotic desires in men. Even the most virtuous women (witness Lucrece) may arouse rapacious desire: their unattainability makes them strange attractors that instigate chaotic rapacity in men like Tarquin. Hence uncontrollable forces (cats, female sexuality – even innocent sexuality) are seen as eternal threats to stability. As Stephen H. Kellert observes in his book on chaos and complexity, today as yesterday, women are often 'likened to wild, disorderly features of the natural', even as the chaos scientist could be likened to the male force out to impose an intellectual order on them.[29] Given its main metaphors for the catalysts of chaos, the strange attractor and the butterfly effect, this seems inevitable. As in John Fowles' *The Collector*, women, not men, are usually compared to butterflies. But the main premise of chaos science is *altogether* different from the old oppositions between (good, male) order and (bad, female) chaos, in insisting that in the nonlinear systems of nature (which are so ubiquitous that the term has been compared to describing all animals that are not elephants as 'non-elephant animals'), order and chaos are inextricably intertwined.

Literary chaos: catalyst or control?

Discussing 'Science and Poetry', back in 1926, I. A. Richards feared that:

> the Hindenburg Line to which the defence of our traditions retired as a result of the onslaughts of the last century will be blown up in the near future. If this should happen a mental chaos such as man has never experienced may be expected. We shall then be thrown back . . . upon poetry. It is capable of saving us; it is a perfectly possible means of overcoming chaos.[30]

But it could be counter-argued, and has been argued ever since Plato made the points in his classic attack on poetry, which I believe is, paradoxically, its best defence, that poetry – in so far as its determinisms not only contain but ordain chaos – can serve and has served the purposes of disrupting smug and tyrannical traditions of sexual, social and political order. The ultimate attractors (male, female, positive, negative) in classic and popular art are *always* 'strange' in one way or another.

For obviously, male and female characters (such as Hamlet and Cleopatra) who exhibit chaotic components are more dramatic, more exciting for an actor to play or an audience to watch, than characters portrayed according to stereotypically, traditionally, culturally ordered gender roles (such as Fortinbras and Octavia). Chaotically, paradoxically, in the context of *Measure for Measure*, the fiery, passionately chaste novice, Isabella (who in the first half of the play cannot be had – or controlled – by any man) is far more exciting to everyone on stage and in the audience than the compliant, supine Mariana. This is why it seems such a let-down when her disruptive, chaotic components are subdued by the playwright-figure, friar-figure, father-figure, husband-figure, Duke who personifies the heavenly and earthly powers-that-be.

Perhaps significantly, chaotic components (seemingly incompatible, often gender-disrupting components) have, without exception, been flamboyantly displayed, rather than played-down, by Hollywood's most celebrated superstars. To give a few examples, Bogart combined cynicism and romantic idealism in *Casablanca* ('I always knew you were a sentimentalist at heart, Rick'); Garbo, with her enigmatic face and androgynous body, combined strength, worldly widsom, unattainability and erotic vulnerability. Tough and tender, the young Elvis looked like Apollo and moved like Dionysius. Like an angel fallen to earth and making ends meet as a call-girl (Julie Burchill's phrase), Marilyn Monroe combined child-like innocence with a knowing, experienced sexuality. And so on. In Shakespeare, the strangely, sexually attractive Isabella combines religious asceticism with a personally uncontrollable power to arouse, 'to move men' (I, iii, 170–2) that neither the icy Angelo nor the previously immune Duke can withstand. The passive, conciliatory Gertrude (who could have been well played by the later Monroe as she appeared in *The Misfits*) has that certain voluptuous something that obsesses male figures as different as the Ghost, Hamlet and Claudius. The most potent of strange attractors in Shakespearian comedy, grey-bearded, white-haired Falstaff embodies qualities generally associated with reckless youth. And all of them serve the drama as catalysts of chaos.

So, of course, does Richard III. The world of his play begins in tenuous order, peace; but as a strange attractor he disrupts it on every scale. Previously compared to chaos incarnate –

Why, love forswore me in my mother's womb
And, for I should not deal in her soft laws,
So did corrupt frail nature with some bribe . . .
To disproportion me in every part,
Like to a chaos, or unlick'd bear-whelp.

(3 *Henry VI*, iii, ii, 153–61)

– Richard subsequently displays extremely seductive powers that somehow seem not impeded but enhanced by his deformity. The dramatic prototype of 'The man you love to hate' (compare Hannibal Lecter as portrayed by Anthony Hopkins in *The Silence of the Lambs*) Richard, especially in Olivier's hypnotic film performance, has an irresistible dramatic appeal. So does Milton's defiant Satan, and so do many quintessential villains embodying the primal appeal of the first of all strange attractors, the seductive serpent in the garden.

Cleopatra, Richard and Iago are likewise associated with serpents, but the serpents Cleopatra is associated with are real, not metaphysical snakes, and she is dramatically associated with the chaos and power of love. By contrast Richard III ('Why, love forswore me in my mother's womb') and then Iago are associated with the chaos that ensues in its complete absence. Richard's schemes unfold 'like to a chaos' that serves a larger order: Queen Margaret's prophecies and curses suggest a relentless historical and metaphysical determinism, a merciless nemesis (an eye for an eye, an Edward for an Edward) that ordains and contains Richard's chaos. By contrast, no system of overriding justice is associated with Iago: his experiments on and tortures of the other characters are as detached from a positive object as those of Doctor Moreau or Amon Goeth. There is a strong suggestion in the play that his demonic godgames are purely a matter of 'sport': 'Pleasure and action make the hours seem short (ii, iii, 369). Iago creatively enjoys making sure that when Othello loves Desdemona not, chaos is come again. In this, yet again, he is very like a playwright determined to turn what otherwise could have been a romance with a happy ending into tragedy (although Shakespeare of course stresses the pity of it and terrifies us with it), even as the Duke in *Measure for Measure* is very like a playwright who suddenly decides to reverse the course of potential tragedy towards comedy.

The positive, life-enhancing components in the portrayals of Falstaff and Cleopatra have affinities with the carnivalesque as classically defined by Bakhtin. But like a photo-negative reversal, the components embodied in Iago suggest a demonic (ultimately negative) determinism as opposed to, say, Prospero's ultimately providential determinism ordaining chaos. Yet the idea of the external force, the virus, the Iago that it would have occurred to no one (Othello, Desdemona, Cassio) to include as a disruptive force in their own deterministic equations (they all foresee a happy marriage and continuing friendship), but which irrevocably alters the otherwise predictable course of action, cannot but arouse pity and terror, since everybody is comparably vulnerable to comparable disruptions. Compare Desmond Cory's account of a strange attractor quoted at the start of this chapter – things may be going around in a nice smooth orbit, but then some unknown factor interferes and pulls the particles out of the pattern; and it all goes haywire. Iago is like a virus that invades and spreads throughout the system. Not so long ago, people unaware of its existence began to be infected by the AIDS virus, and may have innocently infected others, as Emilia transmitted the handkerchief, via Iago to Cassio, quite unaware of the horrific consequences of doing so.

Looked at from this angle, the fearsome and mysterious consequences of butterfly effects (the dropping of a handkerchief) and strange attractors (Iago), as metaphorically operative within it, arguably make *Othello* more interesting than linear critical equations whereby the tragedy was absolutely determined from the outset by the race, gender, class, psychic predisposition or tragic flaws of the protagonist. Likewise in science, it used to be supposed that there was a one-to-one association between earlier and later states, but now it seems apparent that translated into a prediction problem, an input *error* multiplies itself at an escalating rate. The tragedy of Othello is far more poignant, painful and terrifying if, without the input error embodied in Iago, the love between Othello and Desdemona might instead have grown, even as their days did last.

For that matter, if the original equations had absolutely determined the action of *Othello either* one way or another (if, for example, the marriage was doomed from the start on account of, say, Othello's sexual or psychological hang-ups, or on account of the lovers' differences in age, race, and class; or alternatively, if their transcendent love had linearly rendered the relationship impervious to disruption) the consequent tragedy, or alternatively happy ending, would be comparatively pat and predictable. The

more terrifying, and perhaps more accurately metadramatic suggestion that like Othello or Macbeth, we *all* live on the edge of
chaos and may enter transitional 'phase space' at any point as a
consequence of a strange attractor–butterfly effect, is far more com-
pelling and dramatic than the suggestion that unlike the characters
on stage, we in the audience are as immune, invulnerable, and safe
in real life as we are while watching *their* catastrophes unfold on
the stage.

Strange attractors in phase space

In his history of chaos science, James Gleick describes the strange
attractor in ways that could serve as an equally fascinating account
of the impact of the witches in *Macbeth*:

> The strange attractor lives in phase space . . . In phase space the
> complete state of knowledge about a dynamical system at a single
> instant in time collapses to a point. That point is the dynamical
> system – at that instant. At the next instant, though, the system will
> have changed, ever so slightly, and so the point moves.[31]

'Phase space' is thus the place or instant of transition when an
entire dynamical system (like Macbeth the victorious returning general loaded with honours) changes from a given point to a different
state, and so the point moves on.

The phase space the witches inhabit and into which Macbeth
enters is, of course, associated with turbulent weather systems, with
thunder and lightning and rain. The witches can be metaphorically
identified with deterministic chaos generally in so far as their clearly
deterministic prophecies are so equivocal that they ultimately disrupt the very certainties Macbeth himself was so determined to find
in them. From their catalytic point of entry into the world of the
play they exponentially disrupt the psychic, sexual and political
order of things so that predictability and unpredictability unfold
together. They are certainly the strangest, the most alien of all
dramatic attractors: 'They should be women' but their beards make
it impossible for Banquo and Macbeth to interpret that they are so.
Thus, when the boy actor playing Lady Macbeth calls on the
powers that tend on mortal thought to 'unsex me here', he/she

metadramatically identifies himself/herself with the sexually ambiguous witches, and subsequently operates on Macbeth to compel
him from point to point in comparable ways. Macbeth's sexuality
in turn goes haywire: after the murder of an unarmed old man
sleeping under his roof as liege, kinsman, and honoured guest (a
murder ironically undertaken in order to prove himself as much a
man as his wife), Macbeth feels new fears that unman him quite.
Comparable disruptions consequently occur on every conceivable
scale: psychic, climatic, domestic, political. The witches issue equivocal prophecies and everything in the play turns equivocal. Could
Macbeth have moved from point to point in altogether different
ways (like Banquo, or the previous Thane of Cawdor) and finally
finished life with all 'which should accompany old age,/As honour,
love, obedience, troops of friends' (v, iii, 24–5)? The equivocations
in the play suggest that everything can not only be taken in various
ways, but can bifurcate in any number of alternative ways.

The number three, dramatically associated with the witches in
Macbeth, is associated with predictable *unpredictability* in chaos
science; and discussions of three-body systems may explain why a
triangular structure lends a measure of unpredictability to the
drama in general. In the absence of the third force (the strange
attractor, Iago) Othello and Desdemona might have had trouble,
but might well have worked out their differences and settled down.
Octavius and Antony might have remained hostile, but in the absence of Cleopatra . . . As James Gleick puts it:

> The two-body problem is easy. Newton solved it completely. Each
> body – the earth and the moon, for example – travels in a perfect
> ellipse around the system's joint center of gravity. Add just one more
> gravitational object, however, and everything changes. The three-
> body problem is hard, and worse than hard. As Poincaré discovered,
> it is almost impossible. The orbits can be calculated numerically for a
> while, and with powerful computers they can be tracked for a long
> while before uncertainties begin to take over. But the equations can-
> not be solved analytically, which means that long term-questions
> about a three-body system cannot be answered.
>
> (*Chaos*, p. 45)

Or see the conclusions of John C. Sommerer and Edward Ott concerning 'A physical system with qualitatively uncertain dynamics',
in *Nature*, 365, 0442, 9 September 1993:

The notion of determinism in classical dynamics has been eroded since Poincaré's work led to the recognition that dynamical systems can exhibit chaotic behaviour, in which small perturbations grow exponentially fast . . . Practically speaking, the behaviour of such systems is quantitatively non-determined. Nevertheless, as the state of the system tends to be confined to an 'attractor' in phase space, at least its qualitative behaviour is predictable. Another challenge to determinism arises, however, when a system has *competing* attractors towards which an initial state may be drawn . . . We suggest that 'riddled' systems of this kind may not be uncommon. (p. 138)

Shakespeare's plays in which 'small perturbations grow exponentially fast', and in which a one-to-one relationship is likewise challenged when a system has competing attractors towards which its initial state may be drawn (even as Antony is torn between Egypt and Rome) are not the only works of art to suggest that riddled systems of this kind may not be uncommon – witness *Fatal Attraction* and innumerable other artistic examples of 'the eternal triangle'.

It is interesting that in Kevin Fegan's play, *Strange Attractors* (performed at the Contact Theatre, Manchester, in 1994), the three central characters are Three, Nine and Eight. 'Nine' is a hairdresser, associated with imagination, whose mind is flickering towards emancipation (like Ariel?). 'Eight' is her lover, a brutal sewerman, 'an animal' (a kind of Caliban/beast-person) whose incoherent instincts torture himself and others. 'Three' is her distant admirer, who via his video screens is the virtual master of all he surveys (like Prospero?).[32]

The three-body problem in science seems cognate to the ubiquitous triangles that pose comparable problems in literature. In *Paradise Lost*, Satan seemed comparatively stable as second-in-line to God until the introduction of the Son as his superior, even as Macbeth seemed comparatively stable until Duncan's investiture of Malcolm as his heir. Adam's relationship with God is stable until the introduction of Eve, first in a dream, then in reality. Eve's relationship with Adam seems comparatively stable until Satan affects her first in a dream, then in the persona of the serpent. And so on.

In chaos theory, the operation of the catalyst of disorder is often compared to the way a drop of vanilla in pastry dough results, in a very short time and only a few foldings, in its wholesale pervasion of the dough; or to a drop of dye in an American taffy candy machine that with a few turns of the mechanism penetrates the substance all the way down to the molecular structure, making the white candy pink all through, in much the same way Macbeth says his bloodstained hand could 'The multitudinous seas incarnadine,/ Making the green one red' (II, ii, 60–1). As a kind of personification of the green-eyed monster that feeds upon itself, Iago likewise infuses Othello with jealousy as it were down to the molecular level. As Paul Davies points out, the 'hallmark' of the result of a 'change in input' in nonlinear systems (the intrusion of a butterfly effect/ strange attractor) 'is that the results will diverge exponentially fast'. Moreover, as David Ruelle observes, 'as we cool water we see that at a certain temperature it changes to ice in a completely abrupt manner'. 'The freezing and boiling of water are familiar examples of *phase transitions*. These phenomena are in fact so familiar that we may miss the fact that they are very strange indeed.' In the same way, 'the style of a painter might gradually change as the artist gets older. And then the unexpected occurs', even as, 'at a certain temperature, instead of a gradual change you have a sudden jump – from helium gas to liquid helium, or from water to water vapor or to ice'.[33] In literature, the alteration from one state to another may take place with comparable speed, even as jealousy takes over Othello; Leontes is not-jealous one moment, and jealous the next moment.

In science, what is termed 'negative feedback' functions to keep things in check, rather like God's prohibitions in *Paradise Lost*, or like the Good Angel who warns Marlowe's Faustus to proceed no further in black magic. Conversely, 'positive feedback' pushes a system to spiral out of control, even as Satan prompts Eve to taste the fruit, and the Evil Angel prompts Faustus to go forward in the magic arts. In literature, as in life, people may have any number of latent desires or impulses but may not act upon them without some catalyst – in the form of 'positive feedback'. In *Paradise Lost* it is one thing to be tempted, another thing to fall: 'Evil into the mind of God or Man/May come and go, so unapprov'd, and leave/No spot or blame behind' (V, 119) – thus it may be kept in check by negative feedback. The moment when evil – or jealousy or love – is not checked but gains entrance and pervades the entire system is often perceptible only in retrospect, when the alteration has already taken place. At one point in her encounter with the seductive serpent, Eve is 'yet sinless' (IX, 559). Satan then makes an impassioned speech urging her to taste the apple and be as a goddess:

> He ended, and his words replete with guile
> Into her heart too easy entrance won:
> Fixt on the Fruit she gaz'd, which to behold
> Might tempt alone, and in her ears the sound
> Yet rung of his persuasive words, impreg'nd
> With Reason, to her seeming, and with Truth:
> Meanwhile the hour of Noon drew on, and wak'd
> An eager appetite, rais'd by the smell
> So savory of that Fruit. (IX, 733–41)

It is interesting that Milton uses the word 'impreg'nd' to describe the primal 'error in input' implanted by Satan. It is as impossible to be half fallen as it is to be half pregnant. One is either pregnant or not. Or jealous or not – people are rarely only half jealous or half in love for very long.

Satan's persuasive speech penetrates Eve to the heart. In her immediate response she refers to the fruit as 'too long forborne' (IX, 747), and it is clear that she has already and conclusively decided to taste it. All that remains is to justify acting on that decision to herself, and her subsequent speeches amount to an (archetypically?) elaborate rationalization for doing what, in her heart and mind, she is absolutely determined to do:

> What fear I then, rather what know to fear
> Under this ignorance of Good or Evil? . . .
> Here grows the Cure of all, this Fruit Divine,
> Fair to the Eye, inviting to the Taste,
> Of virtue to make wise: what hinders then
> To reach, and feed at once both Body and Mind? (IX, 773–9)

So 'Greedily she ingorg'd without restraint/And knew not eating Death', thus effecting the complete transition from immortality to mortality. Within only 121 lines (from the time she was 'yet sinless' to the instant 'she pluck'd, she eat'), Sin and Death enter and infuse her entire psychological and biological makeup – and irrevocably alter the initial conditions she will transmit to her progeny.

In *Macbeth* the comparable transition from one state ('We will proceed no further in this business') to another ('If we should fail?'

I, vii, 31, 69) occurs during a speech by Lady Macbeth insisting that he is not much of a man if he does not kill the king. Before that he argued that it would be best if they abandoned the plan. After her speech he responds with a question which indicates that he has made up his mind to kill Duncan, and is now primarily concerned with the process and consequences. Future decisions are projected ('Will I or won't I?', 'I have to decide'), but a statement about a future course of *action* ('I will' or 'I won't') actually refers to the past, since it presumes that the decision to do one thing or another has already been made. But the exact moment of decision when the point of no return is crossed is rarely perceivable in the present: there is more often a sudden, certain, instantaneously retrospective knowledge that the decision, one way or another, has already been made, and the only questions left are how to rationalize it to oneself or to others and when – not whether – to act on it. Thus the point moves on. The way Shakespeare and Milton portray the transitions from one state to another – unfallen/fallen, not jealous/jealous, stable/unstable – are nonlinear. There is not a steady linear (moral or temporal) trajectory but a wholesale transition very close to the fast and complete transition from order to disorder in chaos theory. As in chaotic systems, in *Othello*, *Macbeth*, and *Paradise Lost* 'input error multiplies itself at an escalating rate'. By contrast, in a typically non-chaotic system, errors accumulate only in proportion to the time involved, even as a small input error results in a proportionally small, not a disproportionally overwhelming error in output.[34]

Heinz-Otto Peitgen and Peter H. Richter, who produced the original mathematical coffee table book, *The Beauty of Fractals*[35] (Springer-Verlag, Berlin, 1986), point out that like works of art, fractal pictures are simplified versions of chaotic reality. They exaggerate certain things to make them clearer. For example, no real structure can be magnified repeatedly an infinite number of times and still look the same. In nature itself, after only a few iterations a new order takes over that in turn gives rise to new butterfly effects, and so on. Scientists of change have thus learned that the evolution of complex systems cannot 'be followed in causal detail because such systems are holistic: everything affects everything else'. In nature, regular linear orders are the exception, not the rule. Therefore, although the images and imagery of chaos are frankly acknowledged to be visual and metaphorical *approximations* of the dynamics of deterministic chaos, 'Nature's true archetypes' may well be *closer* 'to Ruelle's strange attractors and Mandelbrot's fractals' than to Euclidian geometry or to Plato's stable, unchanging forms.[36] The big question raised here is whether – and what if? – the same dynamical models *might* apply to complexity in art, as well as to natural systems which, through repeating and inextricably intertwined processes of bifurcation and development, may spontaneously and simultaneously give rise to chaos and order, turbulence and coherence.

'Just' representations of general nature: some open questions about chaos and aesthetics

There can be no excellent beauty that hath not some strangeness in the proportion.

Francis Bacon, *Of Beauty*

Hannah. This feedback, is it a way of making pictures of forms in nature? Just tell me if it is or it isn't.

Valentine. (Irritated)   To me it is. Pictures of turbulence – growth – change – creation – it's not a way of drawing an elephant, for God's sake!

Hannah. I'm sorry. (*She picks up an apple leaf from the table. She is timid about pushing the point.*) So you couldn't make a picture of this leaf by iterating a whatsit?

Valentine. (Offhand)   Oh yes, you could do that.

Tom Stoppard, *Arcadia*

'Nothing can please many, and please long, but just representations of general nature.' In his *Preface to Shakespeare*, Dr Johnson thus defended the chaotic ('irregular') elements in the plays on the grounds of their non-literal, metaphorical approximations to, as well as their sometimes literal resonance with, 'the real state of sublunary nature which partakes of good and evil, joy and sorrow, mingled with *endless variety of proportion and innumerable modes of combination*' [my italics].[37] As in the case of Cleopatra, the chaotic components in the plays simultaneously contribute to the pleasure they give, and the sense of nature underlying artifice.

Likewise, as John Briggs observes in *Fractals*, his book on 'the new aesthetic of art, science and nature',[38] in their non-literal mimesis certain works of art 'work like nature'. For instance: in art as in nature, self-similarity, 'which can come in infinite variety', is not created by a slavish permutation of the same form at different scales. 'Rather it is closer to the self-similarity seen when we compare a human hand to a hummingbird's wing to a shark's fin, and to a branch of a tree.' Compare the way Shakespeare, who himself tends to find correspondences 'in all things' – as it were recursively – sends up exactly this form of perception in Fluellen's speech delightedly expounding on self-similar correspondences between everything and everybody from Agamemnon, Mark Antony and the Duke of Exeter (*Henry V*, III, vi, 6–15) to the fish in the rivers in Macedon and Monmouth:

> If you look in the maps of the world I warrant you shall find, in the comparisons between Macedon and Monmouth, that the situations, look you, is both alike. There is a river in Macedon, and there is also moreover a river at Monmouth. It is called Wye at Monmouth, but it is out of my brains what is the name of the other river – but 'tis all one, 'tis alike as my fingers is to my fingers, and there is salmons in both. If you mark Alexander's life well, Harry of Monmouth's life is come after it indifferent well. For there is figures in all things. (IV, vii, 22–32)

We are all Fluellenists in so far as the patterns we perceive in everyday life, in nature as in art, are *themselves* composed of 'an endless variety' of interwoven patterns: see Briggs, *Fractals*, p. 31, where he uses *exactly* the same words Dr Johnson used with reference to 'the endless variety of proportion' in Shakespeare's plays.

For that matter, in their discussions of aesthetics, chaos scientists of different nationalities, generations and religions, in effect ubiquitously – yet quite independently and entirely subjectively – rejoice to concur with Dr Johnson's conclusions about the correspondences between nature and certain works of art. 'In the fractal world' there are irregularities, apparent randomness, patterns inside of patterns, 'sometimes infinite detail, and more and more information the deeper we go', even as their various 'dimensions are tangled up like a ball of twine'. Arguably at least, the same holds true of certain nonlinear works of art that would seem to become infinitely more complex and detailed as you explore deeper and deeper regions of their incessantly recursive 'geography'. By contrast, in the case of linear Euclidian structures, 'magnifying spheres, triangles, squares or lines won't yield up much new information about the object at hand',[39] and the same holds true of certain 'regular' works of art. 'Why', asks the nonlinear physicist Gert Eilenberger, is a determinedly linear 'multi-purpose university building' seen by most people as comparatively boring rather than uniquely beautiful, 'in spite of all the efforts of the architect'?

> The answer seems to me, even if somewhat speculative, to follow from new insights into dynamical systems. Our feeling for beauty is inspired by the harmonious arrangements of order and disorder as it occurs in natural objects – clouds, trees, and snow crystals. The shapes of all these are dynamical processes jelled into physical forms, and particular combinations of order and disorder are typical for them.

Likewise, according to Benoit Mandelbrot, the spare, orderly, linear, reductionist, architecture of the Bauhaus fails 'to resonate with the way nature organizes itself', or with the way people generally perceive and experience the world. Against the Seagram building, Mandelbrot offers the architecture of the Beaux-Arts 'with its sculptures and gargoyles, its quoins and jamb stones, its cartouches decorated with scrollwork, its cornices topped with cheneaux and lined with dentils' because it has important elements that are active and interactive at every scale. As the observer comes closer and closer to it, new details attract the eye.[40] By the same token, with its wonderful intertwined seahorse shapes within seahorse shapes and intricate curlicues within curlicues, the Mandelbrot set itself has a lot in common with an ornate building like St Basil's in Moscow, with its replicated onion domes – or with an intricate oriental carpet – or with jazz – or with kitsch: all of which appeal across cultures.

It is interesting that people in differing societies, who know nothing about mathematics, buy T-shirts, postcards and posters displaying the Mandelbrot set and other fractals (witness 'Strange Attractions', the chaos shop in London), just as tourists unschooled in architecture and from altogether different cultures buy kitschy little copies of nonlinear buildings such as St Basil's. Would they do so if there were no strangeness in their proportions? Or would the perfect face of Nefertiti be any more attractive if one eye were not missing? Might not the missing eye add an extraordinary quality to the perfectly regular face that makes it more, not less, attractive to people who buy little copies of it, like those numinous combinations of animal and human features in statues of Horus and Sekmut?

Even as people of differing nationalities buy duplicates of buildings and statues and paintings produced by past cultures, the combinations of order and disorder so flamboyantly displayed by the most popular film and rock stars have inspired worldwide imitations; witness Garbo look-alikes, Bardot look-alikes, Monroe look-alikes, Elvis look-alikes and Madonna wannabes. For that matter, a possible signature of a complex nonlinear classic – a perfect literary fractal – could be that it will almost *immediately* and then *continually* inspire imitations, ranging from highbrow appropriations and popular spin-offs to comparatively cheap and cheerful and kitschy imitations – like the puppet show based on an opera based on *Paradise Lost*, or the rock musical based on a sci-fi film based on *The Tempest*. Chaotic replications can also take the form of migrations, transplants to different media, different genres, different timelines. Even as Joseph Conrad's *The Heart of Darkness* was transplanted to Vietnam in the film, *Apocalypse Now*, mythic conflicts (such as the Paradise Lost paradigm), with their particular combinations of order and disorder, get transplanted and transported to differing contexts, genres, times and places. The lyrical love (harmony) of Romeo and Juliet was danced and sung against the discord of the feud in Tchaikovsky's ballet, and in *West Side Story*. Nowadays, it would seem comparably relevant to stage the play with a Serbian Romeo and a Croatian Juliet, just as it has recently been staged with Israeli and Arab protagonists.

Arguably at least, the dynamics operative in the nonlinear structures of nature as described in chaos theory, as well as its most evocative metaphors, may prove closer to what most people find aesthetically fascinating and experientially relevant, than comparatively linear aesthetic and ideologically based theories, however well-intentioned, about what people should find artistically and/or ideologically congenial. Order and chaos arising together may resonate beyond their artistic confines. Pure disorder does not. And neither does pure order. This may be why, as Mandelbrot and Eilenberger observe, severely linear architecture has proved only temporarily attractive, and attractive (comparatively speaking) only to a few. There is nothing of the 'strange attractor' in, since there is no strangeness in the proportion of, a purpose-built high-rise shoe box.

Quite independently of chaos theory, Tom Wolfe arrived at conclusions virtually identical to those of Mandelbrot and

Eilenberger. In *From Bauhaus to our House*, Wolfe outlines the ideologically, historically and aesthetically linear assumptions underlying much modern architecture: 'that it should be *non-bourgeois* and have *no applied decoration*; that there was a *historical inevitability* to the forms that should be used; and that the architect . . . would decide what was best for the people and what they inevitably should have.'[41] Then he graphically describes the way rich people and big New York firms, forced by these architectural dicta to inhabit severely linear apartments and offices, spent hundreds of thousands of dollars to alleviate the boredom of absolute order by introducing chaos:

> I have seen the carpenters and cabinetmakers and search-and-acquire girls hauling in more cornices, covings, pilasters, carved moldings, and recessed domes, more linenfold paneling, more (fireless) fireplaces with festoons of fruit carved in mahogany on the mantels, more chandeliers, sconces, girandoles, chestnut leather sofas, and chiming clocks than Wren, Inigo Jones, the brothers Adam, Lord Burlington and the Dilettanti, working in concert, could have dreamed of. (p. 8)

Likewise, people further down the economic scale desperately painted different colours on the doors of the uniform shoe-box council flats that were designed to *divorce* them from 'bourgeois individualism', and then defiantly decorated them with chaotically flamboyant carpets and curtains, fake floral decorations, pictures of animals and shelves full of knick-knacks.

For that matter, in the one and only instance Wolfe cites when people at the very bottom of the scale, the welfare recipients forced to live in it, were actually allowed to deliver their *own* verdict on the impeccably linear housing project designed for them by the prize-winning architect of the World Trade Center, the chant began immediately: 'Blow it . . . *up*! Blow it . . . *up*!'. The city fathers perforce agreed that this was the only solution and blew up the housing blocks with dynamite. By the same token, Wolfe wryly observes, 'nature itself' (deterministic chaos in action) delivered the verdict on huge sports arenas (like the Hertford City Centre Coliseum) with their ideologically mandated flat roofs: 'The snow was too much for them – but they collapsed piously, paying homage on the way down to the dictum that pitched roofs were bourgeois' (pp. 74–5). It could be that artistic, scientific, ideological and political constructions at odds with the independently operative dynamics of deterministic chaos may likewise be doomed not to please many, and not to please long – if not suddenly to collapse.

Conversely, given the most extreme perspective of cultural relativism, it is possible to argue that fractals, the butterfly effect, the strange attractor, and the conceptions of nonlinear dynamics offered by chaos science generally are but culturally produced tropes, 'just' (meaning 'only') metaphors that are no more correspondent to the true state of sublunary nature than the science fictions based on them. But if so, what richly resonant and exciting tropes and metaphors they are! Scientists have found them equally pertinent to the complexities of weather systems, population dynamics, dripping taps, beating hearts and chemical reactions. Creative artists have found them comparably pertinent to their own works and to works of the past, as well as sources of inspiration. And they provide literary criticism with theoretical frames of reference as pertinent to premodern as to postmodern literature, and to widely popular as well as canonical art, even as they have given scientists interpretive tools for describing many of the complexities of the world, from brain rhythms to gold futures.

The metaphors, imagery, and dynamical concepts of chaos science have by now extended far beyond the scientific community because they have simultaneously (and cross-culturally) triggered a strangely combined sense of aesthetic pleasure and experiential recognition in nonspecialists and creative artists alike. They also raise questions. As David Ruelle observes of fractal images: 'These systems of curves, these clouds of points, suggest sometimes fireworks of galaxies, sometimes strange and disquieting vegetal proliferations. A realm lies here to be explored and harmonies to be discovered.' He also observes that 'what is still missing in general is an understanding of how fractal shapes arise.'[42] And the same statement could be made about cognate fractal structures in art. A set of theoretical instructions as to how to construct a play with a dynamic comparable to Shakespeare's or a poem comparable to *Paradise Lost* would probably result in a comparatively lifeless, mechanical and unconvincing play or poem. For that matter, as Tom Stoppard observes (see above, p. 3), chaos science opens up further mysteries by showing that the things people write poetry *about* – clouds, daffodils, waterfalls – to say nothing of 'what happens in a cup of coffee when the cream goes in' are 'as mysterious to us as the heavens were to the Greeks'. And so, arguably, are the spontaneously self-organizing dynamics of complex nonlinear works of art, as well as the spontaneously self-organizing, self-similar, but never exactly repetitive dynamics of the nonlinear artistic tradition itself. No wonder the concepts, metaphors, images and mysteries of chaos have proved irresistibly attractive to all sorts of people (old and young, men and women, scientists and artists) of different nationalities and ideological persuasions. Moreover, if they *do* correspond to the facts, if the real world *is* inherently nonlinear, and they *are*, indeed, 'just' (meaning approximately, comparatively accurate, valid, legitimate, correct) representations of general nature, then their 'real world' implications should be taken into account by all of us.

Looked at either way – as only metaphors, or as more-than-metaphors, megametaphors – they are demonstrably correspondent with what people over centuries have felt to be the most profoundly evocative of all literature's mythical and metaphorical representations of the deterministically chaotic ways of the world.

Notes

1. See John Briggs and F. David Peat, *Turbulent Mirror: An illustrated guide to chaos theory*, Harper & Row, New York, 1989, pp. 109–10. The wonderfully evocative term first appeared in Ruelle and Takens, 'On the nature of turbulence', *Communications in Mathematical Physics* 20, 1971, 167–92. See also David Ruelle, *Chance and Chaos*, Penguin, London, 1993 (first published by Princeton University Press in 1991).

2. See Desmond Cory, *The Strange Attractor*, Macmillan, London, 1991, p. 46. Page references to Cory's book are hereafter cited under Cory, parenthetically in the text.

3. For a very accessible account of attractors, see Arthur Fischer, 'Chaos: the ultimate asymmetry' in *Best Science Writing: Readings and insights*, ed. Robert Gannon, Oryx Press, New York, 1991, pp. 138–57.

4. See Caroline Series, 'Fractals, reflections and distortions' in *The 'New Scientist' Guide to Chaos*, ed. Nina Hall, Penguin, London, 1992, p. 138. The Mandelbrot set reveals the 'set of points in parameter space where a certain type of behaviour breaks down' (p. 147). The same could be said of *Othello* and *Macbeth*.

5. As an addition to the iconography of chaos, it should be noted that cats appear (as it were as strange attractors) in illustrations of alchemy,

since, appropriately, their whiskers form a 'Chi', the initial letter in the Greek ΧΑΟΣ.

6. See Peter Coveney, 'Chaos, entropy and the arrow of time' in *The 'New Scientist' Guide to Chaos* (n. 4, above), p. 203.

7. Contrast the statue scene in *The Winter's Tale*, when art is infused with nature as the ageing Hermione is restored to life. A parallel response to the way in which Cleopatra's departure leaves the world diminished occurs in Karen Blixen's account of the death of a friend in *Out of Africa* (Jonathan Cape, London, 1964, p. 240): 'A presence of gracefulness, gaiety and freedom, an electric power-factor was out. A cat had got up and left the room.'

8. See Karl Popper, *Objective Knowledge: An evolutionary approach*, Clarendon Press, Oxford, 1972.

9. Cultural relativism is highly appropriate to discussions of subjectivity, but it runs into trouble in the domain of non-subjective nature which is governed by chaotic and linear laws that operate quite independently of any cultural considerations. See Richard Dawkins, 'Mad Molecules', *The Sunday Times*, 12 November 1991, section 6, p. 12:

> The cultural relativists who charge scientists with a facile, simplistic or naive realism can be grateful for at least a measure of scientific realism every time they board a jet airplane rather than a magic carpet or a reindeer powered sledge.

Airplanes fly because engineers assume things like 2 + 2 = 4 rather than cultural criteria that are relative and subjective articles of faith as they are 'in the cases of astrology, religion, tribal mythology or Freud'. Dawkins is a strong opponent of arguments that see an essentially benevolent, quasi-religious order in deterministic chaos and complexity. He has evolved a computer model of natural selection from simple rules that generate mutants from a parent and emerge as very lifelike products of a blind, uncaring mechanism. If we human beings are likewise products of a purposeless and pitiless mechanism, this does not mean that we should behave in comparably ruthless and uncaring ways – quite the contrary. See Roger Lewin, *Complexity: Life on the edge of chaos*, Orion, London, 1993, pp. 101–2, and Richard Dawkins, *The Blind Watchmaker*, W. W. Norton, New York, 1987.

10. The elopement of Jessica and Lorenzo posed problems for Nazi productions of *The Merchant of Venice*. One suggested alteration was to make Jessica the product of an adulterous affair between Shylock's wife and a Gentile. But that did not solve the problem, since in the Third Reich the child of such a union would still be classified as a mongrel, a 'Mischling first class' marked for extermination. See John Gross, *Shylock: Four hundred years in the life of a legend*, Chatto & Windus, London, 1992, p. 295. *Othello* was not performed in the Third Reich for obvious racial reasons, and *Antony and Cleopatra* was

deemed too decadent for production. If for no other reason, Shakespeare's romantic lovers deserve congratulations for offending Nazi sensibilities.

11. Love is irrational, but so is patriarchal 'order' in *A Midsummer Night's Dream*: Egeus's preference for Demetrius (Tweedledum) is at least as irrational as Hermia's preference for Lysander (Tweedledee).

12. Chaucer had written brilliantly of Troilus and Criseyde, and Marlowe wrote a play about Dido and Aeneas (to which Shakespeare may have referred in *Antony and Cleopatra*), but it was through Shakespeare that equally matched, equally billed co-starring lovers (Romeo is rarely mentioned without Juliet or Antony without Cleopatra) entered the *mainstream* dramatic tradition. It is important that his dramatic portrayal of equally matched pairs of male and female characters gave rise to the great tradition of co-starring actors and actresses that extended from the Restoration through the heyday of Hollywood (Pickford and Fairbanks, McDonald and Eddy, Garbo and Gilbert, Taylor and Burton) until it was subverted by the succession of 'buddy movies' that arose in the wake of feminism. See Harriett Hawkins, 'Disrupting tribal differences: Shakespeare's radical romanticism' in *Studies in the Literary Imagination* 26 (Spring 1993), 115–24, and Julie Burchill, *Girls on Film*, Virgin Books, London, 1986.

13. See Allan Bloom's tirade against Juliet, Desdemona and Jessica for disrupting tribal/patriarchal order in *Shakespeare and Politics*, University of Chicago Press, Chicago, 1981. Of course they will not, but if every girl carried on the way they did and eloped with – and subsequently had children by – a member of a different clan, race, religion or tribe, although a measure of chaos would obviously ensue, it is hard to see how things would be that much worse than they are now. For an attack on the 'mushy sentimentality', 'softness', and inevitable 'love interest' in Shakespeare's plays see Gary Taylor, *Reinventing Shakespeare*, Hogarth, London, 1990, p. 400. The critical vocabulary describing the wrong kinds of responses to drama (soft, mushy, sentimental, passively yielding to poetry's power of swaying the emotions and moving the heart) has been associated with deplorably unmanly femininity/effeminacy from Plato to the present day. These are the kinds of things about the plays that might appeal to a woman, or perhaps a sissy, but should not be tolerated in serious art or criticism. Still, one might well ask, why not?

14. See Stephen Orgel's brilliant editorial introduction to *The Tempest*, Oxford University Press, Oxford, 1987, pp. 55–6.

15. See Catherine Belsey, 'Shakespeare and the nature of desire' in *The English Review* (November 1993), 4.

16. See Judith Thurman, *Isak Dinesen: The life of Karen Blixen*, Weidenfeld & Nicolson, London, 1982, pp. 118–19.

17. See *Out of Africa* (n. 7, above), p. 205.

18. In a witty column in *The Observer* (29 November 1992, p. 55), Katharine Whitehorn describes a woman of sixty who had put her life entirely in order; but the moment she read that the world's oldest woman was not allowed a glass of port by her doctors, 'something snapped'. Although it was only 11a.m., she poured herself a glass of gin and bought a plane ticket to Paris, having concluded that if you are going to be as well ordered as she had tried to be, you might as well be dead already, and the sixties are our 'last chance saloon'.

19. See William Sleator, *The Strange Attractors*, Heinemann, London, 1991, p. 123. Page numbers are cited parenthetically in the text.

20. For the suggestion that Shakespeare might have played Tiberius in *Sejanus*, see C. H. Herford, and Percy and Evelyn Simpson, *The Complete Works of Ben Jonson*, vol. 9, 1950, p. 252, where they quote John Davies' reference to Shakespeare having played 'some Kingly parts'. Nicholas Rowe first said that Shakespeare played the Ghost in *Hamlet* (see p. 191). See also Stanley Wells, *Shakespeare: A dramatic life*, Sinclair-Stevenson, London, 1994, p. 26.

21. What Alfred Hitchcock famously termed a 'McGuffin' – an object or incident that may seem insignificant in itself but triggers the action – functions as a kind of strange attractor in his films.

22. See Giraldi Cintho, *Hecatommithi*, trans. J. E. Taylor, and reprinted in *Othello*, ed. Alvin Kernan, New American Library, New York, 1963, pp. 171–84. The quotation is from p. 177.

23. See Richard Corliss, 'Ringmaster and Clown', *Time*, 8 November 1993, p. 88.

24. See Stanley Wells (n. 20, above), p. 25. For pre-romantic and romantic idealizations of Shakespeare the Protean poet (independent of the crudities of the stage) that are paraphrased here, see Jonathan Bate, *Shakespeare and the English Romantic Imagination*, Clarendon Press, Oxford, 1986.

25. The same kind of insider reference occurs in *Julius Caesar* when Cassius metadramatically predicts successive performances of its 'lofty scene' in 'states unborn and accents yet unknown' (III, i, 112–14) – such as the ones involved in the present (Elizabethan) production.

26. See Catherine Belsey, 'Disrupting sexual difference: meaning and gender in the comedies', in *Alternative Shakespeares*, ed. John Drakakis, Methuen, London, 1985, pp. 166–90. Art's chaotic elements may influence fashion. There was a vogue for drag among young women in Jacobean London that might, conceivably, have been inspired by popular theatrical heroines swaggering around in doublet and hose, even as Katherine Hepburn and Marlene Dietrich inspired a vogue for trousers.

27. See Susan Niditch, *Chaos to Cosmos: Studies in biblical patterns of creation*, Scholars Press, Chico, California, 1985, p. 105.

28. See Catherine Belsey, *John Milton: Language, gender, power*, Blackwell, Oxford, 1988, p. 66.

29. See Stephen H. Kellert, *In the Wake of Chaos: Unpredictable order in dynamical systems*, University of Chicago Press, Chicago, 1993, p. 156. The association between women and chaotic natural forces is as old as Western literature. In the earliest work of European literature to have women for its theme, Semonides of Amorgos thus describes a woman Zeus made from the sea:

> She has two characters. One day she smiles and is happy . . . But on another day she is unbearable to look at or come near to; then she raves so that you can't approach her . . . and she shows herself ungentle and contrary to enemies and friends alike. Just so the sea often stands without a tremor, harmless, a great delight to sailors, in the summer season; but often it raves, tossed about by thundering waves. It is the sea that such a woman most resembles in her temper; like the ocean, she has a changeful nature.

See *Females of the Species: Semonides on women*, ed. Hugh Lloyd-Jones with sculptures by Marcelle Quinton, Duckworth, London, 1975, p. 43.

30. See I. A. Richards, *Science and Poetry*, Kegan Paul, Trench, Trubner, London, 1926, pp. 82–3.

31. See James Gleick, *Chaos: Making a new science*, Cardinal, London, 1988, p. 145; page references are subsequently cited parenthetically in the text.

32. See Jeffrey Wainwright's review of Kevin Fegan's *Strange Attractors* in *The Independent*, 12 February 1994, p. 48.

33. Quotations are from Paul Davies, 'Is the universe a machine?' in *The 'New Scientist' Guide to Chaos* (n. 4, above), p. 216, and David Ruelle, *Chance and Chaos* (n. 1, above), pp. 122–3.

34. See Paul Davies, 'Is the universe a machine?' (n. 33, above), p. 216.

35. See H. O. Peitgen and P. H. Richter, *The Beauty of Fractals*, Springer-Verlag, Berlin, 1986.

36. See Briggs and Peat (n. 1, above), p. 110.

37. See Samuel Johnson, *Preface to Shakespeare*, in *Shakespeare Criticism: A selection, 1623–1840*, ed. D. Nichol Smith, Oxford University Press, Oxford, 1916, pp. 79, 83.

38. See John Briggs, *Fractals: The patterns of chaos*, Thames & Hudson, London, 1992, p. 30.

39. *Ibid.*, pp. 24–5.

40. See Eilenberger and Mandelbrot as quoted by Gleick, *Chaos* (n. 31, above), p. 117. These conclusions are everywhere confirmed in films and on TV. Linear urban tower blocks are consistently used to show bleak, ugly modern life. Two Russian artists polled a cross-section of Americans about the kinds of pictures they liked, and the respondents favoured outdoor scenes, but not urban scenes. Nor did they want

geometrically linear forms. They wanted water, trees, animals. See 'The People's Choice', *The Independent Magazine*, 30 April 1994, pp. 12–13.

41. See Tom Wolfe, *From Bauhaus to Our House*, Washington Square Press, New York, 1981, p. 98; subsequent page references are inserted parenthetically in the text. As Wolfe observes, among Bauhaus architects (who were, to a man [sic], from the bourgeois class themselves), 'the main thing was not to be caught designing something someone could point to and say of, with a devastating sneer: "How very bourgeois" ' (p. 17). In effect, to scorn everything 'bourgeois' simultaneously identified the scorner with aristocratic good taste and with the proletariat. Comparably concerted efforts were made to distance the British literary intelligentsia from the tasteless 'masses' in general and the 'suburbs' in particular (see John Carey, *The Intellectuals and the Masses: Pride and prejudice among the literary intelligentsia, 1880–1939*, Faber & Faber, London, 1992). 'How very bourgeois' or 'How very suburban' would still be the most damning of insults in certain intellectual circles. As a footnote to a footnote, Tom Wolfe might well find 'the butterfly effect' as described in chaos theory especially congenial: witness how a small effect (an absent-minded turning onto the wrong road into Manhattan) exponentially gives rise to huge effects in *The Bonfire of the Vanities*.

42. Quotations are from David Ruelle's seminal paper, 'Strange Attractors', *Mathematical Intelligencer* 2, 126 (1980), 37–48 and from his *Chance and Chaos* (n. 1, above), p. 178. On chaos and music see Edward N. Lorenz, *The Essence of Chaos*, UCL Press, London, 1993, p. 150:

> Chaos is introduced into music during the process of composing. Unless a piece has intentionally been made devoid of structure, there are likely to be some reappearances of earlier themes. These are often more appealing if they are not exact repetitions, but contain a few unanticipated elements.

See also Ruelle's discussion of informational content, music and meaning in *Chance and Chaos*, pp. 134–5:

> We should not wonder that today's science can tackle only some rather superficial aspects of the problem of meaning. . . . We can measure quantities of information the same way we measure quantities of entropy or electric current. Not only does this have practical applications, but it also gives us some insight into the nature of works of art. [But art, like nature, raises questions that are] too hard for us to answer. Think of musical melodies, they are messages that we feel we understand, yet we are incapable of saying what they mean. The existence of music is a permanent intellectual scandal, but it is just one scandal among many others. Scientists know how hard it is to understand simple phenomena like the boiling or freezing of water, and they are not too astonished to find that many questions related to the human mind . . . are for the time being beyond our understanding.

Select bibliography

Books about chaos and complexity by scientists and historians that are more or less technical and speculative, but generally accessible to non-specialists include:

Briggs, John, *Fractals: The Patterns of Chaos*, Thames & Hudson, London, 1992.

Briggs, John and F. David Peat, *Turbulent Mirror: An Illustrated Guide to Chaos Theory*, Harper & Row, New York, 1989.

Cohen, Jack and Ian Stewart, *The Collapse of Chaos*, Penguin Books, London, 1994.

Gleick, James, *Chaos: Making a New Science*, Cardinal Books, London, 1988.

Hall, Nina, ed., *The 'New Scientist' Guide to Chaos*, Penguin Books, London, 1992.

Lewin, Roger, *Complexity: Life on the Edge of Chaos*, Phoenix Books, London, 1993.

Lorenz, Edward N., *The Essence of Chaos*, UCL Press, London, 1993.

Mullin, Tom, ed., *The Nature of Chaos*, Oxford University Press, Oxford, 1993.

Prigogine, Ilya and Isabelle Stengers, *Order out of Chaos*, New Science Library, Shambhala-Boulder and London, 1984.

Ruelle, David, *Chance and Chaos*, Penguin Books, London, 1993.

Stewart, Ian, *Does God Play Dice? The New Mathematics of Chaos*, Penguin Books, London, 1990.

Waldrop, F. Mitchell, *Complexity: The Emerging Science at the Edge of Order and Chaos*, Penguin Books, London, 1994.

Groundbreaking works in chaos science include:

Feigenbaum, Mitchell, 'Quantitative Universality for a Class of Nonlinear Transformations', *Journal Statistical Physics* 19 (1978), 25–52.

Lorenz, Edward, 'Predictability: Does the Flap of a Butterfly's Wings in Brazil Set off a Tornado in Texas?' (paper delivered at the 139th meeting of the American Association for the Advancement of Science, in Washington D.C. on December 29, 1972), published in Lorenz, *The Essence of Chaos*, UCL Press, London, 1993.

Mandelbrot, Benoit, 'How Long is the Coast of Britain? Statistical Self-similarity and Fractional Dimension', *Science*, 156 (1967), 636–38.

The Fractal Geometry of Nature, W. H. Freeman, San Francisco, 1982.

May, Robert, *Stability and Complexity in Model Ecosystems*, Princeton, New Jersey, Princeton University Press, 1973.

'Simple Mathematical Models with Very Complicated Dynamics', *Nature*, Vol. 261 (1976), 459–67.

Ruelle, David and Floris Takens, 'On the Nature of Turbulence', *Communications in Mathematical Physics*, 20 (1971), 167–92; 23 (1971), 343–4.

Ruelle, David, 'Strange Attractors', *The Mathematical Intelligencer*, 2, 126 (1980), 37–48.

Smale, Stephen, 'Differentiable Dynamical Systems', *Bulletin of the American Mathematical Society*, 73 (1967), 747–817.

The Mathematics of Time: Essays in Dynamical Systems, Economic Processes, and Related Topics, Springer-Verlag, New York, 1980.

James Yorke and Tien-Yien Li, 'Period Three Implies Chaos', *American Mathematical Monthly* 82, (1975), 985–92.

Index

Page numbers in italic refer to pages in the 'Notes' sections.

175